INVISIBLE CRITICISM

INVISIBLE CRITICISM

Ralph Ellison and the American Canon

By Alan Nadel

UNIVERSITY OF IOWA PRESS   Ψ   IOWA CITY

University of Iowa Press, Iowa City 52242
Copyright © 1988 by the University of Iowa
All rights reserved
Printed in the United States of America
First edition, 1988

Typesetting by G&S Typesetters, Austin, Texas
Printing and binding by BookCrafters, Chelsea, Michigan

Library of Congress Cataloging-in-Publication Data

Nadel, Alan, 1947–
    Invisible criticism: Ralph Ellison and the American canon / by Alan Nadel.—1st ed.
        p.   cm.
    Bibliography: p.
    Includes index.
    ISBN 0-87745-190-7
    1. Ellison, Ralph. Invisible man.   2. Canon (Literature).
I. Title.
PS3555.L62515358   1988   87-25071
813'.54—dc19   CIP

*Dedicated to my wife, Amy Perkins,
and my son, Alexander Percy Nadel,
who love words.*

Contents

Preface

t goes a long way back, some twenty years." Thus begins chapter 1 of *Invisible Man*, and thus begins this book on *Invisible Man*, which is being published almost twenty years to the day from the time I wrote, as an undergraduate at Brooklyn College, my first words on Ellison's novel. The assignment was to compare two books, at least one of which had to appear in the syllabus, that is, the canon. The canonized text I chose was *Adventures of Huckleberry Finn*. Because I was poor and for the preceding couple of years had been more or less self-supporting, I chose the second book from a small paperback library I had accumulated two summers earlier, when I worked at near-minimum wage in a book warehouse near the Red Hook docks. It was a place in many ways not unlike—at least as I imagine it—*Invisible Man*'s Long Island City paint factory. Each day just before closing I would duck behind the stacks and slip a book under my shirt. Thus I was first exposed to an array of writers, including Sartre, Moravia, and Ellison.

At the time I wrote that undergraduate comparison between Ellison's work and Twain's, I was primarily concerned that the paper was overdue and, equally, that its completion would bring me that much closer to graduation and therefore to the draft. My literary concerns were secondary; I was wholly ignorant, moreover, of the issues of canonicity, historicity, and cultural criticism this fortuitous comparison suggested. I soon became very aware, however, that many similarities existed between the texts—allusions and swerves—which no one else seemed to have noticed. I had never seen the word "hermeneutics," but I knew some encoded relationship was present; I had never heard of "intertextuality," but I knew that in some way the meaning of the text at hand depended greatly on its relationship to other texts with which it had not been commonly grouped; I had never considered the concept of "rehistoricism," but I knew Ellison's book was pointing toward some gap, some omission, some blindness in the way we read the past or wrote about it. Or at least I think I knew these things, at some level, as I tried to fathom the uncanny resonance I found between two American novels. Perhaps I just dreamed that I knew those things.

If so, as the invisible man's last sentences in chapter 1 say, "it was a dream I was to remember and dream again for many years after. But at the time I had no insight into its meaning. First I had to attend college" (or, in my case, graduate school). As my reading broadened, I found myself returning periodically, with ever-increasing insight, to *Invisible Man* and, through *Invisible Man*, to American literature and American studies. For this I am indebted to Ralph Ellison's prophetic novel. Frequently I was also struck with the sense that I had seen something no one else had. Or if others had seen what I had, they had not understood. Or if they had understood, they were not saying so. Or perhaps I was dreaming. I am indebted, therefore, to Ralph Ellison himself, who read an earlier version of my manuscript and responded with an invaluably generous letter convincing me that, like my original term paper, this work on *Invisible Man* was long overdue.

Gratitude goes also to Vincent Leitch, who helped me sharpen the Introduction; Carolyn Karcher, who gave advice on some aspects of chapter 1; Patricia Harkin, who was similarly helpful with some of the material in chapter 2 (a portion of which appeared in the *Georgia Review*); Andrew Welsh, who read an early version of chapter 3; Donald Gibson, who supervised my dissertation on Ellison; Carol Smith, who was the second reader; and Paul Fussell, who not only read the work with wit and dispatch but also has had, in more general ways, a profound effect on my education. Of course, as Huck might add, I don't blame him none, he didn't mean no harm by it.

Finally, I owe the most intangible debt to my wife, Amy, without whom, for reasons that transcend logic and doubt, this book would not have been.

Introduction

In recent years, the issue of canon formation has attracted a great deal of attention, a phenomenon not incidental to the influence on literary study of poststructuralism, feminism, and ethnic consciousness. At the risk of oversimplifying, we could say that these approaches mandate modes of thinking which urge distance and skepticism, modes which actively call into question the implicit assumptions of any enterprise or institution, and which actively seek to determine the presence and nature of hierarchies. Applying such modes of investigation to the realm of literature makes it hard to take for granted the great authority canons have wielded over the last century. When we look at the hierarchies in literary criticism, at the value systems those hierarchies encode, at the people and institutions they empower, and at the "others" they marginalize, it becomes difficult to view texts as reflecting (or failing to reflect) absolute value from an absolute source. Even the field from which the canonized texts emerge cannot be seen as a totality, either in potential or in fact. Rather, that field exists already in a privileged position created by a series of prior cuts and hierarchies.

Since these prior cuts, moreover, determine at very basic levels the power to speak, to be heard, and to be understood, they in fact control not only what constitutes a canon but also what may affect it. The obvious problem, then, is not that there are no channels for change but that those channels become dysfunctional when they themselves need alteration. To put it another way— a way that parallels the situation of Ralph Ellison's protagonist—how can one be an effective spokesman for change, when speaking effectively means conforming to the very set of rules one wants to change? As that protagonist discovers, this problem exists whether speech means speaking at a ceremonial dinner of "white citizens" or before a northern "trustee," in the office of a black "educational leader" or a white "businessman," at a public "political" rally or a private "committee" meeting. As any structuralist would point out, the speech cannot have meaning independent of a complicated system of social, psychological, and linguistic hierarchies. As any poststructuralist would further note, those hierarchies reflect an arbitrary and tenuous center, thoroughly and always dependent on an already present but unacknowledged other whose crucial presence can only be perceived as absence, as its own invisibility.

The problem, then, of speaking from invisibility, of making the absence visible, pertains not only to public functions but to speech itself, to that act, always both autobiographical and fictional, of describing one's world. Ellison demonstrates this memorably when his invisible and nameless narrator speaks to an invisible and nameless audience, attempting to uncover in their shared otherness the voice which had been encoded into silence, excised from the canon. A first and central claim of my book, therefore, is that *Invisible Man* is deeply framed and informed by the issue of "canonicity," of how to speak from invisibility, of how to speak to and through tradition without sacrificing the speaker's voice or denying the tradition it attempts to engage. I argue that this engagement with tradition is necessitated by a complicated interaction of historical and critical events which effected the erasure of the black's role in crucial parts of American history and of literary history.

Taking a radical approach to the use of allusion, I show that it is one device Ellison employs consistently and effectively to engage the issue of canonicity. To make this case, I examine in detail the ways an allusion can destabilize traditional presumptions. I scrutinize tentative implications a reader draws from the suspicion that something in a text alludes to another text, especially as they impel hypothesizing about the "alluded-to" text. Because allusions require reinterpreting tradition in light of the new work, their effect on the reader's understanding is similar to the effect of reading a piece of literary criticism. In regard to the alluded-to work, allusions do on a semiconscious level what criticism does on a conscious level and what literature does on an unconscious level: alter our sense of tradition.

A systematic use of allusions, which exploits their literary-critical potential, can indeed create a coherent subtext of literary criticism. The subtext Ellison creates, I argue, is one which engages the issues of marginality and decentering, of ethno- and logocentrism, of encoding and interpretation in ways which anticipate much contemporary European theory and much American rehistoricizing in regard to the role of the black in the American canon and our sense of canonicity itself.

No contemporary novelist has had more motivation for wanting to alter that sense than one as systematically excluded, as institutionally invisible, as Ellison was at the time he wrote *Invisible Man*. From his position of otherness, he viewed American literature and American literary history very differently than the members of the literary-critical establishment, circa 1950. Unlike the members of that establishment, Ellison seemed aware of how acute and fundamental a moral problem slavery and its legacy posed for such writers as Melville, Twain, and their contemporaries. And indeed—as his occasional pieces indicate—he could have written a book of literary criticism which explained the ways in which those mid-nineteenth-century writers, unlike their successors, used the black as their symbol of humanity and confronted the moral burden that slavery placed on the "Democratic Experiment." Had he written such a book, he might have entitled it "Love and Death in the American Novel," or "The American Adam," or "Invisible Man." Instead, with Joyce as his stylistic mentor, he wrote a novel which achieves those literary-critical ends through the use of allusions.

In that light—although this book remains committed to the text at hand and manifests that commitment with four chapters devoted primarily to close textual scrutiny—I have tried to keep in sight the larger cultural and theoretical issues reflected by *Invisible Man*.

The harder I work toward that understanding, however, the more I uncover the ways in which the process of understanding itself is centered in spheres of assumptions. At the same time, my discussion keeps finding evidence to discredit the stability of those spheres. Discovering that history—be it social, political, or literary—belongs to whoever owns the erasers is always a disconcerting lesson, regardless of how frequently one learns it. This lesson has, in fact, traumatized some contemporary critics, leaving them in a mire of narrativity told by a theorist, full of signs and structures signifying nothing. And yet the study of the past, which by definition constitutes the lessons of the present, cannot be unlearned. As a result, in writing about *Invisible Man*, as I had in reading it, I often found myself engaged in a discourse which actively verged on discrediting itself. What saved me from such a consummation was the text to which I kept returning, the text whose invisible narrator and highly visible author were dealing successfully with the same problem, that of negotiating between the futility of making presumptions and the fact that reality nevertheless was affected by those futile presumptions.

If I indulge, therefore, in theoretical discussions to examine some turns in American history and criticism, or to explain some of the subtleties in the way an allusion affects the reader, my larger purpose is always to expose some of the ways Ellison situates *Invisible Man* in regard to the American literary tradition, comments on that tradition, and, in so doing, alters it.

INVISIBLE CRITICISM

1. The Origins of Invisibility

O ver the thirty or forty years which preceded the writing of *Invisible Man*, American criticism can be fairly—if somewhat simplistically—divided into two main camps or, to use Grant Webster's term, "charters."[1] The older charter I shall, for convenience, call Progressivist Criticism, a perfect example of which can be found at the conclusion of Van Wyck Brooks' *America's Coming of Age*. Having pointed out the merits of mid-nineteenth-century American writers and acknowledged their limitations, he mourns the fact that no writers have replaced them, a fact he blames directly on the domination of America by big business and industrialism. In industrial, corporate America, he concludes, "intimate feeling, intimate intellectual contact, even humor . . . privateness which holds the string of what we call publicity; these promote that right, free, disinterested publicity which the real gentleman, the real craftsman, the real civil servant has always had in his blood. Socialism flows from this as light flows from the sun" (180). Brooks thus presumes direct correlation between a "successful" society and its art. The argument of his book, the case for socialism, rests on the failure of capitalism as evidenced by the failure of the potentially great mid-nineteenth-century literature to blossom, propagate, and multiply in the late nineteenth and early twentieth centuries. Subsequently, among others, Lewis Mumford in *The Golden Day* (1926) and *Herman Melville* (1929), Vernon Parrington in *Main Currents of American Thought* (1930), and Granville Hicks in *The Great Tradition* (1933) echoed this argument. All of these, further, were indebted to the Beards' voluminous histories.[2]

The other, newer charter, often referred to as New Criticism, Webster appropriately calls Tory Formalism. It includes the critics T. S. Eliot, Ezra Pound, Cleanth Brooks, John Crowe Ransom, and Allen Tate.[3] We can get a clear picture of the difference between these two charters if we compare V. W. Brooks' statement above with the following by Ransom: "The formal tradition in art has a validity more than political, and the latter I am content to waive. What I have in mind is an argument from aesthetics which will justify any formal art, even a formal literature" (*The World's Body*, 32).

Ransom will "waive" political validity because he feels it works against the humanity and compassion that Brooks sees it mandating. For Ransom, the political validity—or economic necessity—consists of using the most efficient means to fulfill a desire, whether that means is a simple machine, or mass production, or rape. Societies that endure and prosper, he believes, frustrate and defer these "economic" activities; this results in manners, rituals, and aesthetics. Socialism for him thus destroys society by replacing deferred gratification with economic (i.e., immediate) gratification. When Ransom considers, for example, the (alleged) equality of the sexes and deritualization of marriage in then newly soviet Russia, the question, as he frames it, is "whether the ideal of efficient animality is good enough for human beings; and whether the economic law, by taking precedence at every point over the imperative of manners, of religion and of the arts, will not lead to perfect misery" (*The World's Body*, 38).

There were, of course, many other differences between the Tory Formalists and the Progressivist Critics, and there were, as well, many differences within these groups. But for this discussion I want to bypass those and focus on one area of strong agreement: both charters hated modern technology. For the Progressivist Critics it represented the monstrosities of capitalism, and for the Tories an assault on religion and the humanities. Both consequently posited an ideal world modeled on some moment in the American past, and both modeled it on antebellum America. For the Progressivist Critics the period was a time when small pioneering and farming communities formed the basic unit of organization, free from the encroachment of industries and monopolies. Lewis Mumford named this age of actual and prototypical communes "The Golden Day." The Tories, many of whom were southerners, also looked to antebellum America, and more specifically to the Old South, as the agrarian ideal which somehow preserved the arts and humanities through the economic self-sufficiency of the farm or plantation. In *I'll Take My Stand* (1930), twelve southern writers, including Ransom, Tate, and Warren, advocated a return to the agrarian tradition. But the book also defended the South—still not quite part of the Union—and indicted the North.[4]

In their misgivings about the outcome of the Civil War, the Progressivist Critics in some ways were in accord with the Tories. The Beards regard the Civil War as a "social cataclysm in which the capitalists, laborers and farmers of the North and West drove from power in the national government the planting aristocracy of the South" (*The Rise of American Civilization*, II:54). To the southerner, they attribute all the virtues of the cavalier. We can see this clearly in their regret over the war's destroying

> the planting aristocracy of the South—a great power which had furnished
> leadership and undoubted ability and had so long contested with the industrial
> and commercial interests of the North. The first paralyzing blow at the plant-
> ers was struck by the abolition of slavery. The second and third came with the

fourteenth (1868) and fifteenth (1870) amendments giving ballots to freed men and excluding from office the Confederate leaders—driving from the work of reconstruction the finest talents of the South. (*A History of the United States*, 336)

This position is echoed strongly by Parrington, who, like the Beards, accepts the myth of the southern cavalier and endorses many of the southerners' critiques of northern industrialism and wage-slavery.[5] I am not trying to suggest that any of these Progressivists endorsed slavery or the arguments against its abolition. Rather, in the interests of demonstrating the economic motivations for political positions, and in the interests of emphasizing the problems of capitalism, big business, and its political arm, the Republican party, they downplayed the moral issues surrounding the Civil War and emphasized the economic. As we shall see, however, from Ellison's point of view, one casualty of such an emphasis is an understanding of the moral function the black served in nineteenth-century American literature.

For it is essential to remember the debt we owe to the Progressivists. Until Brooks and Mumford, there was no nineteenth-century American literature as we know it. It is hard to imagine how unread were Thoreau, Whitman, and Melville in their day. Both *Walden* and the 1855 edition of *Leaves of Grass* were commercial failures. Melville's major successes were his first two books, *Typee* and *Omoo*; when he died years after their publication, *Moby-Dick* was out of print and his obscure obituaries identified him as a minor writer of travel books. As late as 1919, one could buy a first edition of *Moby-Dick* for one dollar. Understanding this, we can see how influential the critics of the twenties and thirties were in shaping the American canon, how much what we think of nineteenth-century American literature was defined by their attitudes which preferred antebellum America to postbellum, despite the presence of slavery.

The Progressivist Critics were particularly influential because they were exploring American literature for the same reason that the Tories were ignoring it: it held the potential of being a proletarian literature. William Empson, in *Some Versions of Pastoral* (1936), explains that this search for proletarian literature was misguided because literature about working people fell into two categories. Either it acclaimed the worker's ability to rise out of the proletarian ranks and thus renounced proletarian life or it exploited an idealized version of working life to reconcile people to the status quo, and thus functioned as covert pastoral. Such a pastoral was the Tories' idealization of the Old South. In his 1977 introduction to *I'll Take My Stand*, Louis D. Rubin makes this clear:

> The tradition out of which they were writing was that of pastorale; they were invoking the humane virtues of a simpler, more elemental, nonacquisitive existence, as a needed rebuke to the acquisitive, essentially materialistic com-

pulsions of a society that from the outset was very much engaged in seeking
wealth, power and plenty on a continent whose prolific natural resources and
vast acres of usable land, forests and rivers were there for the taking. (xv)

One could add to Rubin's remarks that the same pastoral image found
equal acceptance from the Progressivist Critics. Although their antipathy to
the machine accounts for their gravitation toward pastoral, it does not explain
their accepting the Old South as embodying some of those pastoral values. In
order to explain this choice—which had profound effects on American literary history—and show how it structured the canon Ellison received, I analyze
in some detail the institution of the South as it functioned in the antebellum
period and as it adapted in the postbellum.[6] What I hope to show is that the
way power was distributed and order maintained in the South—as that society
developed its regional distinctiveness, protected it in the antebellum era, and
adapted it in the postbellum era—had profound and far-reaching effects on
the role and perception of the black in America. These effects, more importantly, had implications far beyond their obvious manifestations in the areas
of segregation, discrimination, and physical violence. What I want to demonstrate is that a cultural violence—a mandated invisibility—caused by re-
sidual southern practices, in effect, erased the role of the black in American
literature at the same time that the American canon was being formed.

At the center of southern distinctiveness, of course, was slavery. As Carl
Degler points out, the battle over the admission of Missouri showed that the
South was united only by that one issue (*Place over Time*, 39). In addition to
unifying the South politically—to the point of secession and war—slavery
directly and indirectly contributed to many of the conditions which gave the
South its uniqueness. Locking the South into an agrarian economy, for example, it inhibited the growth of cities and thus of industrial and commercial
job opportunities. Paucity of opportunity in turn discouraged immigration to
the South and thereby increased the homogeneity of southern life and reduced the entry of new ideas. This isolationism, which only increased with
the North's increased hostility to slavery, in many ways made the South just
prior to the Civil War an eighteenth-century society in a nineteenth-century
world.

If this anachronistic society fostered in its planter class a paternalistic ideology, similar to that of the English gentry, it did so under conditions that
made such a paternalism increasingly inoperable. James Oakes, in his history
of American slaveholders, explains:

The same forces that diminished [paternalism's] influence in the seventeenth
and eighteenth centuries—the rise of the commercial market, the broad distribution of slave wealth, the diversity of the master class, and the spread of
economic and political liberalism—continued to operate against the effective-

ness of paternalistic ideology in the antebellum South. Yet the nineteenth century witnessed a dramatic rise in the *rhetoric* of paternalism in both England and America, and there was more than coincidence in these simultaneous developments. . . . [Both British and southern paternalists were] enchanted by their nostalgic vision of an older and better age when social relations were stable and harmonious. The perennial complaint, however, was that the patriarchs were failing their paternal responsibilities. Thus paternalism suffered the inevitable fate of an anachronistic world view: as its advocates grew more vocal, its impotence became more apparent. (*The Ruling Class*, 192–93)

The planter class nevertheless enjoyed immense autonomy in which to practice this "impotent" paternalism. Autonomy, of course, emanated in large part from the absolute control the master exercised over his slaves. This was a necessity of a forced labor system, a necessity supported by southern custom and southern law.

Although the laws strengthened the master's autonomy, the converse was not true. In many ways the slave system weakened the legal system. Bertram Wyatt-Brown makes this clear in his insightful study of southern honor:

Policing one's own ethical sphere was the natural complement of the patriarchal order. When Southerners spoke of liberty, they generally meant the birthright to self-determination of one's place in society, not the freedom to defy sacred conventions, challenge long-held assumptions, or propose another scheme of moral or political order. If someone, especially a slave, spoke or acted in a way that invaded that territory or challenged that right, the white man so confronted had the inalienable right to meet the lie and punish the opponent. Without such a concept of white liberty, slavery would have scarcely lasted a moment. There was little paradox or irony in this juxtaposition from the cultural perspective. Power, liberty, and honor were all based upon community sanction, law and traditional hierarchy. . . . (*Southern Honor*, 371)

"A rural class, intensely individual and local in outlook," James Roark reminds us, "planters had always tended to think of themselves as individual sovereigns who happened to give sustenance to the state" (*Masters without Slaves*, 97). This meant that justice and discipline were very much personal matters in practice if not always in theory. In theory, for example, plantation bureaucracy was supposed to create distance between management and labor. Few plantations, however, were able to supersede the human dimension, and the great majority of slaveholders, those who owned fewer than ten slaves, did not have the personnel to implement such a bureaucracy. Slavery thus required a system in which the power to discipline was often both personal and absolute; it affected not only the master's relationship with black slaves but also his attitude toward other whites. And, by setting a tone of behavior, it carried over to nonslaveholding southern whites.

Since the slave system thus encouraged the master to think of himself as outside the law, the South was, not surprisingly, also a very violent region.[7] Dickson Bruce, in *Violence and Culture in the Antebellum South*, has noted, however, that the southern gentleman had complex and ambivalent feelings about violence. Although he accepted it as an inherent part of his life, essential in slave management and in protecting the southern white, he also distrusted it as an unwelcome manifestation of dangerous passions, passions the gentleman was supposed to control. He therefore found elaborate ways to distance himself from the violence that he actively or tacitly endorsed. For example, he always perceived violence as a response and never regarded himself as the initiator.

The southerner also distanced himself from violence through the ritual of dueling. As Bruce and Wyatt-Brown show, the duel was not an event but an extended and ritualized series of negotiations and protocols aimed not at the ultimate demise of one of the two primary parties but at a mutual understanding which would save the life and, more important, the honor of both. Death, they suggest, more often resulted from inept seconds than from expert marksmanship. Since able seconds might use their ambassadorial skills to prevent injury, we might perceive them as making the duel ritual less violent. But in providing the desired distance, I think, they made the duel more permissible and the aura of violence more pervasive. Distanced and ritualized, the duel became less destructive, which was necessary for the practice to survive. Since it epitomized a situation in which violence and the threat of violence became synonymous, it turned a forestalled act of violence into violence universalized as the focus of elaborate threats, challenges, and negotiations, all of which would become meaningless were the threat to disappear or the violence to culminate.

Although more schematic and ritualized, dueling in this way does not differ greatly from the violence of slave control. There, too, the master desired greater distance and employed a universalized threat of violence to defer or render unnecessary individual violent acts. Whether active or potential, however, this violence in both cases emanated from personal not legal codes and was resolved in the hands of the individual, not the state. Under these circumstances, the slaves quite logically perceived discipline as overly capricious. They failed to interpret the personal code of behavior under which the universal threat of violence on occasion became the specific violent act.

As noted, the economic and political forces surrounding slavery made the South both more homogeneous and more anachronistic than the rest of the country. Given the weakened role of law, moreover, in a slave society, the dominance of honor in determining southern behavior becomes understandable. Even those who stood "outside or below the circle of honor must acknowledge its power. Southern yeomen, no less than rich planters, found meaning in honor's demands. Thus, honor served all members of society in a world of chronic mistrust, particularly so in times of crisis, great or small" (Wyatt-Brown, *Southern Honor*, xv).

Much of this southern distinctiveness—the anachronistic beliefs, the isolation and independence of the gentry, the reliance on honor rather than law, the agrarian economy—made the southern planter more similar to the seventeenth- or early eighteenth-century British aristocrat than to the nineteenth-century American northerner or westerner. Or so he would have had himself believe. "As early as the ante-bellum years," Degler notes, "North and South had created a *myth* of difference that went beyond the *facts* of difference" (*Place over Time*, 60). The myth of an aristocracy, nevertheless, both focused the code of southern honor and helped the southerner resist change by looking to the past rather than to the future. In this way, it helped compensate for the unavoidable changes that everywhere threatened southern life.

The writing of the planters during the Civil War, for example, revealed fear of rebellion not only from their slaves but also from nonslaveholding southern whites. The failure of such rebellions to materialize, like the general loyalty of southern whites, attests to the stability of the southern caste system, a stability reliant on the presence of race slavery to mitigate if not eliminate economic priorities. For just as the ritual of dueling helped universalize the presence of violence by reducing the number of individual violent acts, so slavery helped universalize the hope of economic advancement while in actuality helping to concentrate southern wealth. This is the strange quality of American southern mythology—it made caste and aristocracy for whites wholly compatible with freedom and social mobility. The *Richmond Enquirer*, for example, declared: "In this country alone does perfect equality of civil and social privilege exist among the white population, and it exists solely because we have black slaves. Freedom is not possible without slavery" (Oakes, *The Ruling Class*, 111). What I am suggesting, then, is that the southerner ascribed to and defended the slave system not because he was precapitalistic but because he was upwardly mobile.[8] Even someone from the lowest white caste could imagine the possibility of rising to the social pinnacle, a possibility which depended on the preservation of the system as he knew it. Slaves thus became the sign of that system and the reminder of that possibility.[9] This, of course, burdened the slaveowners with dual roles both as nineteenth-century entrepreneurs responsible for fiscal success and as eighteenth-century aristocrats responsible for moral stability. These responsibilities demanded not only efficacious control of the black population but also adherence to codes of public honor, for the public image of aristocrat anchored the private hopes of southern whites.[10]

The implications of these roles, especially in regard to the concept of discipline, can be better understood with the help of Michel Foucault.[11] The American slave system was developed during a time in which, according to Foucault, humans emerged as *subject*. The moral ramification of this emergence was that humans became the source of morality as well as its judge, and that behavior which had formerly been a sign of divine order, of human nature, now became an act of will, a desire to conform or not to conform to standards created by human beings. Punishment similarly was a human obligation—its method, degree, and the choice of the punishable were part of the implicit rules of classification which defined the social order.

The role of the passions also changed. They had been regarded as a natural quality, found to a higher degree in lower animals and to a lower degree in higher animals. The reverse was held true of another natural quality, reason. When order emanated from a divine system, each—passion *and* reason— was accepted as natural; humans happened to be the creatures in the natural scheme endowed with equal quantities of both qualities.[12] As human reason became the source of morality, the passions moved from the role of natural phenomena (to be accepted) to unnatural phenomena—the enemy of reason and hence order and morality—and thus to be resisted, disciplined, punished, excluded. Foucault thus traces the segregation, incarceration, punishment, and treatment of unreason (until Freud) as an attempt to exclude unreason from the discourse of human institutions, to maintain its invisibility.

During the eighteenth century, in other words, the rationalist mind sought justification for action; since actions were no longer part of a divine plan, humans had to classify them and thereby make both implicit and explicit judgment. Morality thus became separate from, but not unrelated to, action. This division of body and soul, which for many thinkers gained prominence by the end of the eighteenth century, created as well the need for a language that unified them by filling the fissure with the discourse of cause-and-effect. Until this happened, enslavement described primarily a condition of the body, external and not judgmental, an act of power, pure in its oppression and economic in its purpose. By the end of the eighteenth century, the emergence of humans as the subject of morality coincided with the need for the South to have a preserving sign of its institution, independent of economic flux, to create in America a condition in which the arbitrariness of enslavement started to be thought of by many as an effect which happened for reasons, the sign of which was race. *Enslavement* thus started to become *slavery*, and a system which had its origins in economics began to serve other needs of a larger institution.

The role of economics in the history of the South and the economic success of slavery are greatly debated issues.[13] This much seems clear: (1) slavery was profitable enough to continue functioning, and (2) noneconomic factors were instrumental in its perpetuation, at least in those parts of the South where it was no longer necessary. But perhaps the most telling insights into slavery come from considering the postbellum South.[14] There we can see rather clearly that the dominating priority was not economic prosperity but the maintenance of the racial caste system rooted in the myth of aristocracy and controlled by the same extralegal codes of white honor. The clearest evidence of this is southern poverty in the century following the Civil War. Roger Ransom and Richard Sutch show that it did not result from the war's decimation, but rather from the South's desire to replicate as much as possible the antebellum racial caste system.

This required the continued primacy of an agrarian economy. Southern whites feared, according to Ransom and Sutch,

> that their social position in Southern society would be eroded by the existence of educated, independent, landowning blacks. They feared, in short, that the Negro might not prove to be inferior. These fears, above all else, created the racial animosities that became so important in reshaping the social and economic institutions of the South. The white southerner was dedicated to putting the black "in his place" and keeping him there. In 1865 the ex-slave's place was, unquestionably, to be in cotton fields. Not in the schools. Not in the cities. (*One Kind of Freedom*, 23)

Despite their desire to tie blacks to agriculture, the whites did not want them to have land. As a result, a sharecropping system emerged in which blacks returned to the plantation as tenants on white-owned land. This system, the direct result of the planter class's refusal to share its monopoly of the land, maintained not only the class but also its control over the lower castes, for the contracts of tenancy required the tenant to work under the direction of the landlord or his representative and allowed the landlord to determine the crop mix (*One Kind of Freedom*, 80). These controls, however, served the planter class's social interests more than its economic interests. Beyond the obvious ways in which it impeded urbanization, industrialization, and immigration, it also deterred agricultural growth. It made capital improvements like investment in better fertilizer or more efficient machinery virtually impossible for the tenant who was kept marginally poor and often in debt by virtue of having to surrender half his crop and often, as well, to buy on credit at exorbitant interest rates. At the same time, it made capital investments by the owner unwise because the owner could only realize half the benefit of any investment. The division of a plantation into small, separately operated units also made it impossible to rotate crops efficiently or, more important, to leave part of an estate fallow.

As the South moved toward the twentieth century, therefore, it moved closer to, not further from, the institutionalizing of power signified by the antebellum South. The isolationism, economic retardation, and caste system resulted from and in turn solidified an agrarian economy in which the land was monopolized by a small upper class and in which racial difference de-

fined the lowest caste.[15] As they had before the Civil War, legal and extralegal
means cooperated to delineate this racial difference and solidify the black as
the concrete base on which the pyramid of social hierarchy rested.

Even before the Civil War, we can find a paradigm for this segregated
society in the treatment of free southern blacks and urban slaves. The urban
slaves often worked and lived outside of their masters' domain. When selling
their labor, moreover, they worked much harder, some exceptionally hard—
so that they provided the community with a great deal more goods and ser-
vices while usually selling them at a lower price than comparable white labor.
In addition, they also relieved their owners of part or all of the expense of
boarding and feeding them while they returned to the community a significant part of their earnings in the form of rent paid and goods purchased, and
in the form of the "commission" paid to the master for allowing the slave to
sell his labor. This rendered slaves in urban areas almost indistinguishable
from free blacks.[16] The consequence of this, as Ira Berlin points out, was that
in most ways free blacks were treated as slaves. Numerous laws explicitly
denied free blacks the rights of citizens; and as the pressures for abolition
increased, the laws became more codified and oppressive. Berlin relates this
directly to the need for the South to preserve its caste system:

> Black slavery provided a floor beneath which no white could fall and laid the
> foundation for racial solidarity in a society rife with class divisions. As long as
> any white, no matter how lowly, could look down on the Negro, those class
> divisions did not seem quite so formidable. Racial unity allowed nonslave-
> holding whites to treasure their liberty and support slavery. While planters
> monopolized the best land and dominated Southern society, they boasted that
> slavery provided the foundation for white democracy.
>
> Under the best of conditions, whites did not like sharing their proudest pos-
> session with blacks. But when slavery became the basis for Southern democ-
> racy, the liberty of some blacks became particularly odious. If some blacks
> were free—could live by themselves, care for their families, accumulate
> wealth, and even own slaves—precisely what was the value of a white skin?
> The free black called into question the racial foundations of Southern democ-
> racy and threatened to undermine racial unity at a time of growing class con-
> flict among whites. (*Slaves without Masters*, 369)

The loss in the Civil War not only expedited the shift from slavery to segregation but also added the element of guilt—guilt not only over slavery but
also over having lost. For the complex reasoning that linked the moral-
religious world with the actual-physical, that related all the parts—caste system, economy, morality—to a paradigm of order—divine order—ought to
have found its final vindication in the triumph of war. As a failed moral test,
then, the war was a source of guilt. But although the war ended the political
construction called the Confederacy, it did not destroy the institution of the

South. The South rather accommodated the guilt of failure by merely segregating the sign of that failure—the ostensibly free slave—making it an otherness, removing it into silence and invisibility in much the way that, in the preceding century, Europe segregated the mad.

But this shift created a new need. Physically free, the black through invisibility determined the limits of the institution. The endurance of the institution, therefore, required new ways of maintaining the invisibility of the black; these were found by moving blacks from physical bondage into silence, as Ellison points out:

> . . . when white men drew up a plan for a democratic way of life . . . the Negro began slowly to exert an influence on America's moral consciousness. Gradually he was recognized as the human factor placed outside the democratic master plan, a human "natural" resource who, so that the white man could become more human, was elected to undergo a process of institutionalized dehumanization.
>
> Until the Korean War this moral role had become obscured within the staggering growth of contemporary science and industry, but during the Nineteenth Century it flared nakedly in the American's conscience, like a raging river revealed at his feet by a lightning flash. Only then is the veil of anti-Negro myths, symbols, stereotypes and taboos drawn somewhat aside. And when we look closely at our literature it is seen operating even when the Negro seems most patently a little man who isn't there. (SA, 46)

Both before and after the Civil War, however, this invisible man, institutionally dehumanized, required a great deal of visible, institutional surveillance and discipline. Even before the war, in many areas, the state had assumed more and more of the responsibility for that mastery. Most southern states, for instance, passed laws requiring free blacks to register and to have a white legal guardian. The individual master's role as discipliner was also greatly lessened by the civil authorities in cities.

Most southern cities had large police forces that attempted to keep strict control on the quasi-free slave population. The police records of these towns show numerous violations (and resulting punishments) of the strict laws governing urban slaves. The great number of violations of laws against slaves' socializing, drinking, smoking, gaming, and so forth, indicate, furthermore, that despite the law and enforcement, such trappings of freedom were a part of urban slave life. The life of an urban slave, therefore, although greatly restricted, was more like that of a freeman in a very oppressive society than that of a slave in a democracy because the arm of the oppression had shifted in large part from the personal master to the impersonal state.

Berlin also points out that the infrequent and capricious enforcement of antiblack laws may have afforded blacks more freedom than a system of strict steady enforcement, but it did so at a huge psychological price, the consequence of which was in certain ways more oppressive than any strict, even-handed enforcement might have been:

> Imperfect, almost random enforcement allowed free Negroes many liberties the law denied, but only at the expense of their security. A free Negro never knew when the law might be enforced. At any time, in any place, any white might challenge his liberty. A routine check of freedom papers could reveal that a free Negro had been improperly manumitted, remained illegally in the state, or worked at an illicit trade. A gathering of friends to celebrate a wedding, to plan an outing, or simply to discuss old times might be broken up by the police, the participants arrested and dragged to the whipping post. Any minor infraction could lead to imprisonment or worse. The irregular enforcement of the law failed to stop offenders, but it constantly reminded free Negroes of the fragility of their liberty. (*Slaves without Masters*, 331–32)

This centralizing of discipline had perhaps the most profound effects on the role of the black. If the postbellum South in many ways replicated the antebellum, in the area of surveillance and discipline it was crucially different in that it shifted these functions from the master to the state. This shift, begun for segments of the black population before the Civil War, changed not only the way the black was to relate to white society but also the way white society was to see or not see the black.

Even during Reconstruction, for example, we see the federal government helping to restore the institutions of the Old South. "The planters' efforts to reestablish a facsimile of the prewar plantation were encouraged by the Freedman's Bureau," Ransom and Sutch tell us. "Having encouraged the Negro to sign [tenancy contracts], the bureau stood ready to assist both in drawing up the contract and in enforcing the agreement when necessary" (*One Kind of Freedom*, 61). In theory, a contract signifies freedom in that it is equally binding on both parties. At the same time, however, it bound the black to a role not very different from that of slave, and, more important, it did so under the endorsement of the liberator, not the enslaver. As such, it signified a more universal white coalition and thus began to define the black's role in postbellum America. The contract was also the sign of a new power structure in which the state intervened in the relationship between worker and master. Instead of condoning or ordaining the master's role, now the state *completed* it, in the name of emancipation. The emancipating powers, in other words, were the first enforcers of the new control which was in fact the old control, redistributed and reconstructed.[17]

The tenancy contract actually moved the planter class closer to the ideal of management prescribed but rarely achieved before the war. That ideal, as noted, recommended distance as the means to efficiency. Here the state provided that distance, and economic incentives could often replace the overseer's whip. These incentives depended, naturally, on the marginality of the southern economy. As long as the South could prevent the economic alternatives that come with urbanization or industrialization, the tenant was bound to his caste. So the retention of the caste system depended on the southerner's valuing it more highly than economic gain.

The development of the segregated South, of course, extended beyond the tenancy contracts. The code of southern honor and the tradition of extralegal violence, as they had prior to the war, continued to affect all walks of southern life and thus to govern race relations strictly. Again the significant difference was that the controls came more from the general white population than from the specific white master. No longer the master's property, the black lost the protection entailed in being his asset. Because the extralegal code of honor which respected another white man's property (or the laws of slavery which protected his investment) no longer applied, the black became the universal slave of the white community and the white began to realize the implicit ideal of southern democracy as the *Richmond Enquirer* had articulated it—that all whites could be masters.[18]

As the southern whites regained control of the courthouses and legislatures, this relationship became more strongly institutionalized through condoned violence against blacks and legislated racial difference. In the 1890s, these legal and extralegal controls manifested themselves with both unprecedented violence against blacks and extensive Jim Crow legislation. If we think of Reconstruction as the period during which the South completed the adaptations necessary to maintain its old way of life, then we can regard the 1890s as its culmination, the successful adaptation of an eighteenth-century mythology for a twentieth-century world.

Perhaps most ironically, that success depended on the South's losing the Civil War. The southern attitude toward the passions, as Bruce points out, did not progress in the nineteenth century to assume positions that on one hand, in the tradition of Adam Smith, downplayed their importance, or on the other, in the tradition of Rousseau, overvalued them: "In politics, Southerners held to classical concerns about passions and to a view which put passion at the center of the political process throughout the ante-bellum period" (*Violence and Culture in the Antebellum South*, 10). The myth of southern aristocracy and its incumbent code of southern honor thus became a way of solidifying hierarchies and controlling the passions by organizing them. The myth of the Old South, in other words, provided order by explaining and/or justifying the use of those passions that the southerner, with his eighteenth-century pessimism, distrusted. As we have seen with the dueling ritual, for example, southern codes and myths did not prevent violence but rather legitimized its role by appropriately distancing it from action. With the Confederacy's demise, the myth of the Old South no longer posed a political problem for nonsouthern society and was thus more free than ever to organize southern passion. When the South's racial caste aristocracy required slavery, it imposed political obstacles to other American regions where other myths and their incumbent practices prevailed.[19] In the postbellum period, the South reformulated its practices in such a way as to allow it to conform to its myth without interfering with the rest of the country. That reformulation took place gradually, and by the end of the nineteenth century it was more or less complete. As the end-of-the-century repression of blacks made clear, the myth was stronger than ever and the perpetuation of the Old South secure for another half century.[20]

This universalizing of discipline also universalized the master's capriciousness. As the free black in the South, after the war as much as before, knew, the best way to lose a legal right was to try to exercise it; the best way to guarantee oppression was to display freedom. This did not mean that blacks could not develop their own culture or family structure, but rather that they could not make their cultural freedoms visible to the white ruling class. The code of southern honor prohibited it. Lynch law, Wyatt-Brown makes clear, was thought to guard well

> the social and racial values upon which white order rested. . . . Even politi-
> cally motivated lynchings—to prevent slaves from developing leadership for
> rebellions or, later, freed men from voting the Republican or Populist bal-
> lots—were ultimately a means to protect white family integrity. Black ad-
> vancements in any aspect of life meant departure from accustomed servitude,
> endangering the white man's honor. Just as before the war insurrectionary
> panics provided mechanisms for dividing the blacks and uniting the whites,
> so postemancipation lynch law set the boundaries beyond which blacks were
> not to go. (*Southern Honor*, 463)

The outbreak of lynching at the end of the century thus became a final sign to a new generation of blacks that they must internalize the fact that the social order of the Old South would admit no tampering.

In this way externalized discipline became internalized. The external power of a given master, demanding labor, present under conditions of enslavement, started to be universalized so as to demand, under conditions of slavery, not only physical but moral restraint. By the time that segregation had fully replaced slavery, therefore, the restraints had become internalized and demanded silence and invisibility.

This is exactly the process that Foucault points out the discipline of the asylum effected on the mad:

> . . . fear no longer reigned on the other side of the prison gates, it now
> reigned under the seals of conscience. . . . The asylum no longer punished
> the madman's guilt, it is true, but it did more, it organized that guilt; it orga-
> nized it for the madman as a consciousness of himself, and as a non-recipro-
> cal relation to his keeper; it organized it for the man of reason as an awareness

of the Other, a therapeutic intervention in the madman's existence. In other words, by this guilt the madman became an object of punishment, always vulnerable to himself and to the Other; and from the acknowledgment of his status as an object, from the awareness of his guilt, the madman was to return to his awareness of himself as a free and responsible subject, and consequently to reason. (*Madness and Civilization*, 247)

The institution of reason demanded the invisibility of unreason, achieved first through incarceration, then segregation, and, finally, institutionalization, so that the mad ultimately internalized their own invisibility as the price for ostensible freedom. The institution of the South demanded the same of its subclass, and we can see how clearly Foucault's statements about the ultimate role of the mad apply to the segregated black:

> Incessantly cast in the role of unknown visitor, and challenged in everything that can be known about him, drawn to the surface of himself by a social personality imposed by observation, by form and mask, the madman is obliged to objectify himself in the eyes of reason as the perfect stranger, that is, as the man whose strangeness does not reveal itself. The city of reason welcomes him only with this qualification and at the price of his surrender to anonymity. (*Madness and Civilization*, 249–50)

> For this new reason which reigns in the asylum, madness does not represent the absolute form of contradiction, but instead a minority status, an aspect of itself that does not have the right to autonomy and can live only grafted into the world of unreason. (252)

> Everything was organized so that the madman would recognize himself in a world of judgment that enveloped him on all sides; he must know that he is judged, watched, condemned; from transgression to punishment, the transgression must be evident as a guilt recognized by all. (267)

We can see in Ellison's early writing a recognition of an analogous situation for the American black. As early as 1944, in an unpublished review of Gunnar Myrdal's *An American Dilemma*, he wrote: "Now, the task of reconciling moralities is usually the function of religion and philosophy, of art and psychoanalysis—all of which find myth-making indispensable. And in this American sociological literature rivals all three: its myth-making consisting of its 'scientific' justification of anti-democratic and unscientific racial attitudes and practices" (SA, 292). And in 1949, Ellison wrote:

> After Reconstruction the political question of what was to be done with Negroes, "solved" by the Hayes-Tilden deal of 1876, came down to the psychological question: "How can the Negro's humanity be evaded?" The problem, arising in a democracy that holds all men as created equal, was a highly moral one: democratic ideals had to be squared with anti-Negro practices.

One answer was to *deny* the Negro's humanity—a pattern set long before 1915. But with the release of *The Birth of a Nation* the propagation of sub-human images of Negroes became financially and dramatically profitable. The Negro as scapegoat could be sold as entertainment, could even be exported. . . . Actually, the anti-Negro images of the films were (and are) acceptable because of the existence throughout the United States of an audience obsessed with an inner psychological need to view Negroes as less than men. Thus, psychologically and ethically, these negative images constitute justifications for all those acts, legal, emotional, economic and political, which we label Jim Crow. The anti-Negro image is thus a ritual object of which Hollywood is not the creator, but the manipulator. Its role has been that of justifying the widely held myth of Negro unhumanness and inferiority by offering entertaining rituals through which the myth could be reaffirmed. (SA, 266–67)

Ellison, in other words, sees an additional shift occurring when a myth created to preserve an institution becomes so pervasive that the reiteration of it becomes economically valuable and—*Birth of a Nation* was a definitive work of art—a determinant of artistic possibility.

This unwillingness to resolve the conflict in keeping with his democratic ideals has compelled the white American, figuratively, to force the Negro down into the deeper level of his consciousness, into the inner world, where reason and madness mingle with hope and memory and endlessly give birth to nightmare and to dream; down into the province of the psychiatrist and the artist, from whence spring the lunatic's fancy and the work of art. . . . imprisoned in the deepest drives in human society, it is practically impossible for the white American to think of sex, of economics, his children or womenfolk, or of sweeping socio-political changes, without summoning into consciousness fear-flecked images of black men. (SA, 109)

The conventions and assumptions of twentieth-century literature, as Ellison sees them, also manifested assumptions which kept the black invisible:

Thus it has not been its failure to depict racial matters that has determined the quality of American writing, but that the writers have formed the habit of living and thinking in a culture that is opposed to the deep thought and feeling necessary to profound art; hence its avoidance of emotion, its fear of ideas, its obsession with mere physical violence and pain, its overemphasis of understatement. . . . (SA, 110)

In the nineteenth century, however, Ellison believes, the American novel at its best was concerned with the basic moral predicament in which slavery put America. "During Melville's time and Twain's, it was an implicit aspect of their major themes, by the Twentieth Century and after the discouraging and traumatic effect of the Civil War and the Reconstruction, it had undergone, had become *understated*" (SA, 165–66). Understatement, however, as Ellison points out, depends "upon commonly held assumptions, and my minority status rendered all such assumptions questionable" (SA, 112).[21]

Perceiving all of this, Ellison's task became to obviate the understatement by basing it on assumptions that he could share with all Americans, assumptions that he found grounded in an American tradition of Melville and Twain and, subsequently, forced into invisibility. We can see this at work even in the inscription to the book *Invisible Man*, which quotes Melville's "Benito Cereno": "'You are saved,' cried Captain Delano, more and more astonished and pained; 'you are saved: what has cast such a shadow upon you?'" The understatement comes in the editing of the quote; one must go back to the text, must reread Melville, to find the answer to Delano's question: "The Negro." He has been left out of the quoted section, so that his invisibility makes this brief Melville text *appear* enigmatic.

The "experimental attitude" of *Invisible Man*, therefore, Ellison views as an "attempt to return to the mood of personal moral responsibility for democracy which typified the best of our Nineteenth-Century fiction" (SA, 111), for although Ellison views protest as an element of all art,

> . . . it does not necessarily take the form of speaking for a social or political program. It might appear in a novel as a technical assault against the styles which have gone before, or as a protest against the human condition. . . . The protest is there, not because I was helpless before my racial condition, but because I *put* it there. If there is anything "miraculous" about the book, it is the result of hard work undertaken in the belief that the work of art is important in itself, that it is a social action in itself. (SA, 142)

Ellison, in other words, was not trying to reject tradition but to return to it, a tradition forced into invisibility not only by American literature but, as we have seen, by American criticism. His objective was to use the technical innovations of the modern novel to alter tradition as he received it, to reinterpret the American canon.

Any attempt at "reinterpretation," of course, suggests the validity of one interpretation over another. From a contemporary perspective, however, this is a very problematic assumption. The idea that a text has a single "true" reading is for the most part, albeit to the regret of some, passé. Recognizing that the answers we get from examining a text are structured by the questions we ask, contemporary critical theorists impel us to examine the conditions which create our questions and the tacit assumptions which those questions reflect. Semiotics, the study of how we interpret signs, leads us therefore to an exploration of what context informs our interpretation (sometimes to the point of proving interpretation itself impossible). As a result some critics believe the state of contemporary criticism to be dangerously relativistic. Gerald Graff, for example, in *Literature against Itself*, locates the source of this relativism not in the postmodern critics but in the modernists, whose love of science brought to the relationship between "reality" and the humanities not a new sense of precision but rather an extension of the theory of relativity.[22] In trying to capture the taxing complexities of a "reality" viewed through the insights of Einstein, Freud, Marx, and Darwin, moreover, Graff finds the modernists doubly culpable: they created and invoked literary conventions so demanding as to distance most readers from their meaning—a situation which in turn emphasized the role of critic as interpreter and deemphasized his or her role as evaluator. For Graff, the logical outgrowth of these conditions was the postmodern shift in the source of meaning from the text to the critic or reader. Whether Graff is right or wrong about the dangers of such a shift, he correctly describes the current state of critical self-consciousness. A kind of wisdom, perhaps, it is a hesitant wisdom (often expressed in annoyingly unhesitant terms) that comes from our unavoidable awareness of alternatives—cultural, sociological, psychological, economic, philosophic—which create endless possibilities in the search for meaning, in the interpretation of signs.

The formalizing and institutionalizing of this type of doubt, of course, makes an agenda for social change difficult, if not impossible, and certainly it distances writing from action. For rather than being a factor in changing the future, the written word becomes an artifact of the already-present. Yet those who have acted blindly at one time or another on manifestos for change might not find this shift to be inherently dangerous. Before following signs, they might not object to understanding more fully what those signs signified; nor might they object, before choosing an alternative, to considering possibilities, however endless those possibilities might seem.

Ralph Ellison's narrator, at the end of *Invisible Man*, is in a role analogous to that of a postmodern critic. Having blindly followed one version of reality and then another, he has stopped to examine the artifacts of his experience—an accumulation of notes, documents, and icons in his leather briefcase—and concluded that interpretation only confirms the version of reality which has already shaped the interpretive questions. The narrator tells us in the epilogue:

> When one is invisible he finds such problems as good and evil, honesty and dishonesty, of such shifting shapes that he confuses one with the other, depending upon who happens to be looking through him at the time. Well, now I've been trying to look through myself, and there's risk in it. I was never more hated than when I tried to be honest. Or when, even as just now, I've tried to articulate exactly what I felt to be the truth. No one was satisfied—not even I. On the other hand, I've never been more loved and appreciated than

when I tried to "justify" and affirm someone's mistaken beliefs; or when I've tried to give my friends the incorrect, absurd answers they wished to hear. (432)

In giving the "absurd answers they wished to hear," the narrator was conforming his speech to an implicit set of assumptions. Yet without some implicit set of assumptions, no meaning of any sort is possible. This is true on the level of linguistics, as de Saussure has made clear, and true in addition on larger social and cultural levels. Always raw data "means" only within shared frameworks for meaning, frameworks which in fact predetermine what constitutes "raw data," how it is collected, and how it is organized.

Frank Kermode has distinguished the raw data in literature from its interpreted meaning by identifying two kinds of reading: carnal and spiritual. In *The Genesis of Secrecy*, Kermode locates the practice of finding a text's secret message in the tradition of Biblical exegesis. This practice of *hermeneutics*, named after the Greek messenger of the gods, Hermes, involves viewing the text with a set of assumptions that will reveal the text's secrets; this results in what Kermode calls a "spiritual" reading to accompany the carnal. The practice of hermeneutics, however, implies a necessary circularity. For although the secret meaning of the text determines the assumptions necessary to reveal that secret, it also is the product of those assumptions. If we change assumptions, therefore, we reveal a different secret.

This lesson in hermeneutics, fundamental to any postmodern interpretation, again sounds strongly similar to the one that the invisible man discovers in his hole, by virtue of becoming invisible. As Marcus Klein points out,

all of his advisers and all of these mementoes have the same veiled, complicated advice for him: of a something unique in Negro life, of something in Negro life hidden, mysterious, and willfully obscured, a something kinetic and not fixed. Negro life contains the necessity for hiding, duplicity, treachery, for adopting shifting roles which the real reality goes on beneath. And the perfect metaphor for all the advice he has received is invisibility. ("Ralph Ellison," 132)

Ellison's protagonist, however, does not seem to have reached this position deductively, as, say, Derrida or Barthes have, via Kant, Nietzsche, de Saussure, and others, but rather inductively, having lived among the kin of Hermes. Hermes, as Kermode tells us,

is the patron of thieves, merchants, and travelers; of heralds and what heralds pronounce, their *kerygma*. He also has to do with oracles, including a dubious sort known as *kledon*, which at the moment of its announcement may seem trivial or irrelevant, the secret sense declaring itself only after long delay, and in circumstances not originally foreseeable. Hermes is cunning, and occasionally violent: a trickster, a robber. So it is not surprising that he is also the patron of interpreters. Sometimes they proclaim an evident sense, like a herald; but they also use cunning, and may claim the right to be violent and glory in it. The rules of their art, and its philosophy, are called "hermeneutics." The word itself, after centuries of innocent use, turns out to have secret senses; for it is now thought by some to connote the most serious philosophical inquiry, to be a means whereby they effect a necessary subversion of the old metaphysics. Even in its more restricted application, which is related to the interpretation of texts, the word covers a considerable range of activity, from the plain proclamation of sense to the oracular intimations of which the true understanding may be delayed for generations, emerging in historical circumstances quite unlike those in which the oracle spoke. Such operations may require the professional use of stealth or violence. (*The Genesis of Secrecy*, 1)

In all the literature noting the folk, classical, and mythological strains in *Invisible Man*, surprisingly, only one critic has identified Hermes—this trickster, underground man, and original runner—as precursor. In 1983 Houston Baker noted the relationship between Jim Trueblood and phallic tricksters, including Hermes ("To Move without Moving," 837). Yet in much of the criticism the implied figure of Hermes looms.

Robert Bone, for instance, evokes the figure of this hidden messenger when he tells us that in Ellison's work one senses "an unseen reality behind the surface of things. Hence his fascination with guises and disguises, with the con man and the trickster. Hence the felt dichotomy between visible and invisible, public and private, actual and fictive modes of reality" ("Ralph Ellison and the Uses of the Imagination," 96). Ellison, like Louis Armstrong, Bone reminds us, uses his cunning and stealth to adopt the role of secret messenger:

> Ellison writes of certain jazz musicians: "While playing in ensemble, they carried themselves like College professors or high church deacons; when soloing they donned the comic mask." Louis Armstrong, as Ellison reminds us, has raised masking to the level of a fine art. Musical trickster, con man with a coronet, Elizabethan clown, "he takes liberties with kings, queens, and presidents". . . .
>
> In his own prose, Ellison employs various masking devices, including understatement, irony, *double-entendre* and calculated ambiguity. There is something deliberately elusive in his style, something secret and taunting, some instinctive avoidance of explicit statement which is close in spirit to the blues. His fascination with masquerade gives us two memorable characters in *Invisible Man*: the narrator's grandfather, whose mask of meekness conceals stubborn resistance to white supremacy, and Rinehart, whom Ellison de-

scribes as "an American virtuoso of identity who thrives on chaos and swift change." (98)

Bone is far from the only critic who feels the invisible man's mercurial nature is best epitomized by his ability to become Proteus Bliss Rinehart, the "SPIRITUAL TECHNOLOGIST." Tony Tanner notes:

> After being taken for a number of contradictory Rineharts— from gambler to Reverend—the narrator suddenly understands and appreciates the significance of this figure. "His world was possibility and he knew it. He was years ahead of me and I was a fool. . . . The world in which we lived was without boundaries. A vast seething, hot world of fluidity, and Rine the rascal was at home. Perhaps *only* Rine the rascal was at home in it." The realization makes him feel as though he had just been released from a plaster cast; it suggests what life on the surface never suggested: "new freedom of movement." "You could actually make yourself anew. The notion was frightening, for now the world seemed to flow before my eyes. All boundaries down, freedom was not only the recognition of necessity, it was the recognition of possibility." This is as succinct an expression of the discovery earned in this book as one could wish for. But what follows is also important. "And sitting there trembling I caught a brief glimpse of the possibilities posed by Rinehart's multiple person-alities and turned away." I stress this because although the narrator learns his most important lesson from the spectacle of Rinehart he does not wish to emulate him. ("The Music of Invisibility," 86–87)

Tanner fails to see, however, that the invisible man, not Rinehart, is the more mercurial of the two, because the invisible man has even more identi-ties than Rinehart in that he can be everything Rinehart is and he can also not-be Rinehart. A chaos of possibilities available to the invisible man (if not available, their rejection would be meaningless), Rinehart physically repre-sents the thesis, in antithesis to which "invisibility" forms the novel's ultimate dialectic. But that dialectic merely echoes more concretely, more emblemati-cally, earlier alternatives. At every stage, the narrator's imagery links the in-visible man to the oppressor who has selected a role for him to fulfill; at every stage he verges on accepting that role, on accepting someone else's defini-tion—no matter how incompletely understood—of himself.

The figure of Rinehart, I think, is not so important as the invisible man's ability to become him—or not. In acquiring this ability, he fully becomes the marginal man, the crosser of borders, who contains secrets and uses disguise. For, most important, the figure of Rinehart is about secrecy, his identity an interconnection of secrets, a self-contained structure of secrecy, which the invisible man learns to interpret. In acquiring the secret, furthermore, he becomes the secret's sharer, its messenger and its "interpreter" in another sense. If the shift from interpreter meaning *decoder* to interpreter meaning *encoder* seems paradoxical, it is a paradox integral to the figure of Hermes, that is, the paradox of hermeneutics about which I have been speaking.

That paradox is revealed in another form in *Invisible Man*'s widely noted relationship to folk material. Although Floyd Horowitz asserts that the invisible man chronically plays the role of "Brer Bear" ("Ralph Ellison's Modern Version of Brer Bear and Brer Rabbit," 21–27), O'Meally indicates that he also plays the role antithetical to Brother Bear's dupe, that of Brother Rabbit, the trickster (*The Craft of Ralph Ellison*, 79). Blake asserts, moreover, that he plays these roles and others that relate to folklore in tales that represent the slave's point of view and in tales that represent the master's ("Black Folklore in the Works of Ralph Ellison"). Blake views what she perceives as Ellison's attempt to merge slave mythology and plantation mythology as contradictory and, ultimately, as undermining the strains of black folk culture. Where Blake finds subversion and contradiction, however, I find a lesson in hermeneutics and the lurking figure of Hermes constantly defying us to fix the message of a tale.

William Schafer comes particularly close to seeing the relationship between the trickster and secret messenger when he reminds us:

> It is a commonplace to note that Negro humor is at once a means of catharsis and a form of "code" communication. Wit and reflexive irony have been staples of Negro jokes, songs and folk tales for centuries. During slavery times, comic tales formed a mythology for a largely illiterate and scattered captive culture; they provided relief from suffering and degradation and a binding force or sense of identity for the blacks. . . . Humor in its simplest and most direct forms pervaded black culture, developing from the language itself—arising from neologic dialects and slang terms on through a rich and complex folklore still only partially appreciated. Humor permeated secular music, from field shouts and blues through party songs and jazz; all the forms of black music reveal acute wit and self-analysis. ("Irony from Underground," 22)

We see signs of Schafer's own hidden assumptions in the phrase "still only partially appreciated"—we might ask: by whom? Certainly they were fully appreciated by those who encoded the messages, and still are by those who can decode them. Those ignorant of the hidden message, those with carnal knowledge but not spiritual—the body but not the soul—continue to remain outside the secret, still not appreciating the joke because they are, by virtue of their ignorance, its butt. The difference between Schafer's set of assumptions—his hermeneutic—and Ellison's becomes even more evident as Schafer goes on to explain that "Ellison has used all the resources of folk humor, black slang and the 'underground' viewpoint of the Negro as his literary material. The imaginary synthesis of non-literary attitudes and ideas is a testimonial to Ellison's skill in coping with a largely unexplored subculture"

(22). Again we can ask Schafer: "unexplored by whom?" But we know the answer because we are able to infer Schafer's meaning not from the information in the text but from the set of assumptions they imply. Those assumptions limit the possible "explorers" to exclude, for instance, microbe hunters and moonwalkers.

My intention in belaboring the obvious here is to suggest one of the reasons something seems obvious is that it operates within a set of assumptions—rarely articulated—implied by the text and assumed by the audience so quickly that the text virtually interprets itself. When we strip away those assumptions, we delimit the possibilities. This, I would contend, is what *Invisible Man*'s narrator does by approaching American life and culture from what Schafer calls "the 'underground' viewpoint of the Negro." From that viewpoint, of course, one might challenge Schafer's distinction between literary and nonliterary material. Although Schafer may see Ellison as synthesizing "non-literary attitudes and ideas," someone with a different set of assumptions might consider folk material highly literary.

I have dwelled on Schafer's statements not only because they provide exempla for a discussion of hermeneutics, but also because the content as much as their analyses reveals the connection between Hermes and Ellison's protagonist. Schafer rightly understands that slaves, like all oppressed groups (e.g., early Christians), practiced encoding and thus created what Kermode would call spiritual texts out of carnal, requiring a descendant of Hermes to guide us across the margins of discourse and turn our blindness into insight.

The question remains, however, how we can know if any given text has a secret, and the paradox is that we only know by discovering signs which reveal that secret. It is the solution which differentiates puzzle from chaos, and only after the puzzle ceases to be a puzzle do we know it was one, instead of random carnage. But perhaps the same puzzle can be assembled two different ways, revealing two different pictures, one with square borders containing curved pieces, and one with round borders holding angular parts. By sorting and assembling according to the form we infer earliest, we determine our results. To carry this metaphor just a bit further, let us assume that from our experience with similar puzzles, we know that no finished puzzle uses all the pieces, or that some puzzles have pieces missing. We never know, then, if we have discovered all the possibilities—all the secrets of the puzzle—nor do we know whether the secrets were discoverable. This is the position of the modern reader, who may, in an act of faith, cast some critic, theory, or philosophy in the role of Hermes, the god who will reward that faith with the key to decode a secret message. What a semiotician, like *Invisible Man*'s narrator, comes to know is that Hermes can also be the trickster who disguises the secret. Horrifyingly, from some points of view, this may suggest that the narrator has abandoned social action for interpretation: "I believed in hard work and progress and action, but now, after first being 'for' society and then 'against' it, I assign myself no rank or any limit, and such an attitude is very much against the trend of the times. But my world has become one of infinite possibilities" (435).

Yet this insight does not remain divorced from social action, for the epilogue concludes with the assertion that the narrator's hibernation is over, that even an invisible man might have a socially useful function. As many critics have indicated, that conclusion comes from the process of retelling the tale. The act of writing or telling becomes an act of interpreting which will return the narrator to action. To this extent, the narrator remains similar to modernists rather than postmodernists. As C. W. E. Bigsby astutely points out, "if history is indeed fiction, Ellison does not press this perception to the logical limits explored by Pynchon, Coover or Kosinski, for where they see a relativism which breeds only irony, an irony which reaches out to include the fiction which contains it, Ellison is drawn to a liberal model in which the individual invents himself through his dialogue with society" ("The Flight of Words," 96). Others remain unconvinced, however, about the outcome of that dialogue. For Addison Gayle, the novel's ending is flawed because "Ellison's protagonist chooses death over life, opts for non-creativity in favor [sic] of creativity, chooses the path of individualism instead of racial unity" (*The Way of The World*, 213).

The question of "racial unity," of the "appropriate" stance for Afro-American literature has—as all questions structure answers—structured much of the *Invisible Man* criticism, almost from the book's publication. At its core is the more basic debate over the appropriate relationship of modernism to Afro-American values. For many critics modernism is necessarily opposed to ethnicity or folk culture, and "Afro-American modernism" is necessarily a contradiction in terms. Modernism was, after all, the argument goes, the invention of fascist, racist, elitists. They wrote, furthermore, for an elite readership, creating difficult languages and complicated conventions which rendered their works far less immediately accessible than the classics from which they drew. Although they adapted or alluded to myths, they did so in such a way as to divorce them from their broad cultural origins. Such techniques, the argument follows, are inherently antithetical to the goal of speaking for the oppressed or disenfranchised who have limited access to the oppressor's "culture" and, perhaps, ought not in any case desire to emulate it.

In an essay entitled "The Survival of Black Literature and Its Criticism," John Oliver Perry expresses a version of this view:

> To deal with those forces of modernism and postmodernism, black literature needs strong programs of defense and offense. Paradoxically, however, developing new theories to resist assimilation by the dominant culture may contribute to overwhelming the most distinctive qualities of black art. Though black critics and artists can wield the tools of modern literary technology as

well as anyone . . . few of them would deny that one strength of black cul-
tures lies in abjuring elaborate self-conscious tricks and conjuring instead with
techniques from the preliterate folk tradition, where spontaneous, or at least
extemporized individual forms incorporate communal or ritual structures.
Can black writing freely develop that tradition? (170)

Like Graff, Perry sees modernism and postmodernism as a reactionary con-
tinuum, one he considers antithetical to the folk culture of suppressed minorities. In the work of James Joyce—whom Ellison claims as stylistic mentor[23]—we can, however, see the ways in which modernism, folk culture, and
ethnic identity embrace one another.

Robert List in his book *Dedalus in Harlem* suggests that Joyce was Ellison's
stylistic mentor because Joyce experimented with literary technique in order
to assert ethnic identity as a member of an oppressed culture (or race). To
support this claim, List demonstrates the influence on *Invisible Man* not only
of *A Portrait of the Artist as a Young Man* but also of *Ulysses* and *Finnegans
Wake.* The importance of List's implications extends beyond the direct connection between Ellison and Joyce, because seeing *Invisible Man* in the tradition of *Ulysses* and *Finnegans Wake* alters considerably the critical expectations we bring to Ellison's text. They mandate a heightened awareness of
Ellison not only as an American writer and as an ethnic writer but also as a
very self-conscious modernist. They suggest we approach *Invisible Man* with
the same critical apparatus that we would bring to a passage from *Ulysses*—a
consciousness of historical, philosophical, and psychological backgrounds, an
awareness of theme and leitmotif, and above all a sensitivity to a language
which creates and disassembles hierarchies through echo, allusion, and
parody as it juxtaposes strains of catholic and eclectic literary and ethnic traditions. Like Joyce, Ellison employs modernist techniques to establish his
ethnic identity, and the more we examine his text as a modernist text, the
more it reveals that black American identity.

Although we do not need Harold Bloom to tell us that, for an artist, tradition always connotes authority, thinking about the relationship between ethnic identity and Joyce's stylistic rebellions helps us see the limitations of Irving
Howe's famous charge that Ellison had not been true enough to black experience.[24] A more sophisticated version of that charge was made by Susan
Blake, more recently: "Ellison's adaptation of Black folklore, however invol-
untarily, exchanges the self definition of the folk for the definition of the
masters" ("Black Folklore in the Works of Ralph Ellison," 135). Both criticisms seem, in the light of List's book, like claims that Joyce was not true
enough to Irish experience.

The value of List's approach becomes apparent when we examine his treatment of the Peter Wheatstraw scene in *Invisible Man* (chapter 9). Peter
Wheatstraw is a black pushcart man with a cart full of blueprints, whose

folk singing reminds the invisible man of home, and whose irreverent street talk challenges the invisible man into accepting his racial identity. Robert O'Meally identifies the source of Wheatstraw's blues songs and tells us:

> Peter Wheatstraw, strolling in Harlem, helps the slow-to-learn hero make a vital connection: southern black folk experience must not be discarded in the North. . . .
>   The Harlem bluesman's song also prepares the hero for the disappointment he must face when he learns that Bledsoe and the trustees have conspired to "keep him running." Here the blues not only serve as an antidote for pain but seem to describe with humorous exaggeration the quality of his luck: "Feet like a monkey, Legs like a maaad bulldog!" (*The Craft of Ralph Ellison*, 88)

List, however, shows the folk elements, as Ellison employs them, allude strongly to *Finnegans Wake*, that Wheatstraw's language (not to mention his name) is full of Joycean puns, and that Ellison's text uses Jungian archetypes and reflects a Viconian sense of history. Wheatstraw's phrase "Oh goddog, daddy-o," for example, not only uses folk idiom but also alludes to the fall of the Father-God (198–201). If we expect this subtlety of craft from Ellison, we can begin to see how strongly Ellison's Afro-American identity is manifest through his modernism, not in spite of it.

Yet all this modernist technique has, I have suggested, culminated in the narrator's assuming a postmodern stance, as interpreter of signs, outside of time, framing experience with a new set of questions. Although this would seem to support the contention that postmodernism follows from modernism rather than reacts to it, the interpretations impelled by the narrator do not end in mere relativism. Instead they alter the reader's understanding of history, culture, and literature by exposing the invisible assumptions which structure that understanding. Using the stylistic techniques he learned from studying *Ulysses* and *Finnegans Wake*, Ellison constructed an intense network of allusions in contexts which force the reader to reinterpret their historical or literary referents. Ellison, however, does not create a deconstruction but rather reconstructs a coherent alternative to the "accepted" ways of reading American history and literature in 1952.

2. Translating Tradition

Since much of my study of *Invisible Man* relies not only on a complex understanding of Ralph Ellison's use of allusion but also on an understanding of allusion in general, it is necessary now to take an extended look at that literary device so heavily employed by Ellison's stylistic mentors, Eliot and Joyce. This is especially necessary because surprisingly little has been written about theory of allusion.[1] Ziva Ben-Porat sums up the situation remarkably well when she says, "The paucity of theoretical discussion of literary allusion stands in strikingly inverse proportion to the abundance of both actual allusion in literary works and the focus on particular allusions in many critical writings" ("The Poetics of Literary Allusion," 106). This is particularly surprising in light of all the contemporary work relating linguistics to literature.[2] One could make the case that implicit in this work or derivable from it is the idea that all language is allusion, that "allusion" accurately describes the relationship between the "signifier" and the "signified."

If we wish, however, to focus on practical literary criticism—wish to consider the world made up of many things, of which literature is a part, and language is a part, but neither the consuming whole—then it may be useful to make some finer distinctions. I want to limit this discussion, therefore, to literary allusions and examine descriptions of the process by which readers make meaning through attending to allusion.[3] For that reason it may be useful to look at this problem in intertextual relationships as it has been framed by some modern and contemporary critics.

Reuben Brower's *Alexander Pope—The Poetry of Allusion* is a good starting point.[4] For Brower, allusion is a way of embracing the past and blending it with the topical. Citing the Augustan sense of balance between the novel and the traditional, Brower lauds those poets who successfully achieve this blend. Dryden's poetry, he says, "brought the larger light of European literature and European past into verse of local public debate" (127).

His mode is allusive in a wide variety of ways: in close imitation or parody of other writers, in less exact references to language, styles, and conventions of

other literatures—Classical, Biblical, and French—in drawing on the large
materials of philosophy and theology, in playing of popular parallels between
contemporary religious and political situations and those of ancient history,
sacred and secular. Through this mode Dryden makes his "affirmation of
Europe." (8)

This paragraph gives us a concise survey of the forms of allusion, and, more
important here, suggests that an allusion is an act of affirmation, an appeal to
recognized values in the face of transient experience. The contemporary
writer affirms affiliation with the past, and the result is that "thanks to Dryden
the tone of Augustan poetry is less parochial than it might have been: it is
resonant with echoes of other literary worlds, of larger manners and events"
(*Alexander Pope*, 11).

The Continent—both a historical and a physical entity—with its *larger*
manners and events, sheds its *larger* light on the "modern." The past, in this
way, becomes the constant against which modern life can be measured and
criticized: "Let us consider more particularly how this mode worked, how and
why epic allusions offered Dryden a way of expressing important values. In
ironic contexts, the more or less close imitations of epic introduced a standard
of manners and actions by which the exploits of politicians and poetasters
might be measured" (*Alexander Pope*, 10).

Because criticism—social, literary, religious—grounded solely in contemporary standards lacks the heft of more universal authority, allusions not only
identify a work with the "larger" past, but also measure the "smaller" present,
and thereby eliminate some of the relativism involved in making judgments.
Dryden's satire, therefore, measures life not only in the dim light of contemporary standards but in the larger light of tradition, and universality is all-
important because it makes the topical endure.

Since writing a poem which refers to the larger past secures for it the in-
definite future, the skillful use of allusion enlarges the immediate work; but
in another way, it diminishes the immediate work. For the act of affirmation
is also an act of subordination; implicit in the affirmation of the past is the
sense that the past is a standard to which the present ought be adapted. When
a work brings tradition into it, therefore, it also enters into that tradition, so
that the attempt to embrace the past is also a call to be embraced by it. The
past, in other words, remains the knowable constant applied to the unknow-
able—unfolding—work, and thus tradition is static.

One can easily see how this static vision could come under criticism from
any of a number of contemporary critics and theorists. But it may be more
useful here to compare Brower's view of tradition with the view held by someone normally considered an antagonist by postmodern critics, T. S. Eliot. In
Eliot's famous essay "Tradition and the Individual Talent," I think we can see
a crucial difference between his view of the past and the role it plays and

Brower's.[5] Both men see it as essential to the creation of "new" art, and they both see it as enlarging in essential ways the scope of the artist's work. Brower's sense of the relationship, however, is more schematized. The juxtaposition of old and new causes us simultaneously to see more intensely local issues as well as their more universal implications; the traditional and the modern are discrete components which the reader's experience synthesizes. For Eliot, the synthesis occurs earlier. As Eliot tells us:

> the historical sense involves a perception, not only of the pastness of the past, but of its presence; the historical sense compels a man to write not merely with his own generation in his bones, but with a feeling that the whole of the literature of Europe from Homer and within it the whole of the literature of his own country has a simultaneous existence and composes a simultaneous order. This historical sense, which is a sense of the timeless as well as of the temporal and of the timeless and of the temporal together, is what makes a writer traditional. And it is at the same time what makes a writer most acutely conscious of his place in time, of his own contemporaneity. (*The Sacred Wood*, 49)

In many ways, we can see this is little different from the kind of praise Brower gave Dryden. It certainly expresses the interdependence of the local and universal. But the chief difference is the location of the simultaneity. Rather than the *work* containing the discrete components, the *artist* contains them. In his "bones" reside "a sense of the timeless as well as of the temporal and of the timeless and of the temporal together." Unless we consider this repetition redundant, we can assume that Eliot is reaching for some very fine distinctions. He is making us aware, I believe, of a paradoxical condition that precedes artistic creation but is essential to it. The artist cannot have a developed historical sense by accident. Although we all have some sense of our time, which is historical, whether we know it or not, we cannot develop, enlarge, perfect it, without making distinctions, without compartmentalizing and categorizing. One cannot develop a sophisticated historical sense without knowing, for example, the difference between Renaissance and Roman drama, or without recognizing some basic allusions or parallels. But "newness" is, for Eliot, an essential quality for a work of art.

To arrive at this newness which manifests the past, the artist must, therefore, both invoke and overcome his or her historical sense. He or she must know the difference between the past and the present so well as to be able to afford not to know it. The making of something new requires a breaking down between time present and time past, so that tradition, for Eliot, means the manifestation of the past in the new. The artist, through the simultaneous awareness and suppression of this historical sense, synthesizes tradition and contemporary experience, and that experience thus enters into tradition.

This approach has one very important implication. Brower emphasizes the way the modern work is intensified, extended, universalized; but if, as Eliot suggests, the new work, simultaneous to its creation, manifests tradition, then since the tradition has a new component, it is no longer the same tradition. Its own manifestation has altered it. For, when we deal with the concept of tradition, we see that *only its own manifestation can alter it*.

We can see the difference between Brower's view and Eliot's in another way: Brower, unlike Eliot, seems to separate the critical and the creative arenas. For Brower, therefore, the term "tradition" functions differently in each. In criticism, tradition is a descriptive quality that identifies the way we perceive the past and categorize its traits. In that sense, certainly Dryden alters tradition and Pope extends the altered tradition. But within the artistic work, "tradition" means a series of reference points against which the contemporary is measured. The way of perceiving the past, therefore, is not based on a static view of it, the "permanence" that Matthew Arnold stresses, but on a dynamic view wherein the perspective always alters so long as there is to be any artistic activity.[6]

Allusions form a constant, for Brower, against which the present is measured, a balance between the stable background and the dynamic foreground. Brower, for example, makes much of the use of the word "happy" in a section of *The Dunciad*. The context recalls the Virgilian ideal and the deflated eighteenth-century use. Again the allusion provides the constant in the context which is adaptive and ironic in complex ways. Pope thus restores some of the complexity to the shepherd's song (*Alexander Pope*, 33–34).

But if we think of the new usage as changing the meaning of the word "happy," not just for the contemporary usage but for all of its usages, if we think of it as altering the original source of the allusion, we see the stress that Eliot's sense of tradition places on our consciousness. We have a vision in which the foreground can alter the background, and the eye must approximate its measurement in the tension between the changing two.

Against this background—a background which sees a fissuring in the attitude toward the past, the interrelation of old and new—two more recent examinations of the meaning of self-referentiality in literature make an interesting comparison. Both Northrop Frye and Harold Bloom seem to be excavating this fissure in tradition with very different results which help define the contemporary limits within which the concepts of self-referentiality and allusion function. In dealing with tradition, it is these limits which must be negotiated for Ellison to find a way of embracing the past without affirming its received interpretations. If the circumstances of American literary and historical discourse had relegated him to a position of invisibility, he had to alter those circumstances in some way, not just present his own reaction to them. This is not possible, I try to show, if we view the past from the interpretive perspective of either Frye—who alienates the individual artist by institution-alizing tradition—or Bloom—who alienates the artist by isolating the re-sponse. If my readings of these two critics are correct, then both their ap-proaches do not provide means for Ellison to speak from invisibility but means by which that invisibility becomes reinscribed.

Frye rarely uses the word "allusion," but his theory of "displacement" as articulated in *Fables of Identity* and *Anatomy of Criticism* comes so close to being a theory of allusion that it deserves serious examination here. Frye views literature as a self-contained universe, dealing not with reality but with con-ventions of reality. Literature, in other words, never refers to the amalgam of experience we generally call "the real world"; it refers, rather, to other stories:

> Literature may have life, reality, experience, nature, imaginative truth, social
> conditions or what you will for its *content*; but literature itself is not made out
> of these things. Poetry can only be made out of other poems; novels out of
> other novels. Literature shapes itself, and is not shaped externally: the *forms*
> of literature can no more exist outside literature than the forms of sonata and
> fugue and rondo can exist outside music. (*Anatomy*, 97)

That self-contained world, therefore, is heavily, is perhaps exclusively, self-referential. "Literary shape," Frye tells us in his essay "Myth, Fiction and Displacement," "cannot come from life; it comes only from literary tradition, so ultimately from myth" (*Fables*, 36). There exists for Frye, in other words, an ultimate source of images and narrative structure, but it is not only a source meaning a pool from which to draw, but also a source meaning a generating cause. Speaking of G. K. Chesterton's poem, "The Donkey," he says, "the allusion to the first Palm Sunday is not incidental to the poem: it is the whole point of the poem: it is, once again, its formal cause" (*Fables*, 46).

Literature, therefore, seems to be not only self-contained but also self-generating. Frye thus appears thoroughly to ignore the author. And in certain ways the role of the author is, if not ignored, then overshadowed by the gen-eral flow of movement of literature, which forms, for Frye, a cycle or a num-ber of cycles.[7] Each amounts, basically, to a kind of literary climate which supplies the body of material—world of literature—from which an author can draw, and thereby limits the possibilities for adaptations. This is aug-mented by a social climate, outside the world of literature, which defines the audience's expectations. The author adjusts that from which he or she can draw to that which is expected. These adaptations (e.g., of genre, mode, treatment) are necessary so that the audience can suspend its disbelief. The author thus uses hidden myths—indirectly mythologizes—and the method of that indirection is "displacement," "the techniques a writer uses to make his story credible, logically motivated or morally acceptable—lifelike, in short" (*Fables*, 86). The prime function of criticism, then, is to discover the displaced myth and thus "understand the corresponding place that a work of literature has in the context of literature as a whole" (*Fables*, 37). In this way we shall move from what Frye calls a "criticism of 'effects' " (i.e., New Criticism) to "a criticism of causes, specifically the formal cause which holds the work together" (*Fables*, 37).

It is possible, therefore, to say that myth criticism is the identification of allusions, but the term "allusion" generally implies, and certainly does for Frye, an author's conscious reference to a literary precursor. Frye is interested, however, in showing that, acknowledged or not, conscious or not, all authors owe this debt, all of the time. Obviously, conscious, overt allusions help support his case for literature's state of literary indebtedness. But these allusions support it *so* obviously that they can be taken for granted. Both the interest in and validity of Frye's argument, therefore, rest on the discovery of the covert. For this reason, Frye finds that discussing parallels in imagery between Eliot's *Ash Wednesday* and Dante's *Purgatorio*, in view of the explicit and avowed debt of the poem to the *Purgatorio*, "may not seem very significant. It is all the more interesting to compare the treatment of the 'winding stair' image in Yeats, as there, whatever influence from Dante there may be, the attitude taken towards the ascent is radically different" (*Fables*, 61).

Frye here is differentiating between the meaning of an image and the attitude toward it. He wants to show that the meaning transcends the attitude, which he shows best by identifying the image not in the context of the works in which it is found but in the context of a tradition which supplies the source of the image and, therefore, its meaning. The critic's job is to identify the covert image and relate it to its original form—its archetype—in the source myth. An overt allusion, especially to something very old and basic— Oedipus, Adam and Eve, Thor—does a large part of the critic's work.

In this light, Ellison's allusions to the tricksters and dupes, in the forms of Brer Rabbit and Brer Bear, become displacements of the low-norm *eiron* in the satiric counterpart to the comedy of escape—the picaresque novel, which is "the story of the successful rogue who, from Reynard the Fox on, makes conventional society look foolish without setting up any positive standard" (*Anatomy*, 229). Whether or not *Invisible Man* has elements of the picaresque novel (certainly it does), Frye's critical approach emphasizes them at the expense of the specific conditions that created the Brer Bear and Brer Rabbit versions of the *eiron*. Indeed, those animal figures may be connected to earlier animals of myth and fable, or—since Frye asserts symbolic equivalence between worlds animal, mineral, vegetable, human, and divine (*Anatomy*, 141)—the tricky slave of Roman comedy, but they also manifest the specific marks of oppression and consequent encoding created by the racial caste system deeply embedded in the legal and extralegal institutions of the South. The slave in Roman comedy who wins his freedom ceases to be in an ironic position; he is not merely *ostensibly* free, not, like the free black in the South, a slave without a master.

Of course, following Frye, we could say that the irony of trickster victories in *Invisible Man* merely shows that ours is a more ironic age and, therefore, the Ellisonian tricksters are more ironic displacements of slaves in Roman comedy or satire. But it is exactly that difference that separates Afro-American experience from its precursors; it is exactly the obscuring of that difference which enables a critic to equate the slaveholding South with the Roman empire and label them both as nominally "conventional." If Frye is right, moreover, a work which appears to make no allusions is just as heavily allusive as, for instance, *The Waste Land*. Frye sees the archetypal images and patterns as few, the displacements as many, and as many times removed. *Anatomy of Criticism* thus functions to identify, as systematically as possible, the various archetypes and the various ways in which they can be displaced, making the book analogous to a diagnostic physician's handbook of diseases and symptoms. The New Critics, then, are like doctors who treat the symptom rather than the disease. They treat a patient with sores and another and another, but they have no idea what an epidemic is, nor what smallpox is. This is what Frye means by criticism of effects rather than causes.

Frye wants to go, in other words, to the cause, but the idea of a "cause," like the idea of "displacement," entails assumptions about tradition. The first assumption is that there is an original source, a point of origin from which all flows. The second assumption is that the source has, by virtue of its primacy, a sacrosanct, or at least inviolable, integrity. The displacements are ever changing, are synonymous with change, while the archetypes are synonymous with permanence. The second assumption brings us back again to the idea of tradition and its relationship to the allusive present.

Frye's view of tradition seems to be somewhere between the static one implied by Reuben Brower and the dynamic one presented by Eliot. The word "tradition," like the word "allusion," is one Frye tends to avoid, but he does have a keen sense of the past, sees it as a unified whole, and sees the body of mythology as being altered by new works. This alteration in fact forms the very soul of literary activity. The story of the Fall moves through history, being altered in each age and genre. On the other hand, these alterations cause one another to happen in a predictable order, which is cyclical. All these alterations, therefore, ultimately produce no change. Frye has, in essence, taken Eliot's awareness of the dynamism of the past-in-the-present and used it to argue the opposite. For when one focuses on the *process* of change, rather than the *product*, change becomes a constant, as do the predictable points dependent on the constant cycle of change.[8]

Like Brower, Frye sees "tradition" as having great authority: "Agamemnon is one of the founding fathers of our literary society: that is why an allusion to him has the tremendous evocative authority of our whole literary tradition behind it" (*Fables*, 46). Although Frye does not quite make clear what he means by "tremendous evocative authority," Frye's sense of allusiveness, in a way oddly similar to Brower's, provides a way of measuring the contemporary in the light of tradition.

Frye's referents, furthermore, are even more stable than Brower's because they are in no way dependent on society. No age or opinion has changed them and none will or can. An age merely displaces them, which is both a radical alteration and no alteration at all. By accepting Frye's premises we enter into a world of displaced absolutes, with the degree of displacement, therefore, providing a measurement of the present age. A displacement, then, is a form of allusion that changes the original in ways more drastic than Brower ever attributed, certainly, to Pope and, almost as certainly, to the device of allusion. In displacement, the referent is disguised almost beyond recognition. But the "almost" is crucial, because once the recognition takes place, the whole disguise is penetrated and we discover the original in its pure form. We then have a reliable measure for the present: X is romantic displacement of myth A ∴ X is the product of a romantic period; Y is a low mimetic displacement of the same myth; Z is an ironic displacement. Looking up from the microscope, after examining these three slides, our diagnostician says: these are all pox—small, chicken, and cow. No new strains, no mutations alter the generic category. The discovery of frog pox or big pox would not change the archetype, the "poxness." The laws of physical nature are always at work: "The archetypal critic studies the poem as part of poetry, and poetry as part of the total human imitation of nature that we call civilization. Civilization is not merely an imitation of nature, but the process of making a total form out of nature, and it is impelled by the force that we have just called desire" (*Anatomy*, 105).

Within the framework of this cosmology, we can lose not only Ellison but also the authors to whom he alludes. Consider, for example, Ellison's allusions to *A Portrait of the Artist as a Young Man*. At the beginning of the prologue, the invisible man describes an incident in which he bumped into a blond, blue-eyed stranger who, in response, called him an insulting name. "I sprang at him, grabbed his coat lapels and demanded he apologize . . . I pulled his chin down sharp upon the crown of my head, butting him as I had seen the West Indians do, and I felt his flesh tear and the blood gush out, and I yelled, 'Apologize! Apologize!' " (4). The "Apologize! Apologize!" echoes strongly Stephen Dedalus' opening monologue in which the childhood images of guilt and retribution combine in nursery rhyme form:

Pull out his eyes,
Apologize,

Apologize,
Pull out his eyes.

Apologize,
Pull out his eyes,
Pull out his eyes,
Apologize. (8)

In the invisible man's prologue, as in Dedalus' monologue, the cries for apology combine with the threat of blindness. The invisible man's invisibility is a function of blindness, and the novel is full of images of distorted vision, blindfolds, and other forms of sightlessness. Unlike Joyce, however, Ellison locates these traits in the antagonist not the protagonist. To the extent that the invisible man, too, feels guilt and retribution, in the context of the prologue, the allusion to Joyce helps establish a sense in which the invisible man serves as a mirror of the world around him. To put it another way, the allusion helps us to see *Invisible Man* as a portrait of society as a young man, a point made at the end of the novel when the narrator says to the reader, "Who knows but that, on the lower frequencies, I speak for you?" (439). This fulfills the implications of the altered Joyce allusion by making explicit the suggestion that the search for artistic individuality is also a social not only a personal issue.

This is one of many ways, furthermore, in which the novel demonstrates its oft-repeated assertion that the end is in the beginning. The narrator tells us in the prologue about his own narration that "the end is in the beginning and lies far ahead" (5), and at the end of Tod's funeral oration he says, "that's the end in the beginning and there's no encore" (343). The last sentence of chapter 25 again returns to that idea: "The end was in the beginning" (431). The phrase also alludes to T. S. Eliot's "East Coker," the second of his *Four Quartets*, which begins "In my beginning is my end" and concludes "In my end is my beginning." Like the *Four Quartets*, *Invisible Man* uses paradigms from music as an organizing structure and then integrates musical time with historical and personal. Like Eliot, Ellison implies a quest's cyclical nature by virtue of the way memory alters time, so that, as the opening of the *Four Quartets* says, "Time present and time past / Are both perhaps present in time future, / And time future contained in time past."

This understanding of time is fundamental to modernism, and *Four Quartets* is far from the only work to show this influence of Freud and Einstein. The famous last passage of *The Great Gatsby*, for example, has Nick ever moving forward into the past, which is, of course, the general motion of Proust's *Recherche du Temps Perdu*, a motion hermeticized by the structure of *Finnegans Wake*. Joyce perhaps more than any other modernist understood the complexity of time and its relationship to literature. He grasped the infinite possibilities in puns, allusions, echoes, and parodies to condense and expand literary time.

In Frye's vision, however, the subtlety of these devices would be lost in an interest of tracking down the mythic implications. The issue of guilt and retribution would be low-mimetic variations on the Icarus/Daedalus myth, which itself is a variant on the story of pride and the Fall. "Eagle" and "eye" become references to bird and sun symbols which combine with water images to give the book its epiphany, that is, proof of redemption. Since, for Frye, "epiphany" is the "symbolic presentation of the point at which the undisplaced apocalyptic world and the cyclical world of nature come into alignment" (*Anatomy*, 203), it is not surprising that he reads literature for its revelation of the informing myth:

> Learned mythopoeia as we have it . . . in James Joyce, for example, may become bewilderingly complex; *but the complexities are designed to reveal and not to disguise the myth.* We cannot assume that a primitive and popular myth has been swathed like a mummy in elaborate verbiage, which is the assumption that the fallacy of reduction would lead to. The inference seems to be that the learned and the subtle, like the primitive and the popular, tend toward a center of imaginative experience. (*Anatomy*, 117; emphasis added)

The inference is that civilization can be regarded as a version of nature so that the same rules of mutation and causality apply if we are able to identify correctly the corresponding coordinates.[9] Frye seems to believe that finding these coordinates is generally possible, for he says: "We said we could get a whole liberal education by picking up one conventional poem, *Lycidas*, for example, and following its archetypes through literature. Thus the center of the literary universe is whatever poem we happen to be reading. One step further, and the poem appears as a microcosm of all literature, an individual manifestation of the total order of words" (*Anatomy*, 121). From one poem, in other words, we can clone all of literature. Note how this presumes that there is no difference between "all of literature" when Milton wrote *Lycidas* and all of literature today. Literature is not only, therefore, unchanging but reducible to a small number of components, like the physical elements set out in the periodic table.

And this is, perhaps, why Frye's theory is so problematic: the metaphor of the scientist is, after all, only a metaphor. Ideas have no physical properties and, therefore, cannot retain them, nor can they be shown to fit into physically predictable patterns or to be mutually exclusive. Ideas neither occupy space nor respond to the physical environment. Nature, on the other hand, not only regularly produces observable phenomena, but also loses part of its past: petals shed, leaves rot, snow melts. Since ideas, however, have the potential for infinite overlap, the assertion that they fit into a large consistent scheme relies more on faith than on reason.

Perhaps present ideas can change the way we regard old ideas. Frye half says this: "Wherever we turn in literature, it is the same story: every fresh contact with 'life' involves a reshaping of literary convention" (*Fables*, 48). But Frye backs off from the full implications of the word "reshaping" so that a "reshaping of literary convention," by the end of the passage, based on the examples cited, becomes *the convention of reshaping*. The emphasis is not on the reshaping but on its conventionality. Perhaps, however, conventions are reshaped in the true sense. Perhaps it is possible to reshape anything beyond recognition. If so, how do we fit the new aberration into our scheme? More important, what are the crucial qualities (i.e., those which must be retained) if we are to identify the new version with the original? What I am raising is the traditional metaphysical quest for essence (at the time that Frye wrote *Anatomy of Criticism*, it was particularly popular to call this an "existential" question), and I raise it here not to answer it or even to explore it, but to illustrate the kind of mire into which Frye's presumption of an inviolable archetype leads. His theory of displacement is exceptionally valuable in seeing relationships between works, but it suffers, I think, under the demands of his rigid cosmology. Perhaps any use of an allusion alters the old in a new way. Perhaps because ideas don't have to oblige physical law, can superimpose upon one another and/or yield, destroy or undermine one another, their potential is greater than anything physical. Can't they be molded through a constant series of modifications and criticisms, and, most important, doesn't every use modify the whole ever so slightly?

To read Ellison through Frye, therefore, makes it virtually impossible to see tradition as altered, not only because of Frye's theological cosmology but also because of his critical practices which reify that cosmology. Since his investigation does not test and prove the sacrosanct status of the past—and ultimately the Word—but presumes it, his anatomy creates a taxonomy and critical vocabulary to insulate and defend that status, appropriating any possible challenge in the profane world by giving it a sacred classification. The informing myth indeed comes from Genesis, but it informs Frye's enterprise, not all of literature's. Frye plays the role of Adam, who by naming all the creatures large and small exercises authority delegated by God and thereby affirms God's dominion forever. Henceforth, humans can neither create nor destroy, only resist or comply, misconstrue or understand. No author or critic can change the eternal elements or the cyclical plan in which they function; they may merely assume one of the roles Frye in the name of the Word has identified. Canons, too, obey divine ordinance and are not subject to reinterpretation. To identify Tod Clifton as a Christ figure in *Invisible Man* (as I do in chapter 3) would show that Ellison was affirming the universality of the Christ myth and that I was making that universality visible. No matter how sharply Ellison alters the myth, no matter what implications I draw from those alterations, for Frye the immutable essence would remain the same and the deviance would reside in Ellison, whose alteration could be classified under the rubric of irony as, nevertheless, an affirmation.

If Frye sees clearly the allusive nature of literature, he can reconstitute
alteration as affirmation because, I believe, he belittles the effect allusiveness
has on a reader. Harold Bloom, at the other end of the spectrum, is interested
in this allusive nature *only as it affects the reader*, especially the poet-as-
reader, or the reader-as-poet. Bloom, in fact, makes no distinction: all readers
are potential poets (i.e., have poetic impulses) and thus are in the position of
rivalry with any work they read. That rivalry, according to Bloom, creates a
response in the poet/reader that is determined by his or her psychological
complexion. In all cases, however, this response takes the form of a misreading (or "*misprision*") of the original work: "To the poet-in-a-poet, a poem is
always *the other man*, the precursor, and so a poem is always a person, always
the father of one's Second Birth. To live, the poet must mis*interpret* the
father, by a crucial act of misprision, which is the rewriting of the father" (*A
Map of Misreading*, 19).

If we think of this rewriting as a type of displacement, we can see Bloom as
very close to Frye, and he seems to be echoing Frye when he says "poems are
neither about 'subjects' nor about 'themselves.' They are necessarily about
other poems; a poem is a response to a poem, as a poet is a response to a poet,
or a person to his parent" (*Map*, 18).

The difference, however, between Bloom's "response" and Frye's "displacement" is the profound difference between relativism and absolutism. As noted
earlier, the concept of "displacement" implies the existence of a pure original
and an impure version; "response," however, implies a form of equality between the earlier and later work. Displacement, furthermore, implies a static
relationship because it suggests that the new work is a container. A response,
on the other hand, is an active attempt to differ with an original, to alter it,
to make the author's position clear in relation to it. Any classical rhetoric tells
us that a good response will address all of the opponent's points, conceding
some, attacking others. A response, thus, contains the original, but not pas-
sively, so that the nature of a response is not the original argument that it
contains, but the attempt to undermine that argument. Seeing this basic difference between Frye and Bloom, we can see why Bloom thinks that Frye
"has Platonized the dialectics of tradition." For Bloom:

> There are no longer any archetypes to displace; we have been ejected from the
> imperial palace whence we came, and any attempt to find a substitute for it
> will not be a benign displacement but only another culpable trespass, neither
> more or less desperate than any Oedipal return to origins. For us, creative
> emulation of literary tradition leads to images of inversion, incest, sado-
> masochistic parody. (*Map*, 31)

Bloom's interest, then, is in helping us understand the psychological dynamic which a poem manifests, which is the unique relationship between

two poets. This relationship, furthermore, is the same kind as that which takes place for all readers and manifests itself as literary criticism:

> If to imagine is to misinterpret, which makes all poems antithetical to their precursors, then to imagine after a poet is to learn his own metaphors for his acts of reading. Criticism then necessarily becomes antithetical also, a series of swerves after unique acts of creative misunderstanding. . . . Every poem is a misinterpretation of a parent poem. A poem is not an overcoming of anxiety, but is that anxiety. Poets' misinterpretations or poems are more drastic than critics' misinterpretations or criticism, but this is only a difference of degree and not at all in kind. There are no interpretations but only misinterpretations and so all criticism is prose poetry. (*Anxiety*, 93–95)

Bloom's relativism is acute. If poems are the dynamic of their interaction with other poems, there is no firm point of reference. "There are *no* texts," Bloom tells us, "but only relationships *between* texts. These relationships depend on a critical act, a misreading or misprision, that one poet performs upon another, and that does not differ in kind from the necessary critical acts performed by every strong reader upon every strong text he encounters" (*Map*, 3).

Poems are the response, in other words, of the poetic impulse in the reader to interact with, enter the closed club of, the already written, which by its nature is elite. All readers, therefore, are critic/poets, differing from great critic/poets merely in degree, merely in the strength of the creative impulse to carve a niche for themselves. Since all readers are critic/poets, ultimately anything said about a poem can only be another poem, that is, the manifestation of the critic/poet's attempt to penetrate the closed circle. It can never be credible other than as a manifestation of psychological phenomena, the interplay of anxiety and repression, which Bloom's map of misreading allows us to correlate with the tropes at work.

It is impossible, then, to say that a piece of criticism changes the way we see a piece of literature, because the change is fomented not by the criticism but by the reader, who in the act of reading is forever and unavoidably fomenting change, even in the process of identifying the types of change others have fomented. To identify the changes is the reader's way of dealing with them, just as to ignore the changes is a way of dealing with them. The Oedipal struggle, for Bloom, is a given, as are the alternatives for dealing with it. Literature is one arena where that struggle takes place, and in that arena rhetorical devices are weapons.

Allusion, according to Bloom, is one of those weapons used best by Bloom's exemplary strong poet, Milton, in whose control allusion "as a covert reference became . . . the most powerful and successful figuration that any strong poet has ever employed against his strong precursors" (*Map*, 126).

Pointing to what Angus Fletcher terms Milton's "transumptive" style,[10]
Bloom shows how Milton compresses allusions to many referents—Virgil,
Tasso, Spenser, Ovid, Homer, the Bible—so as to force them to comment on
one another. Such a juxtaposition, however, and such a commentary are only
possible from the perspective of Milton's present. The effect of these transumptive allusions, Bloom tells us, is "to reverse literary tradition, at the
expense of the presentness of the present. The precursors return in Milton,
but only at his will, and they return to be corrected" (*Map*, 142).

Bloom is keenly aware of the "correcting" effect allusive juxtapositions create for the reader; but given his relativistic stance, there seems no way of
asserting this correcting effect as more than the psychological dynamic of the
work in which it is found. Bloom, in other words, sees allusions as a form of
criticism, as a way of altering our view of an earlier work, but he does not
recognize the validity of criticism per se. It is only a weak form of poetry, so
that there is indeed no separate genre known as literary criticism, no texts at
all, only responses.

If we accept, however, that there is such a thing as literary criticism—
works that comment on other texts with the intent of enhancing or refining
our understanding of those texts—then Bloom's form of criticism, brilliant
and fascinating as it might be, is only of tangential interest because it constantly takes our attention away from the text and focuses it on the psychological ordeal of the author-as-reader-as-author. Bloom even tells us that for
us to accept another's analysis of a prior text is a sign of our own weakness.
For us to accept Bloom's analysis of Wordsworth's poetry, for example, means
not that we have arrived at some understanding but that we have given in to
Bloom.

Like Frye, Bloom has thus created a closed version of tradition, but with a
crucial difference. He has substituted himself for Frye's God. Whereas for
Frye the dominant paradigm comes from the narratives of the Bible, for
Bloom it comes from a narrative of Bloom's own creation, one in which
authors constantly reenact, with their symbolic fathers, a rivalry of the sort
Freud finds in the Oedipus myth. All we need to do is to give in to Bloom,
accept his narrative as the genesis of literary creation, and everything else
makes sense. In the same way that Frye plays Adam in the name of God, we
can play Adam in the name of Bloom and identify any author's style in a
rivalry relationship to any other author's style.

In order to apply a Bloomian analysis to Ellison, therefore, we must first
presume the Bloom narrative, then see whether we can demonstrate that Ellison, within the auspices of that narrative, demonstrates in relation to a
"strong" author some of the misreading devices Bloom describes. If not, we
can simply dismiss Ellison as "weak" and therefore inconsequential. For the
canon-according-to-Bloom belongs to the "strong"—that is, those who confirm
Bloom's narrative by employing the devices he describes. If Ellison feels he is

invisible, the reason has nothing to do with social or literary institutions, nothing to do with critical blindness, and everything to do with Ellison's failure to fulfill a role described in Bloom's narrative-of-strength. On the other hand, showing that Ellison does fulfill one of these roles also proves that he should be canonized. Ellison's right to visibility thus depends on how we describe his relationship to, for example, Eliot or Joyce. Rather than summarize Bloom's six acceptable descriptions, I merely note that almost any of them could be used to explain Ellison's relationship to his precursors, but each at a price—the same price—Ellison's racial and ethnic heritage, his identity. Like his own revered Freud, Bloom creates the psychological intervention so that he may define normalcy—the code of reason by which the madman may gain acceptance.[11] So long as Ellison's allusions are read in relation to the norms of canonicity set up by the code of Bloomian intervention, they cannot but be read as a valorization of that code. Invisible no more, Ellison no longer need blame that invisibility on the blindness of the critics; he has merely to renounce—or we as Bloomian critics could do it for him—what he has termed the social significance of his "experimental" style.

The comfort in this approach is that it rids us of worry about the canon, or the social and cultural implications of our "aesthetic" criteria, or those cast into otherness by institutionalized practices. If Frye reduces literature to one text, Bloom simplifies it to none. All we have are reactions: all the important ones are covered, most of the strong poets are known, and the others can be discovered. We need never again fear change. Society, history, and the text itself have been forever marginalized in the name of Freudian Oedipal psychology. All that remains is a story of struggle. In the reader's interplay of resistance and submission to a text, for Bloom, rests that text's meaning, its *only* meaning.

Whether a work has one meaning, however, as Frye asserts, or many readers, as Bloom asserts, both see the problem of meaning logistically rather than dynamically. They believe that the meaning of a text can be tracked down and identified. And Bloom's map—despite his avowals of subjectivity—is intended as an analytic tool for achieving that end, as much as is Frye's anatomy. Perhaps, however, this tracking down of meaning is an impossible task, precluded by the fact that tradition, and hence literature itself, is always in flux. Although it may be impossible ever to produce something genuinely new, we continually perceive things as new. The point is that perceived newness *is* newness, and everything is unavoidably new, even when it is highly unoriginal.

The question this raises (a question I think implicit in "Tradition and the Individual Talent") is: what happens to the meaning of a work when we apply a new framework to it, a new framework necessitated by a new work? We might want, for example, to interpret Dryden's *Aeneid* by identifying a genre called the "Augustan Classical Epic." Pope and Dryden, more than any other writers, create the genre's traits in the way they alter an earlier understanding of both the classical epic and the English epic, but since they both contribute to the creation of the new genre by which they are to be interpreted, doesn't Pope's contribution affect the way we interpret Dryden and, therefore, before Pope wrote, was it possible to find the same meaning in Dryden that we find after? The unique example—Pope's one-of-a-kind translation of Homer—affects even the most limited genre. If Pope hadn't translated the *Iliad*, but Dr. Johnson had, our understanding of the limited genre and hence its members, for example, Dryden's *Aeneid*, would be changed.

In our conscious activity as readers and critics, we constantly form interpretive frames inductively, which brings us to a tautology: we base our knowledge on what we know. What we know, however, constantly changes and what changes it is the introduction of something new, the thing-we-hadn't-thought-of. The new context for the old, therefore, as Eliot sees, forces us to see the differences in both and defer our understanding of the present until we alter our understanding of the past. Here Eliot seems, I think, to have an unlikely ally, Jacques Derrida. It is interesting that Derrida, who is so interested in the interplay of these differences, ignores the concept of allusion. He probably does so because the concept violates his understanding of writing. He does not see two texts, one new and one old, but one entity that is always already there, both as presence and absence, and our language is the interplay of traces from that writing. There is, therefore, no capacity for two texts, only a limiting and delimiting of possibilities within a single text. This play of traces he calls *différances* (a pun, in French, which combines the noun forms of the verbs "to differ" and "to defer").[12] Applying this concept, however, is a useful tool in understanding the way the present alters the past, because the interplay of traces impels a rejection of the linear metaphor by which we structure time:

> . . . protention is as indispensable as retention. And their two dimensions are not added up but the one implies the other in a strange fashion. To be sure, what is anticipated in protention does not sever the present any less from its self-identity than does that which is retained in the trace. But if anticipation were privileged, the irreducibility of the already-always-there and the fundamental passivity that is called time would risk effacement. On the other hand, if the trace refers to an absolute past it is because it obliges us to think a past that can no longer be understood in the form of a modified presence, as a present-past, the absolute past that is retained in the trace no longer rigorously merits the name "past" . . . it may be said that its passivity is also its relationship with the "future." The concepts of *present, past,* and *future,* everything in the concepts of time and history which implies evidence of them—the metaphysical concept of time in general cannot adequately describe the structure of the trace. (*Grammatology*, 66–67)

Derrida understands, then, that our sense of an absolute past is metaphoric. In referring to it, we are acknowledging that it is that which, by definition, has been lost. Were it not lost—were it "here," so to speak—it would be the "present," not the past. But, of course, it is here, both as a referential concept and as a body of data partially described in terms of that referent. Allusions to the past, then, are both the retention of things no longer here and the acknowledgment that the retention is conditioned by loss, by absence. The allusion to the past, thus, is all we shall ever have of it and becomes one with it. Yet that acknowledgment is also an alteration. [13] Derrida, of course, would be likely to challenge the term "alteration" because it implies a point of origin when things were whole, were unaltered. But for Derrida, the "alterations" were always already there. As the quoted passage indicates, there was never a point when the concept of past was not inextricably linked to the present. Yet, still, that recognition of "pastness" calls forth a special structure or qualification, a conditioned absence, an only partial retention. Whether this conditioned absence was always already present, or not, seems less important, however, than whether the use of past tense summons that absence *into consciousness*. For in so doing it makes us acknowledge differences. And these differences force us paradoxically to say X is not what it was, but was what it is. The allusion to the past alters the past in that it makes us see differences.

Again, if the idea of past is antithetical to Derrida's schema, the concept of tradition must be, especially tradition as a set of original points against which the present is measured. Eliot's sense of tradition as dynamic also might be antithetical to Derrida's schema because, for Derrida, the writing is static in that it represents the always-already-there. Yet Eliot perceives, as does Derrida, the continuing sense of rearrangement that writing mandates. Whatever terminology, whatever metaphysical presumptions, differentiate the two, both point us toward an understanding that the acknowledgment of differences alters the entire arrangement, that our sense of time is just a metaphor, and that perception is not a linear progression, a process of addition, but of rearrangement of the whole.

Perhaps it would be useful here to call forth Einstein's understanding of a limited universe in which matter and energy are never lost, destroyed, or created. They merely metamorphize and rearrange. Matter takes the form of energy, energy of matter; the universe is always already there. The conversions of matter into energy and energy into matter are constant and extensive in our bodies and in the world around us. Sometimes we call these rearrangements something new—a cooked meal, flowers in the yard, a newborn child—but whatever we call them, they exist as a form of interplay within determined limits. If we call that universe from which all language is derived "writing," we can see how Derrida's view of the cerebral parallels Einstein's view of the physical. And we can also see how compatible, in ways, it is with Eliot's understanding of the interplay between tradition and creation.

Meaning thus becomes a continuous process of rearrangement, a reordering of known quantities. As much as it might be useful, then, to pretend otherwise, Hirsch's distinction between "meaning" and "significance" does not work. The relationship of a work (and word) to the outside knowledge a reader has *does* affect that work (or word's) meaning. Although I am not saying that all readers bring their own meaning to a text or create their own meaning, I am saying that the meaning is slightly altered by the significance each reader attributes to or infers from the text, based on that reader's selective, limited knowledge. It does no good, furthermore, to posit an ideal reader—one with complete knowledge of all possible significance, all possible meanings. Even if such a reader could be shown to exist, this state of total knowledge could only have been arrived at by passing through states of partial knowledge, during which the reader constantly readjusts his or her understanding. And the fact that we cannot move instantaneously from no knowledge to all knowledge indicates that knowledge acquisition is a process; and since interpretation is predicated upon it, interpretation is always in dynamic flux.

This is quite different from being subjective. Perhaps meaning is not analogous to substance but to energy. Consider sunlight: we cannot see it, but that does not mean that the sun or the light is a subjective creation. We infer it, rather, from its protean manifestations in our limited field of vision. As our field of vision changes, as our memory grows, we discover new manifestations, new meanings for sunlight. Our art and history and science have thus explored the meaning of sunlight for thousands of years. Would it not be an act of the most blatant hubris, then, to think that we finally have complete understanding of sunlight? That is an act of subjectivity perhaps as great as assuming that any understanding is wrong or that all we need understand is that the light comes from the sun. Bloom's misprisions and Frye's reductions, in other words, share with Hirsch's "objectivity" a faith in scientific method which is limiting and which the dynamically allusive nature of language and of literature both facilitates and undermines.

Readers experience dynamically and put on the mask of scientist—psychologist, anthropologist, linguist—retrospectively as critics with well-tested, well-honed theses. This is only natural, as we understandably demand of critics that they have points to make and that they make them thoroughly and expeditiously. This unfortunately tends to ignore the ancillary effects of reading, which are, however, not only inherent to the process but also perhaps essential to understanding. For it is my belief that readers, even novices, when they suspect they perceive an allusion, even when this perception is naive or ill-founded, are forced to make mental accommodations which alter for them, however slightly, tradition as they know it.

In order to understand fully the way Ellison exploits this capacity of allusion, it is necessary to look more closely at the way an allusion can function.

The term "allusion" is inextricably linked to a concept of simultaneity. It identifies a point in rhetoric when we are made aware, through one or more of numerous devices, of a parallel. Walking on a wooded path, we suddenly glimpse railroad tracks through a thinning of the trees. At the instant of glimpsing, they seem exactly parallel to our path. How far the parallel extends, it is impossible to see. Even the ostensive parallel at this point may be an illusion created by our angle of vision. It may turn out to be an odd and irrelevant coincidence that the rail path and footpath come near at all. Although, at the moment of glimpsing, we do not know the relationship, our imagination is lured by potentials. A clearing would be useful, particularly at the top of a hill, over a broad open plain. We could see where these tracks lead and how they relate to our footpath. If the destination of the two turns out to be the same, perhaps we can get there faster by walking along the tracks.

This logistical approach to the experience of perceiving an allusion is perhaps a bit simplistic, but it does make clear, I think, one essential element of our perception of an allusion—the sense of departure from the primary path which *precedes* our sense of direction. To call this sidetracking—given the metaphor with which I have begun—would be a facile pun but also an inaccurate one. For we do not know whether we are being sidetracked, being assured of the main path, or being shown a short cut.

If we focus, then, on readers as they perceive an allusion, as they consider and digest it in the process of understanding a text, we can see that allusions impel a reconsideration of the alluded-to text. Because readers have no idea of an allusion's limitations, they must readjust—at least in the form of a tentative hypothesis—their understanding of that which had been alluded to, and they must readjust as well their sense of all relevant associations to accommodate their hypothesis. To some extent all allusions, therefore, function as a covert form of literary criticism. Although some authors minimize and others exploit an allusion's literary-critical potential, the potential is inherent in all allusions because it arises from the readers' experience of understanding the self-referential world of literature.

I begin my examination of the role of allusions in that world with a very special and limited case, a case in which the literary texts—the primary and the referent—are so parallel as often to raise the question of whether the "simultaneity" I posed as requisite is not "simultaneity" at all, but rather "synonymousness." The case I mean is *translation*.[14]

Unquestionably there is a parallel text, but many translators strive to present the exact equivalent. By intention, to the extent that they succeed, they are denying allusion. Rather than make us aware of an alternative text, they are trying to make us *un*aware of it. Those translators who strive for fidelity are implicitly saying, "This is not *like* Tolstoy; it *is* Tolstoy." And for

readers who do not have Russian, these translators cannot help but be partially right. There is no *War and Peace* but the one received through translation. If that translation is, in fact, highly allusive the reader has no referent
(in this case the Russian original) and therefore cannot experience it as such.
This helps demonstrate exactly how borderline a case of allusion "translation"
seems to be.

That is exactly why I have chosen to begin with it. Translations highlight
that moment of departure and simultaneity, those points at which we have a
clear sense of two texts and an equally clear sense of a conscious, extended
relationship between them.

Brower, for instance, calls Pope's *Iliad*, for the Augustans, "a grand allusion
to Homer" (*Alexander Pope*, 127). Brower bases this opinion on the idea that
the educated Augustans had both a sense of Homer and a sense of Augustan
life, so that they could recognize the adaptation of Homer to the necessities
of the Augustan audience. Because Brower, implicitly, does not see the present as affecting the past in such a way as to call the standards of measurement
into question, his approach to Pope's *Iliad* becomes particularly interesting.
Although Pope is obviously changing Homer (Brower explains at great length
the nature of some of the changes), Pope is also purporting to present Homer's
original. So, in this case, we have a text which parallels its referent very
closely, yet also uses its context and what is associated with that context to
create the fabric of a new text. The referent, in keeping with Brower's theory,
supplies the standard against which the adaptations can be measured. And
certainly the referent subsumes its immediate context; the Homeric tradition,
in other words, is larger than Pope's translation. Calling Pope's *Iliad* an allusion to Homer, therefore, is consistent with Brower's approach.

But we must also realize that Pope is changing Homer, on the most *prima
facie* level, by changing the language, the syntax, and the scansion; in a larger
sense by changing the sensibility and inserting local issues and values. The
work, in other words, is an interpretation, a way of reading Homer, a piece
of literary criticism. Homer's *Iliad*, therefore, is more than just the subject of
Pope's interpretation.

By looking at the case of translation, we may perhaps get some clearer idea
of the dynamic Eliot has in mind when, in "Tradition and the Individual
Talent," he sees new works as changing old. At its core rests the interplay
between creation and criticism. Pope is at once trying to write something new
and trying not to. He is being faithful to the *Iliad*, as he sees it, and having
to see the *Iliad* through him, we see new meanings in Homer. Pope's Homer
changes the Homeric tradition, ever so slightly perhaps, as any piece of criticism does, but still changes it. And only as allusion can we praise both the
original and the adaptation at the points where they differ. Recognizing an
allusion allows us numerous pleasures in reading. One of them is that it

makes tradition dynamic—Homer is revivified because he is not the same. I do not mean only that Pope's text differs from Homer's, but also that the original Homer is different because we see him differently in the light of Pope's allusions. In this way, Pope is writing literary criticism. This is made more explicit, furthermore, by the footnotes Pope includes at various points to explain why he has made certain choices in translating.[15] These passages are interpretations of Homer. They are, in other words, explicit criticism, which becomes implicit criticism in the poetic text.

Douglas Knight rightly realizes even larger implications in the relationship of Pope's translation to tradition:

> The tradition of heroic poetry, and in particular the work of Virgil and Milton, is a constant voice in the translations. Zeus becomes a Jove and almost a Judeo-Christian god; the heroic situation becomes one of finite human participation in the final and divine order of things; and the chief poetic absorption is with this dynamic participation of man's freedom in his fate. Traditions and developments of insight which are the major achievement of the *Aeneid* and *Paradise Lost*, yet at the same time the major bond between them and the *Iliad* and *Odyssey*, are for Pope a means of reinterpretation, a road to the past which is equally a road to the present. Homer may legitimately be seen in the light of Virgil and Milton because of the debt they owe him; for Pope (who is in debt to them all) the proper homage to Homer, and the living justice he deserves, are expressed by exploring and transmuting his major kinds of order without doing violence to them. ("Translation: The Augustan Mode," 204)

Knight understands that the translation reorders the entire landscape of the English sense of epic poetry, so that it becomes not only a reinterpretation of Homer, but of the epic genre as defined by, and handed down through, Virgil and Milton. Since Knight is essentially implying that Pope is translating Homer while alluding to Virgil and Milton, we can see that the distinction between allusion and translation begins to blur. But we can also see how much a whole tradition is altered by the introduction of a new element.

This helps us understand why Ezra Pound calls translation a form of criticism.[16] And Brower would generally agree, because he himself has said that "the study of translation . . . is one of the simplest ways of showing what is expected at various times in answer to the question 'What is Poetry?' " In his essay "Seven Agamemnons," he shows how various passages of Aeschylus' play reflect the poetic values of their translators:

> The eighteenth-century translator, as we saw, solved his difficulty by elimination, by rejecting words and actions which would be at variance with the contemporary code of aristocratic behavior. The result was a uniformity of tone which the modern translator cannot achieve, for one reason because he has

no corresponding assurance as to what constitutes aristocratic manners. He
can only be honest in a blundering democratic way.

But this honesty pays some dividends. The reader's attention is directed primarily to what is going on, to what is happening. (193)

The same may be said if we call these translators critics. Their acts of interpretation, focus, stress, omission, and simplification interpret the original in
terms of their age and its values.

Yet the act of translation is also creative. In addition to retaining and interpreting, it emulates one creative process and performs another; it enters directly into a tradition and immediately alters that tradition. As John Hollander
observes, "translation has come to the brink of identification with the process
of literary invention as such, with respect to both the practice, and to the role
of the practitioner. (The job of the poet outlined in T. S. Eliot's 'Tradition
and the Individual Talent' is strangely like that of an Ideal Translation)" ("Versions, Interpretations, Performances," 209). Hollander sees translation as a
"version." Each version of a play, each staging, has to have the matrix of some
bias. Hollander understands the partial nature of any translation. Focusing
on *Othello*, he shows that one version may try to recreate the play per se, as
it was for the Elizabethan audience, another to recreate, through contemporary analogies, the *experience* of the play for the Elizabethans. By the same
token, as choreographers Martha Graham and Jose Limón did, in their respective versions, interpreters can change the medium and edit the story,
while retaining part of the original skeleton and retaining a theme, or stressing
a theme, or altering a theme. We could easily, I think, say the Graham and
Limón pieces heavily allude to *Othello*, without changing our sense that they
are interpretations or, I think, interfering with Hollander's sense that they are
analogous to translations.

Similarly, the request for some inalterable referent is analogous to the demand for the impossible version. For, although the referent in an allusion
may be the standard of measurement, it is not a constant, because the allusion
not only refers readers to a standard but also forces them to interpret and
redefine that standard. Here we can see the interplay between past and present
that Eliot suggests. An allusion refers us to a standard, a constant, but the
process of making the references makes that standard less constant, alters it.

Pope's *Iliad* tells us about potentials in reading Homer's *Iliad*. We could
argue that these potentials were of greater interest to the Augustans than they
are to contemporaries; the potentials found in Joyce's way of reading Homer
are more interesting for us. But these are historical questions. My point is
that both Joyce and Pope find new potentials in reading Homer, the way
Freud does in reading Oedipus, and even today we can have the experience,
as Keats did, of first looking into Chapman's Homer.

If tradition demands interpretation, furthermore, the paradigm of translation can be seen as dominating our understanding of meaning in the self-referential world of language and literature. I think we can see, in fact, that what I started out positing as a special case of allusion is, in another sense, also the general class which contains "allusions" as a subset. If all language can be viewed as a form of allusion, in other words, it can also be viewed as a form of translation. George Steiner makes a very convincing case for this:

> The schematic model of translation is one in which the message from the source-language passes into a receptor language via a transformational process. The barrier is the obvious fact that one language differs from the other, that an interpretive transfer, sometimes, albeit misleadingly, described as encoding and decoding must occur so that the message "gets through." Exactly the same model—and this is what is rarely stressed—is operative within a single language. (*After Babel*, 28)

The self-referentiality of any literature, in other words, is no different from the self-referentiality of any natural language. Still, within prescribed limits, there are always newly discovered potentials for variation. This constant reordering, this protention and retention, is requisite to both allusiveness and translation. Without this constant reordering, as both Eliot and Derrida see, we would have neither a sense of the old nor a potential for the new. This is exemplified in general by the way literature must exploit tradition, a very particular example of which can be found in the apparently inexhaustible possibilities for literary translations:

> As every generation retranslates the classics out of a vital compulsion for immediacy and precise echo, so every generation uses language to build its own resonant past. . . .
> In short, the essence of art and literature, the reality of felt history in a community, depend on a never-ending, though very often unconscious, act of internal translation. It is no overstatement to say that we possess civilization because we have learned to translate out of time. (*After Babel*, 30–31)

"To translate out of time" is to be aware with Eliot that the past is "altered by the present as much as the present is altered by the past"; it is to understand the protention and retention inherent in our use of language; it is to see that what rises out of our consciousness as something new is a reordering of elements, a realization of potentials already present. But that realization of potentials takes the appearance of discovery. We are made aware, in other words, of a potential for language or art when we see that potential take concrete form. Only after Thespis did we understand the potential that had rested all along in the chorus; the advent of "tragedy," in other words, revealed the potential of the dithyramb. In that its presence made us aware of new potentials in old material, "tragedy" was a form of commentary, a piece of literary criticism telling us about the potentials of the choric song. Both the song and the genre of tragedy, as a result, could never be seen as they would have been, independent of one another. The whole tradition of Western tragedy, unavoidably, forms a body of self-commentary and self-interpretation in that it reveals potentials in its antecedents. Although these potentials may have been awaiting discovery, their discovery changes our conscious understanding by giving additional meanings to the same material.

The allusive nature of any literary tradition, then, is also its vitality, because it is the source of constant reinterpretation, the same type of reinterpretation that is necessitated by interlingual (and intralingual) translations. Steiner calls this, very appropriately, "interanimation," and his remarks on it apply, I think, equally well to the concept of allusion:

> "Interanimation" signifies a process of totally attentive interpretation. It tells of a dialectic of fusion in which identity survives altered but also strengthened and re-defined by virtue of reciprocity. There is annihilation of self in the other consciousness and recognition of self in a mirroring motion. Principally, there results a multiplication of resource, of affirmed being. "Interanimated," two presences, two formal structures, two bodies of utterance assume a dimension, an energy of meaning far beyond that which either could generate in isolation or in mere sequence. The operation is, literally, one of raising to a higher power. If we consider these attributes, it will be immediately apparent that they reproduce the terms proposed throughout this study to define and characterize translation itself. Intensely focused penetration, the establishment of mutual identity, through conjunction, the heightening of a work's existence when it is confronted and re-enacted by alternate versions of itself—these are the structural features of translation proper. Even where it relates to works remote from one another in language, formal convention and cultural context, "interanimation" will show itself to be one further derivative form, one further metamorphic analogue of translation. If this has not always been obvious, the reason may be that the area of relations covered by this rubric is so immediate to and so ubiquitous in our culture. (*After Babel*, 452–53)

So far I have only shown that allusion, like translation, requires interpretation. Now I want to examine the difficulty in limiting the reference of an allusion to explore the hypotheses that readers must formulate in light of these difficulties, and the effect of those hypotheses on their understanding of the alluded-to text.

In one of the few theoretical discussions of allusion in print, Carmela Perri states:

> In alluding, although the aspects of connotation are unexpressed in the allusion-marker, these are tacitly specified. . . . the character who says to her

jealous husband, "I will not have you misinterpret my handkerchief," refers to the play *Othello*, but tacitly specifies the attribute associated and its interpreter: the false evidence of a husband's blinding jealousy. A similar aspect of connotation is meant by the sentence, "I will not have you make me into a Desdemona." It is not Desdemona the acknowledged beauty, the inhabiter of Venice, the disobedient daughter, etc., that is meant by the allusion, but merely one of her qualities: the innocent victim of her husband's jealousy. ("On Alluding," 296)

I find Perri's approach here problematic. Let us consider, for instance, one of the connotations that Perri dismisses: "Desdemona, the acknowledged beauty." Perhaps the woman in Perri's example is homely and she is saying that the husband is overestimating her general attractiveness, that his specific jealousy is a misestimation not only of a specific event but also of the larger relationship between the wife and her social milieu. Or perhaps the wife is indeed beautiful but does not perceive herself as such, so that in making the allusion to Desdemona she is intending to point out her husband's overvaluing of her appearance, but reveals instead her own undervaluing of it. The meaning of the allusion, then, is not the same for the character making it as for the reader. The character, moreover, may have a misunderstanding or eccentric understanding of Shakespeare's play. She may be pretentious, and betraying her ignorance, or deranged and revealing her distortion of reality, or perhaps she is a uniquely gifted critic giving a fresh interpretation to the handkerchief scene's meaning.

Subsequent events in the story will help us judge which of these interpretations is valid. E. D. Hirsch, in other words, would solve this interpretive problem by saying we need more information about the author's intentions.[17] Unlike Perri, he does not find the immediate text sufficient. While he sees it as supplying some of the needed information, he also sees a need for discovering the author's intentions by looking at his other works, and all of this in the light of additional generic conventions. With this information at hand, we can start to estimate the "probability" that the author's intention included "Desdemona the acknowledged beauty."

There are, however, two problems with this approach. The first arises at the moment readers first recognize the allusion. As readers, they simply do not have enough information to discount readily a number of possible connotations that they would discount retrospectively or, perhaps, with the aid of research. As student, critic, or scholar, in other words, we may increase our "odds"; but as readers at the initial reading, the best we can do is to call forth as many possibilities as we can and await further information. We may even rest on one set of connotations, but we do so very tentatively, for the pleasurable compact of reading is that we are always open to moments of acquisition and surrender—in which we recover and discard implications brought to the surface by the text. So as we read we are always forced to make probable interpretations based on inadequate information. I do not mean to imply, however, that there is anything wrong with reconsiderations based on more information or that there is something sacred about the first reading. Since almost all criticism, however, reflects that moment when the critic feels he or she has an interpretation that is valid, we often overlook the fact that the critic has passed through a period of uncertainty and has discarded numerous hypotheses. That stage of limited uncertainty, which we all pass through, does not discredit subsequent stages but does, I believe, have ancillary effects of some importance, which I shall be examining at length.

I want to look first, however, at another problem in applying Hirsch's approach to discover the probable connotations of an allusion. The first problem is that probability, in the immediate context of first readings, doesn't apply because we don't have enough information to judge the probability. The second is that, from the long view, probability never applies to the specific case: if there is a one-in-fifty-thousand chance of catching a rare disease, the odds are as equally meaningless for the general, uncontaminated population as they are for the few victims. To tell victims that it was highly improbable that they became sick serves no purpose.

Similarly, if we can show that, based on every kind of possible information, there was a 99 percent probability that Shakespeare intended X, we have no way of knowing that this example is not the 1 percent exception. It is improbable that we should have even one writer of Shakespeare's genius. The very existence of the play *Hamlet* is an astoundingly fortuitous improbability. How, then, can we base an interpretation on probabilities? For *Hamlet* is like all other artistic works in that their individual creations are improbable, even when they are highly conventional. There is a great problem, therefore, even with the most sophisticated type of probability interpretation, in that it discounts, in considering an artistic creation, the same kinds of improbabilities that are most closely associated with creativity: innovation and genius—the very qualities most manifest in those works worth discussing.

Another problem is that such an approach distinguishes the critical activity from the creative in a way that T. S. Eliot, for example, found thoroughly untenable. For Eliot every entry—critical or creative—into the canon of knowledge reorders the entire landscape. The paradigm for consensus criticism, on the other hand, is scientific, wherein the work is an object analyzed by many tools. The dynamic acts of the imagination upon which artistic work is predicated thus become alien to the critical realm, even though in Coleridge—one of the fathers of the modern understanding of the imagination—we have blatant evidence that this dichotomy is false: *Biographia Literaria* both asserts and stands itself as evidence that the imaginative and critical activities are profoundly and essentially intermixed. The "multiety in unity" Coleridge found at the core of beauty is the improbable complexity necessary to stir the imagination as much as it is the capacity to understand that improbable agitation. The willing suspension of disbelief, in other words, is a resonance in the imagination with the improbable, a resonance which for Coleridge echoed the eternal. The greatest works, it seems to me, are those which continue to put readers in resonance with the improbable, continue to admit new interpretations.

Instead of seeing the critic as scientist, perhaps we should see him or her as a magician. I do not mean someone with supernatural powers but rather someone who performs tricks. The magician does not discover natural law but breaks it. He does not tell us what we believe to be true but what we know to be untrue: glasses of water can disappear, and rabbits can come out of empty hats.

But the magic trick is not wholly untruthful. While it promotes its lie, it also reveals something new about reality, about the capacity of glasses and water, rabbits and empty hats. They can be made to appear unbound by their natural limitations. The magic trick tells us, therefore, as much about the real potential of the material as it does about the illusion. The fact that we know the magician has lied, that he hasn't actually materialized a rabbit out of thin air, allows our double vision wherein we experience simultaneous deception and revelation.

If we view critics as magicians of sorts and accept that they intend to deceive us, we can marvel at the boldness and novelty of their undertaking while discovering anew the rich potential of the material on which they work. Any criticism shows, to some extent, the potential of the literature to admit the discussion, and tests the critical vocabulary which facilitates that discussion. If we assert, for instance, that the Marquis de Sade is a moralist or that *Troilus and Cressida* is a pastoral, we would most probably have to be somewhat dishonest, but we would also be testing our understanding of moralism and pastoralism and the limits of the language we use to describe them in literary contexts. These are real pursuits, directly related to practical criticism and the kinds of truth-claims literature can make and we can make about literature, in spite of the fact that it is constantly in flux.

I have pursued this line of thought at length because it reflects strongly on the concept of allusion in this way: if the value of criticism is that by imaginatively creating new "tricks," it legitimately finds new potential in old material, the value of allusions is that they imbue the old material with wider potentials. But this is only so if we do not take for granted, as Perri does, the referent's marked qualities.

We can see this in *Invisible Man* if we look at some Eliot and Whitman allusions. When Emerson's son invites the invisible man to the Club Calamus, Ellison is clearly alluding to Whitman's homosexual Calamus poems as a way of suggesting that young Emerson is homosexual. This is a standard use of allusion, one in which the alluded-to provides a known quality which enhances or explains the text, but Ellison also uses Whitman in more complex ways. Marvin Mengeling has demonstrated that Homer A. Barbee's speech about the Founder rephrases Whitman's elegy for Lincoln, "When Lilacs Last in the Dooryard Bloomed":

> All the Whitman symbols are there: the lilac, the star, and the thrush—the bells and the funeral train—but, and I do not think that this point can be emphasized too heavily, Ellison employs them for almost entirely opposite reasons than did the bard of American poetry. . . . Ellison is much less concerned with poetic potentials than with more pessimistic ideas, for the reader is quick to recognize that he uses these same symbols of the lilac, star, and thrush to measure the great irony and bitter disillusion of racial betrayal brought about after the death of another great fighter for emancipation, the beloved Founder—Ellison's picture of a black and mythical Lincoln. ("Whitman and Ellison," 68)

Mengeling seems to desire a kind of fixity—what Iser calls "the permanence idea"—from the allusion. But how are we to know whether the Founder is Ellison's black Lincoln, or merely Barbee's?

Barbee, both blind and stumbling on Bledsoe's feet, uses the language of American optimism to describe the Founder. He has, in other words, integrated his speech with Whitman's, adapted Whitman's imagery to his own purposes. But what are those purposes? Are they the same purposes that Bledsoe has in requiring the invisible man to attend the service? Both Whitman's optimism and his faith in democracy are indeed called into question when his language is used to the corrupt ends of Bledsoe. Whitman, like many other writers of what Lewis Mumford called "The Golden Day," had been adapted and adopted by twentieth-century critics as an example of the innocence of antebellum America. More and more, however, we see that Whitman's poetry was far from innocent, that the persona he created existed not in ignorance of America's failings but as a challenge to them. Whitman understood the tenuous nature of democracy, and therefore he exhorted that "democracy," as though it needed constant encouragement to live. Most of his greatest works, however, were about death, almost as if, in a country which celebrated the individual, mass vitality could be made to compensate for individual mortality. Whatever Whitman missed, it was not the American sins of suffering, bondage, insensitivity; otherwise his efforts to transcend them would be trivial.

Still, his failure fully to confront evil made his language adaptable to the purposes of propagandists like Barbee and Bledsoe. Seeing Whitman's language so closely applied to the Founder, a man strikingly similar to Booker T. Washington,[18] thus tells us more about the interpreters of Whitman than about the Founder or Ellison's view of the Founder. The allusions to the elegy for Lincoln force us to notice, therefore, the differences rather than the similarities between the real emancipator and the ersatz, and the differences as well between Whitman and Barbee. It might also make us ponder, to some degree, interpretations of Whitman and the assumptions which those interpretations reflect. For when Barbee in Bledsoe's interest uses Whitman's language to make the Founder look like Lincoln, Barbee becomes an interpreter of Whitman's poetry as much as of the Founder's life, and we have to consider what assumptions structure his interpretation.

The meaning of the allusion, then, may be found in the oscillation between the two texts which stimulates a reader's imagination in a way that causes him or her to see both texts anew. Wolfgang Iser, in *The Implied Reader*, comes closer than Perri to realizing the agitating effect allusions have on readers. For Iser, literature, in general, is an imaginative stimulus which causes the reader to fill in gaps:

> The participation of the reader could not be stimulated if everything were laid out in front of him. This means that the formulated text must shade off, through allusions and suggestions, into a text that is unformulated though nonetheless intended. Only in this way can the reader's imagination be given the scope it needs; the written text furnishes it with indications which enable it to conjure up what the text does not reveal. (31)

Iser uses the term "allusion" here clearly in the general sense as any form of reference, not just the reference to a literary text. The problem of reading thus becomes the problem of locating the material in any context other than that supplied by the text itself. This is the basic problem of identifying and placing in perspective a text's referents. Since no text can exist completely independent of reference to some aspects of reality, and yet since no author can possibly reveal all the referents for even one limited scene, Iser posits that authors reveal their referents in an inverse manner, in an act of what he calls "negation": "Expectations aroused in the reader by allusions to the things he knows or thinks he knows are frustrated; through this frustration, we know that the standards and models alluded to are somehow to be transcended, though no longer on their own terms" (37). Iser, in other words, is acutely aware of the role the reader plays as mediator between what the text reveals and what it does not. He also understands reading as a process, a process that demands constant reconsideration.

Examining the Homeric parallel in *Ulysses*, he notes:

> There is clearly no formulated connection between the archaic past and the everyday present, so that the reader himself is left to motivate the parallelism indicated as it were by filling in the gaps between the lines.
>
> The reader is provoked into a process of recognition, for recognition, like grouping, is part of his natural disposition and is an elementary activity in reading. As he recognizes the implications of the allusion, he tries to equate

them with the events now being set before him, but he finds they do not actually coincide. There is just enough common ground to make him aware of
the differences, and the process of equating and differentiating is one that will
be both disturbing and stimulating. (228)

This suggests Ziva Ben-Porat's definition of a literary allusion, which she,
unlike Iser, distinguishes from general allusions. Ben-Porat defines a literary
allusion as "a device for the simultaneous activation of two texts" which "results in the formation of intertextual patterns whose nature cannot be prede-
termined" ("The Poetics of Literary Allusion," 107). Ben-Porat thus narrows
Iser's understanding of literary allusion in that she distinguishes it from general allusions, but she also broadens the understanding in that she sees that
all literary allusions require this mental oscillation, that the quality of simultaneous activation is not peculiar to reading *Ulysses* but to reading allusions.

   Derrida might further assert that the experience is characteristic of all reading in that all words create recognition of *différance* not greatly dissimilar
from Iser's "equating and differentiating." Iser treats the effects, however, as
an author's strategy, while Derrida treats them as a property of language. Making sense of something as problematic as language is, as Derrida shows, a
monumental task, so monumental in fact that it is relatively easy for him to
prove it almost impossible. The reader must conduct a constant test for meaning, a constant hypothesizing: what is the context for this word? how does it
refine my previous understanding? It seems an impossible task, and yet we do
it, for the most part, constantly, and for the most part automatically. Without
realizing it, in other words, we continually settle on tentative understandings
and accommodate all we know to them.

   This reshifting of the mental landscape is inherent in the act of learning,
but it is usually subconscious. As new usages broaden or refine a word's connotation for us, we rarely feel obliged to reject formally the old meaning and
substitute the new one with additional qualifications *a*, *b*, and *c*. Although
no one probably still maintains a purely Lockean view of human understanding, I suspect many of us still cling, at least in part, to the metaphor of a
tabula rasa, think of our knowledge as discrete entries in an elaborate filing
system. Harboring this concrete metaphor, we find it hard to see how new
entries alter old ones. There are of course instances when, even with the most
fundamentally Lockean beliefs, we admit these alterations; we cross out an
old entry and write in a new one. In psychotherapy, such revelations occur;
and sometimes in debate or rational argument we are persuaded to substitute
a new understanding for an old.

   When the argument is printed and concerns literature, we call it literary
criticism. And often we find a critical article convincing, meaning that it
impels us to substitute a new understanding of text A for an old one. Because
the argument is formal, the point is clearly stated, and we know exactly what

we are being asked to accept and what it will replace in our "storehouse" of knowledge. We can therefore acknowledge the substitutions without rejecting our concrete understanding of the way we contain knowledge. It is a good deal harder, however, to see how *any* piece of knowledge modifies the *whole.* If the information we take in is not tagged so as to tell us which index card to pull and correct, we find it hard to believe that any change in what we already know can take place. Yet I believe it does at a subconscious or semiconscious level, and the great value of Derrida is that he not only shows us why and how this is so, but also makes a strong argument for the idea that were it not so—were we not constantly readjusting everything we know (recognizing difference and deferring understanding)—we could not make sense of anything. But that constant readjustment *must* take place subconsciously. Derrida, therefore, constantly tries to make us aware of exactly that which we must do, without being aware of it, in order to function.

Derrida's assertions, as a result, seem to belie empirical evidence. Earlier, I compared Derrida's understanding of "writing" to Einstein's understanding of the physical universe. It is perhaps useful to consider here that Einstein's formulations also tended to belie empirical evidence: we don't feel packets of light energy arriving and stimulating us at the rate of 186,000 miles per second. Rather, we *see objects,* those that generate or reflect light. Similarly, we don't consciously perceive the complicated set of interrelations that convert utterance to sign to meaning, don't follow the play of the trace, but rather we think in units like word, sentence, idea.

The unique quality of allusions is that they add a level of complexity and therefore demand more conscious attention, thus forcing a normally subconscious activity toward consciousness. They make the hidden dynamic in literature—the flux of rearrangement—more vivid, in the same way that literary criticism attempts to. If, for instance, in reading a novel one comes across a character named "Oedipus Jones," a number of possibilities emerge. Readers who recognize the name Oedipus may start to see similarities between the Oedipus myth and the story they are reading. But, of course, simultaneously they know this is not the Oedipus myth, not Sophocles' play nor Freud's treatise; it is something other, some new work. The divergence from the original may be a great deal further than is the case with most translations; the parallels are less clearly marked; nevertheless, some may exist.

In our hypothetical story, suppose that Oedipus Jones has left home, is uncertain about his parentage, has a volatile temper. Are there other similarities? There seems to be no warning or prophecy, no riddle to solve, no slaying, no older woman. Perhaps these will appear later. The finding of similarities, then, is also the discovery of differences. The Oedipus myth for each reader presents a checklist of characteristics, and for each item on the checklist the reader answers two questions which are the same question. Is it similar? Is it different? The differences, however, do not answer the questions but extend them. For although the answer to the general question "Is it different?" is always "yes," the answer to the specific questions is always "wait and see." Perhaps Oedipus Jones solves a riddle *after* he marries his mother-figure. Then in the process of acknowledging a similar event we also acknowledge a dissimilar order of events. Since the new text is always already different from the original, we face constant interplay of differences causing us to defer our understanding.

But this process has another dynamic, too. Since we know that every allusion presents differences always already present, we know the original is changed, is not being presented as it originally was. By virtue of its new context, by virtue of its being an allusion, it becomes both old and new. The presence of an allusion, therefore, forces us to ask how it is being changed. We cannot do otherwise seeing "Oedipus Jones" and still treat the name as an allusion.

There is, of course, always the reader who has never heard of Oedipus or who discounts the name at the outset in the way that someone seeing the name Peter Jones would not stop to wonder what the character had in common with Saint Peter. But for readers who recognize an allusion, or *think* they do or, even better, *suspect* they do, the process of exploring differences seems unavoidable, and with this process comes a deferral, because until readers understand how the original text has been changed they cannot understand the current text. Reuben Brower is partially right, therefore, in asserting that tradition—the alluded-to work—forms a standard for measurement, but it is a standard which emerges through its own alterations. The author of our hypothetical text, by using the name "Oedipus," is altering the myth by putting it in a new context, but only the altered myth—altered by the story that has made it different—becomes a measuring point in that story. Thus, as Eliot understands, a sense of tradition is a comparison "in which two things are measured by each other." If Eliot focuses on the self-referentiality of literary texts, then he comes to occupy a middle ground wherein he has isolated some of the problems Derrida sees as ubiquitous in language as they affect the world of literature *per se*, so that for him the interplay between what the reader brings to the text and what the text brings to that sensibility is the means not for bringing the reader into the reality of the text but for bringing the text into a tradition.

My interest in all this is not simply to explain Eliot's enigmatic remarks. I am interested, rather, in showing how Eliot, if understood in the light I have suggested, helps explain the reader's response to an allusion. At the moment of sighting, the deferral/differentiation is not simply that which Derrida would say is inherent to all language. The entrance of that tradition in the form of a referent text doubles the deferral, defers the deferral, so to speak.

Allusions, then, help us become aware of other problems in the text we deal with subconsciously. It is not that the text fails to transmit meaning but rather that it does so in spite of numerous problems which, for the most part, we overcome as fast as they arise. This does not seem remarkable if we consider that we actually "see" upside down and backward as a necessity of the optics of the human eye, yet our brain learns to unscramble the message so quickly we do not realize it, so quickly for some people that they can figure out in less than a second where a small hard ball hurled at over ninety mph from only twenty yards away will be in relation to their bodies; they also have time left over to decide if they want to swing at that ball with a bat, act upon that decision, and often succeed in hitting the ball. Just as Dr. Johnson's throbbing toe undermines Bishop Berkeley's cosmology, so Willie Mays makes a sham of Derrida.

He makes a sham of Derrida, that is, if we insist on taking Derrida literally. If, however, we see Derrida's work as a reminder of the pitfalls of language we regularly overcome and sometimes do not (Willie Mays sometimes struck out), he is to reading what the slow-motion close-up replay is to baseball. Normally the ball seems to have been a continuous extension of the pitcher's motion, but in the slow-motion close-up we see that the pitcher's motion was comprised of many separate motions, his arm, elbow, wrist, and fingers all rotating and flailing in harmonious discord. The ball, too, which normally seems to take a straight path, can be seen to spin, waver, and buzz as though it were following the threads of a rough, narrow corkscrew; as it crowds the plate, furthermore, it appears inexplicably to tremble then rise. Just then the bat enters the picture to solve all the logistical uncertainties of the fastball.

Despite that solution, however, what remains is the awareness of the problems, the intricate ways in which we must defer understanding while we presume to be gathering it. This awareness both warns readers of pitfalls and facilitates greater appreciation of reading. Allusions thus facilitate the understanding of literature without the slow-motion close-up of external criticism. If they don't grind the text to a meaningless halt, a morass of deferral, they force the reader to reshuffle it in terms of literary tradition, and literary tradition is the referent set most responsible for its meaning. Allusions therefore occupy a strange halfway position between full critical arguments and common language, to form subtle open-ended arguments. As our examination of intralanguage translation has shown, even common language mandates interpretation.

Literary criticism focuses that interpretive energy onto a specific text and/ or a specific aspect of that text. Allusions supply the focus without fully developing the argument. As I illustrated with the case of "Oedipus Jones," the suspicion of an allusion forces the readers to do, on a semiconscious level, what common language forces them to do on a subconscious: defer understanding and reinterpret. This is exactly what literary criticism asks them to do on a fully conscious level.

Literary allusions, in other words, are a covert form of literary criticism in that they force us to reconsider the alluded-to text, request us to alter our understanding of it. Like all literary criticism, of course, allusions may be dismissed as silly, or irrelevant or misinformed or obvious. Of the thousands of articles on *Hamlet*, only a few could alter readers' understanding greatly; some might affect the way they regard a specific scene or word, and a great many would probably be dismissed completely. Some works, further-more—*Hamlet* is a perfect example—seem more impervious to the call for reinterpretation. This is largely by virtue of the abundance of criticism. It is not that *Hamlet* has so clear and inviolable a central meaning as that the numerous interpretations tend to hold each other in check, in part because, by their partial overlap, they tend to stabilize the center. More importantly, however, they create so large a universe, so vast a "*Hamlet* tradition" that any one new entry is unlikely to change the whole greatly.

So, too, for allusion: a widely alluded-to line, scene, name, or work ac-quires some stability. No one allusion is likely to alter drastically our interpre-tation, but a creatively novel usage always *might* have a significant impact. In the same way, reading a fifth or tenth translation of the *Iliad* will not change greatly our understanding of the book, yet people still believe that it can to some degree. Otherwise, no one would bother to write, publish, or read a new translation of Homer. In this sense we can see again how perfectly allusions function as a form of translation and therefore impel reinterpretations.

It is important to note, finally, that the power to impel reinterpretation is not dependent on a bright, informed, or astute reader. Readers simply trying to understand what they read, when they suspect the presence of an allusion, are forced to question the author's intention, which means examining their own sense—however limited or naive—of the alluded-to text, of literary tra-dition. How much they will gain from that reading experience differs with the reader; in the same way that some critical articles can be too sophisticated for a specific reader, some allusions can be. Some readers, on the other hand, can be too sophisticated to respond to ill-conceived or careless allusions. But allusions always have the potential to function as criticism, and the present thus can alter the past.

Ellison demonstrates this, for example, at the beginning of chapter 2, using a Joycean juxtaposition of allusions, to the end that Iser has noted. In describ-ing the college he attended, the invisible man states:

> Oh, long green stretch of campus, Oh, quiet songs at dusk, Oh, moon that kissed the steeple and flooded the perfumed nights, Oh, bugle that called in the morning, Oh, drum that marched us militarily at noon. . . . (28–29)

This Whitmanesque revelry is tempered by the doubts expressed later in the paragraph:

Why is it that I can recall in that island of greenness no fountain but one that was broken, corroded and dry? And why does no rain fall through my recollections, sound through my memories, soak through the hard dry crust of the still so recent past? Why do I recall, instead of the odor of seed bursting in springtime, only the yellow contents of the cistern spread over the lawn's dead grass? (29)

And in the next paragraph:

. . . the school a flower-studded wasteland, the rocks sunken, the dry winds hidden, the lost crickets chirping to yellow butterflies.
    And oh, oh, oh, those multimillionaires! (29)

The sterile, arid "Waste Land" images culminate in a paraphrasing of Eliot's "o o o o that Shakespeherian Rag." In this way Ellison links the "oh"s of Whitman's optimism with the "O"s of Eliot's pessimism.

This juxtaposition is a typical example of the technical manipulation characteristic of some aspects of modernism. It is densely allusive, reiterates motifs, and is structurally dependent on musical rhythms. Ellison uses it to comment on, and thereby call into question, interpretations of Whitman's and, more generally, Transcendentalism's apparent optimism.

As Melville, in *The Confidence Man*, and Hawthorne, in "The Celestial Railroad," contended, the Transcendentalists tried to make people believe that one could be successful, in both this life and the next, without ever confronting evil. For Melville and Twain, the American evil, which the Transcendentalists refused to confront, came to be symbolized by slavery, and the black man became a symbolic moral burden. But the authors who pointed out this burden were ignored, and American institutions became Emersonian in outlook.

In *Invisible Man*, Ellison makes a surreal trip through contemporary institutions, showing that the idyllic dream propagated by the Transcendentalists is actually a nightmare. The invisible man journeys through college, New York, the Men's House, and paint factory, the Brotherhood, and the streets of Harlem. In each place almost inadvertently—and certainly in spite of all he had been taught—he rips away the Transcendental façade and reveals the unfaced evil at the core of things, the Waste Land. Thus, the movement from the Whitman allusion to the Eliot indicates both Ellison's theme and technique. The themes come largely from nineteenth-century writers; but for the technique of using copious allusions to broaden the scope of his work, Ellison is indebted to Eliot and Joyce.

To understand the full potential of these allusions, however, readers and critics owe some debt to the contemporary examinations of hermeneutics and deconstruction.

With all this in mind, we can now look at the way Ellison exploits the literary-critical potentials of allusions to revise the interpretive assumptions that structured the canon which emerged during his childhood and which reflected the social hierarchies that rendered him invisible. Specifically, I examine his use of Tod Clifton as a Christ figure and his allusions to Lewis Mumford's *The Golden Day*, Melville's *Benito Cereno*, Emerson's essays, and Twain's *Adventures of Huckleberry Finn*. In all cases, I look at the ways assumptions determine interpretation and contrasting traditional assumptions with those impelled by acknowledging Ellison's allusions. In this way I hope to demonstrate that not only the text is being interpreted but also ideas about tradition, canon, and literary history.

3. Tod Clifton: Spiritual and Carnal

I want to approach *Invisible Man* by asking a simple question: who is Tod Clifton? Perhaps the simplest answer is "a character in *Invisible Man*." That answer, like any other answer, as simple as it may be, implies assumptions. The first, of course, is that I am asking a literary question. Otherwise, the answer might come from a Who's Who directory, a phone book, or the FBI files. The first assumption, then, is a necessary context, without which the question is meaningless. That context is implied by the question's appearance here, in a book of literary criticism focused on *Invisible Man*. Given that necessary context, however, the answer seems trivial. Recognizing the context thus creates expectations about the sufficiency of the answer, expectations the answer I gave leaves unfulfilled.

A more fulfilling answer might go on to say that Clifton appears in the last third of the novel. He works for the Brotherhood as Harlem director of youth and he befriends the invisible man, who has become the Brotherhood's newly appointed Harlem organizer. Together they plan a campaign against evictions which includes street-corner speeches. At one rally they are accosted by black separatists led by Ras the Exhorter. In the fighting, Ras has the opportunity to kill Clifton but instead tearfully exhorts him to abandon the Brotherhood, where, Ras feels, he functions as the puppet of white masters. Clifton, angered, knocks Ras down and leaves. Some time after this event, the Brotherhood transfers the invisible man out of Harlem, only to recall him when Clifton disappears. Clifton reappears in midtown, selling Sambo dolls. When a policeman repeatedly pushes Clifton while arresting him for illegal peddling, Clifton punches the policeman and is gunned down. The invisible man, who has witnessed the shooting, then organizes a public funeral for Clifton which precipitates riots in Harlem.

Is this outline of Clifton's actions a more sufficient answer? If so, rendered as it has been, with the flatness of a crib sheet, comic book, or opera program synopsis, it is hardly more interesting. One reason for its dullness is that I have attempted to omit any details which might suggest interpretation. I have tried to give, in other words, what Kermode would call a "carnal" reading, by which he means one hinting no secret meaning to Clifton's presence, no meaning which would be revealed through interpretation.

Next we can try to decide whether the text requires anything more than a carnal answer to the question of his identity. The first clue that it does is the inordinate repetition of Clifton's name. Although Clifton actually only appears in two chapters (three if we count his funeral), his name is mentioned in each of the nine chapters from the point of his introduction through the epilogue; in all, it is mentioned well over 150 times.[1] Clifton's behavior, moreover, leaves much to be explained. We know almost nothing about his origins; we don't know why he disappears or why he chooses to reappear selling Sambo dolls. Like the invisible man, we can only formulate assumptions to help answer our questions and thus interpret Clifton's behavior. The invisible man's search, of course, differs from our own in that he is still a character, like Clifton, created by a text. Yet from his limited position he replicates our hermeneutic enterprise (as he suggests in the final words of the epilogue: "Who knows but that, on the lower frequencies, I speak for you?").

Many critics, from their broader vantage, have attempted to complete the narrator's inquiries by supplying interpretations of Clifton's significance in the novel. Their interpretations, like all interpretation, result from trust in some system of beliefs outside the text which explains what the text does not.

Most critics attempt to explain the puzzle of Clifton's decision to sell Sambo dolls, which precipitates his death. The simplest explanation is that Clifton, in the words of Barbara Christian, "goes nuts" ("Ralph Ellison: A Critical Study," 363). Christian supports this interpretation by citing an earlier piece of the text in which Clifton states that "a man sometimes has to plunge outside history . . . otherwise he might kill somebody, go nuts." Christian's pieces clearly fail to interlock with each other or with the other parts of the narrative. Clifton equates going nuts with killing somebody, not with being killed, and he sees plunging outside of history as the alternative to going nuts, not the consequence of it. The invisible man, too, regards Tod's actions as plunging outside of history, and Tod's decision to do that structures much of the invisible man's subsequent interpretation.

Kirst tells us that Clifton's behavior indicates that the invisible man's grandfather was wrong, that "aggression through compliance is a potentially self-destructive tool. It demands that one violate his inner nature; the virtual suicide of Tod Clifton is its logical outcome" ("A Langian Analysis of Blackness," 23). This interpretation is interesting in isolation, that is, if we choose to see the entire novel as a dream fantasy meant to help the invisible man decode his grandfather's initial injunction. If, however, we expect the parts of the novel to cohere in any other way, Kirst's explanation fails because it doesn't explain why Clifton, who has not heard the injunction and does not seem implicitly to be following it, should elect to convert himself into an emblem to solve someone else's riddle.

Others view Clifton as a victim of his own conscience and/or the white manipulators. For them his peddling of dolls represents an admission of guilt, or a spiritual or psychological death with self-destructive overtones.[2] Unclear about Clifton's motives, the interpreters reach no consensus about what his relationship to the dolls signifies. Some suggest that Clifton has come to accept the inevitable dehumanization and exploitation of blacks. Another adds that the dolls also symbolize the invisible man, dancing on Brother Jack's string.[3] These critics are failing to account, in their readings, for the string's being black, or they are failing to explain what in the text allows us to convert a picture of a black man (a *very* black man) manipulating a black-and-orange doll with a black string into a sign of white manipulation of blacks.

Eleanor Wilner focuses on that thread "that the narrator, like the white people whose vision he shared, had been always too blind to see—that black identity that threaded its way, hidden, through all the oppressed past, the possession of those picaresque black men who manipulated the mask of the slave, but never merged with it, men who were never entirely the captives of their historical role, and who kept pride alive against a better day" ("The Invisible Black Thread," 249). Attributing this meaning to the black string effectively discounts other interpretations, but it also renders Tod's actions, for Wilner, indecipherable, and she concludes that "there is no way to resolve the various roles Tod may play in this work since they tend to work against each other" (253), yet she does suggest that Tod might

> serve as a kind of *alter ego*, a man whose integrity leaves nothing out. It is Tod, not the narrator, who opposes Ras, but at the same time admits to being tempted by his emotionally releasing rage; and it is Tod who turns, as the last act of his life, against the authority which has always opposed and oppressed him. It is Tod, then, as has been shown, who carries the black identity, and the human dilemma; he may be the vicarious bearer of the narrator's repressed identity, placed at a distance from himself, observed in the infinite way of the dimly comprehended inner truth, and destroyed in the very way that the narrator fears his emotions would destroy him. (256)

We need, then, a spiritual reading that will reconcile Wilner's insights about Clifton to the details in the text which, nevertheless, render him indecipherable to her. Jonathan Baumbach suggests the beginnings of one by identifying Tod as martyr-saint. In hawking the Sambo dolls, he asserts, "Clifton was not so much mocking the Brotherhood's attitude toward the Negro as he was parodying himself" (*The Landscape of Nightmare*, 81). Baumbach's argument implies that he understands the crucial quality of a "parody" is not its sameness to something else but its difference. Only through its differences can we tell parody from parallel, and yet, paradoxically, only by noting parallels can we begin to suspect that we are reading a parody. Jonathan Culler notes that "in calling something a parody we are specifying how it should be read . . . making the curious features of the parody intelligible" (*Structuralist Poetics*, 152). One key, then, to a coherent "spiritual" reading is the recognition of a generic structure, one which asks us to interpret not by trying to extend parallels but by trying to identify the ways in which we cannot. Baumbach focuses on the difference between Clifton's play and Jack's: "Clifton makes only *paper* Negroes dance; it is Jack and Tobitt who treat flesh-and-blood Negroes as if they were puppet Sambo dolls" (*The Landscape of Nightmare*, 83).

Similarly, Clifton's plunging outside history also acquires significance through the concept of parody. Clifton's ostensibly nonhistorical act is recorded in police records and in newspapers, and it effects riots similarly recorded in historical documents. His acts thus mock the Brotherhood's "history" in which his acts go unrecorded: "Deceived by the bogus historians of the Brotherhood, Clifton has 'plunged outside history,' though in punching the white policeman he demonstrated that he had not quite 'turned' his back! [Clifton] became a heckler of the Brotherhood, of the Negro, of the white man's treatment of the Negro, of himself, of the universe" (*The Landscape of Nightmare*, 81). Understanding the significance of Clifton's final scene, Baumbach views Clifton's death not as a self-destruction but as purposeful

> sacrifice to a culpability too egregious to be redeemed in any other way, and, at the same time, a final gratuitous act of heroism. In giving himself up to be murdered, Clifton takes on the whole responsibility for the Brotherhood's betrayal of the Negro. If by his sacrifice he does not redeem the hero from his own culpability, he at least through his example sets the possibility of Brother _____'s redemption. (80)

With a nod to Baumbach and homage to Hermes, I would like to suggest my "spiritual" reading of the Clifton chapters.

The first thing that we learn about Tod Clifton is that he is not on time. The invisible man arrives at a meeting of the Brotherhood at which all are present except Brother Clifton.

> "Well," Brother Jack said, "you are on time. Very good, we favor precision in our leaders."
> "Brother, I shall always try to be on time," I said.
> "Here he is, Brothers and Sisters," he said, "your new spokesman. Now to begin. Are we all present?"
> "All except Brother Tod Clifton," someone said.
> His red hair jerked with surprise. "So?"
> "He'll be here," a young brother said. "We were working until three this morning."
> "Still, he should be on time—Very well," Brother Jack said, taking out a

watch, "let us begin. I have only a little time here, but a little time is all that is needed. . . ." (273–74)

The numerous references to time which differentiate Tod from the invisible man might seem trivial in a "carnal" reading, but we already know that "time" is one of the keys to the narrator's hermeneutics. As he informed us in the prologue, "invisibility, let me explain, gives one a slightly different sense of time, you're never quite on the beat. Sometimes you're ahead and sometimes you're behind. Instead of the swift and imperceptible flowing of time, you are aware of its nodes, those points where time stands still or from which it leaps ahead, and you slip into the breaks and look around" (7). In the prologue, from the vantage of his invisibility, the narrator tells us, further, of the yokel who stepped inside the scientific boxer's sense of time, and of his own stepping inside Louis Armstrong's sense of time. Under the influence of a reefer, that musical time became historical time which itself subdivided into folk history, literary history (with echoes of Melville, Hawthorne, Poe, and Faulkner), and, finally, personal history. So Tod's not being on time—on the Brotherhood's time—prepares us for his contemplation of plunging outside of history, his decision to do so, and even his emulation of the boxing yokel as he shifts out of his role as humiliated black peddler and transforms into a graceful, dancerlike boxer to step inside the policeman's sense of time.

This accentuated difference between Tod and the invisible man at the moment of their meeting, however, is also an accentuated similarity between Tod and the narrator, twenty years later, who also has plunged outside of the Brotherhood's time. By comparing Clifton's introduction with the narrator's, in other words, we can see Clifton is set up as something the invisible man will become. Other details underscore this suggestion. Clifton was about the same age as the invisible man and "was moving with an easy Negro stride out of the shadow and into the light" (274). That motion replicates the general motion of the invisible man from his preinvisible days to the time of the narration in a room covered with lights.

Tod differs from the ginger-colored invisible man, however, in that he is "very black," even though his description shows distinct signs of miscegenation:

> . . . he possessed the chiseled, black-marble features sometimes found on
> statues in northern museums and alive in southern towns in which the white
> offspring of house children and the black offspring of yard children bear
> names, features and character traits as identical as the rifling of bullets fired
> from a common barrel. And now close up, leaning tall and relaxed, his arms
> outstretched stiffly upon the table, I saw the broad, taut span of his knuckles
> upon the dark grain of wood, the muscular, sweatered arms, the curving line
> of the chest rising to the easy pulsing of his throat, to the square, smooth
> chin, and saw a small X-shaped patch of adhesive upon the subtly blended,

velvet-over-stone, granite-over-bone, Afro-Anglo-Saxon contour of his
cheek. (274)

Tod seems to have acquired hybrid bone structure while retaining deeply
black skin. He looks like an artist's ideal not of an African but of a uniquely
Afro-American black—ideal in that he had infused American traits without
diluting his blackness and without any unnaturalness, a point stressed by the
reminder that "his head of Persian lamb's wool had never known a straight-
ener" (277).

The other detail that suggests a secret in the text is the "X-shaped patch of
adhesive" on Clifton's face. A few paragraphs later it is called the "cross of
adhesive on the black skin." Clifton bears this cross as the result of his confrontation with Ras, and it foreshadows another confrontation, one which
deeply troubles Tod. Keeping in mind Baumbach's view that Clifton's death
is self-willed and sacrificial, when we see that physically he suggests some
natural but impossible ideal at the same time as he foreshadows the path that
the invisible man will follow and the enlightenment he will achieve, the cross
gains significance. Taken together with the associations with the East (Persia)
and the lamb, the cross seems to suggest that Tod is a Christ figure.

This tentative hypothesis, nevertheless, has problems, the most notable at
first being Tod's proclivity toward violence, of which the cross is also a sign: it
covers a wound he got in an encounter with Ras. When someone at the
meeting warns, furthermore, that Ras "goes wild when he sees Black and
white people together," Tod responds, " 'We'll take care of that,' . . . touch-
ing his cheek" (276). Tod thus associates his wound and his cross with fighting
Ras, as he had earlier with being late for the Brotherhood meeting. Tod's
cross, in other words, signifies his difference from both Ras and the Brotherhood, each of whom tempt him in different ways.

Although we don't know how Tod was recruited into the Brotherhood, we
do know how the invisible man was, and we do know that his initial interest
arose from a need for money. Guilty about accepting Mary's support after his
accident compensation money ran out, he decided to call Brother Jack, who
had offered him a job as spokesman. At the meeting where the offer is made,
Jack, whose red hair is often noted, appears very much a mysterious stranger:
"There was something mysterious in the way he spoke, as though he had
everything figured out—whatever he was talking about. Look at this very most
certain white man, I thought. He didn't even realize that I was afraid and yet
he spoke so confidently" (221–22). And Jack's offer to the invisible man
echoes traditional Satanic appeals: " 'You are wise to distrust me,' he said,
'You don't know who I am and you don't trust me. That's as it should be. But
don't give up hope, because some day you will look me up on your own
accord and it will be different, for then you'll be ready. Just call this number

and ask for Brother Jack. You needn't give your name, just mention our conversation.' " (222). When the invisible man responds, he is very rapidly taken to a party at a building named "Chthonian" (an "expensive-looking building in a strange part of the city" [277]), where the elevator moves "a mile a minute" (288) but leaves the invisible man uncertain "whether we had gone up or down" (228). The woman who greets them at the apartment door has an exotic perfume and "a clip of blazing diamonds on her dress." Jack's constantly pushing the invisible man forward adds to the onerous quality of the scene, which is underscored by a nightmarishly "uncanny sense of familiarity" (227).

> Then I was past, disturbed not so much by the close contact, as by the sense
> that I had somehow been through it all before. I couldn't decide if it were
> from watching some similar scene in the movies, from books I'd read, or from
> some recurrent but deeply buried dream. Whatsoever, it was like entering a
> scene which, because of some devious circumstances, I had hitherto watched
> only from a distance. How could they have such an expensive place, I wondered. (228)

His pact concluded for the sum of $300 and the promise of $60 a week, the invisible man returns to Mary's and goes to sleep, preparing to leave the next day for his new quarters and new identity. Before falling asleep, he hears the clock tick "with empty urgency, as though trying to catch up with time. In the street a siren howled" (240). The clock in Mary's house thus seems out of synchronization with the world outside where the siren beckons, the world of Jack's watch and history which Tod, three years earlier, had entered, no doubt with similar promises of power and similar monetary rewards. The recruitment scene is indeed familiar in literature, film, nightmare, and, as well, in the experience of the invisible man's black brothers.

The similarity between Tod's relationship with Jack and his relationship with Ras becomes clearer when Ras tempts Tod. Although the scene has the same motifs as the invisible man's Chthonian initiation, it emphasizes power a great deal more than money. Both scenes, however, have a Satanic red cast over them—in the Chthonian apartment created by Jack's red hair and the "Italian-red draperies that fell in rich folds from the ceiling" (228), in the street confrontation created by the red neon "CHECKS CASHED HERE" sign, which glowed mysteriously over the whole scene (279–84).

Ras has the opportunity to kill Clifton but instead asks Clifton to join him: "I saw his face gleam with red-angry tears as he stood above Clifton with the still innocent knife and the tears red in the glow of the window sign. 'You *my* brother, mahn. Brothers are the same color; how the hell can you call these white men *brother*?' " (280). The word "brother" suggests Ras is vying with Jack, in an analogous way, for Tod's loyalties, and the word "hell" along with the red glow emphasizes the Satanic similarities. This emphasis gets even stronger when Ras refers to Tod as "a chief, a black King!" (281). Ras repeats this theme (". . . you wan the kings among men! . . . I will do it now, I say, but something tell me, 'No, no! You might be killing your black King!' " [282], and the scene resembles one of Christ's temptations as the speech concludes with a reiterated exhortation for Tod to join Ras:

> "So why don't you recognize your black duty, mahn, and come jine us?"
> His chest was heaving and a note of pleading had come into the harsh voice. He was an exhorter, all right, and I was caught in the crude, insane eloquence of his plea. He stood there, awaiting an answer. And suddenly a big transport plane came low over the buildings and I looked up to see the firing of its engine, and we were all three silent, watching.
> Suddenly the Exhorter shook his fist toward the plane and yelled "Hell with him, some day we have them too! Hell with him!"
> He stood there, shaking his fist as the plane rattled the buildings in its powerful flight. Then it was gone and I looked about the unreal street. They were fighting far up the block in the dark now and we were alone. I looked at the Exhorter. I didn't know if I were angry or amazed. (282–83)

At this point the invisible man intervenes and, after they argue, Ras appears similar to a fire-spitting devil: "He spat angrily into the dark street. It flew pink in the red glow" (283).

Although we could interpret this scene to affirm our hypothesis that Clifton is a Christ figure, in so doing we would have to discount specific details that confound that reading. If the scene concludes with Tod's rejection of Ras' temptation, for example, it does so with violence. Tod rejects Ras as he does the policeman later, not with articulate refutation or ascetic restraint, but rather with a swift 180-degree turn: "And before I could answer Clifton spun in the dark and there was a crack and I saw Ras go down and Clifton breathing hard and Ras lying there in the street, a thick, black man with red tears in his face that caught the reflection of the CHECKS CASHED HERE sign" (284). Another problem with casting Ras as the devil is that Ras casts the invisible man in that same role, calling him "a reg'lar little black devil" (280). The invisible man is, moreover, an agent—a paid agent—of Brother Jack's Chthonian organization, working on Brother Jack's time.

After he strikes Ras, Tod seems perplexed, but the invisible man calls him away from his self-doubting or remorse:

> And again, as Clifton looked gravely down he seemed to ask a silent question.
> "Let's go," I said. "Let's go!"
> We started away as the screams of sirens sounded, Clifton cursing quietly to himself. (284)

Clifton's questions thus remain silent as the sounds of sirens surround his self-cursed state. The invisible man, too, heard sirens when other members of the Brotherhood first noticed him at an impromptu street rally, just as he heard them again after he decided to join the Brotherhood. Because these lures to self-destruction surround the Brotherhood's temptations, the language of the text makes it hard for us to discount Ras' charge that the invisible man is a devil.

How then are we to interpret the conversation that follows this meeting?

"Where'd he get that name?" I said.

"He gave it to himself. I guess he did. *Ras* is a title of respect in the East. It's a wonder he didn't say something about 'Ethiopia stretching forth her wings,' " he said, mimicking Ras. "He makes it sound like the hood of a cobra fluttering. . . . I don't know . . . I don't know . . ."

"We'll have to watch him now," I said.

"Yes, we'd better," he said. "He won't stop fighting. . . . And thanks for getting rid of his knife."

"You didn't have to worry," I said. "He wouldn't kill his king."

He turned and looked at me as though he thought I might mean it; then he smiled.

"For a while there I thought I was gone," he said. As we headed for the district office I wondered what Brother Jack would say about the fight.

"We'll have to overpower him with organization," I said.

"We'll do that, all right. But it's on the inside that Ras is strong," Clifton said. "On the inside he's dangerous."

"He won't get on the inside," I said. "He'd consider himself a traitor."

"No," Clifton said, "he won't get on the inside. Did you hear how he was talking? Did you hear what he was saying?"

"I heard him, sure," I said.

"I don't know," he said. "I suppose sometimes a man *has* to plunge outside history . . ."

"What?"

"Plunge outside, turn his back. . . . Otherwise he might kill somebody, go nuts."

I didn't answer. Maybe he's right, I thought, and was suddenly very glad I had found Brotherhood. (284–85)

Ras here is compared to a snake, Tod to a king, and both Tod and the invisible man regard Ras in the kind of language used to caution against the devil. Ras, furthermore, had called the invisible man a mongoose—the natural predator of snakes—which would identify the invisible man as a disciple of Tod, affirming his need to ward off Ras' serpentine subversions. Tod, nevertheless, seems to reject the Brotherhood as well.

One can see why Wilner was confused about how to interpret Tod's role. As we build an hypothesis around some details in the text, others seem to undermine it. The first point to be made, however, is that allusions, like parodies, work not through their sameness but through their differences. So the first question we can raise is not whether Tod is a Christ figure, but rather, being identified with Christ through a number of signs in the text, how does he differ from the referent of the allusions? To put it another way, how is Ellison using Christ and Satan images?

We need to remember that the invisible man is not the narrator but a person whom the narrator has renounced or distanced himself from. The crucial difference between them is that the invisible man did not know how to interpret signs, did not know that in limiting his possibilities to other people's versions of reality, he was yielding up his identity. I do not think, moreover, that it would be an inappropriate pun, in this context, to call his ethnic identity his soul. The name that Tod knows him by, after all, was not the one his grandfather knew him by, but the one given to him when he accepted Jack's offer, by a white woman who drew it from an envelope kept in her bosom. Although he has given his soul, then, for money and the promise of power, as yet unable to read the signs, he remains unaware of the terms of the exchange. When the scene above concludes with an affirmation of faith in the Brotherhood, as though it were different from Ras' black Satan idolatry, the irony emerges out of the disparity between the invisible man's carnal reading and our spiritual one.

Yet Ras is no more astute than the invisible man. His entire offer to Tod was motivated by his belief that Tod was pure African. We know, however, that, although very black, Tod has Afro-Anglo-Saxon features. If the invisible man is blind to the Brotherhood's true composition, Ras is blind to Tod's; if the invisible man fails to see he is manipulated by whites, Ras fails to see he is manipulated by blackness. Both of them lure Tod for the wrong reasons, and just as Tod turned around to hit Ras, some time earlier he had also turned on and struck a white member of the Brotherhood (298). Tod thus seems to know and manifest what the narrator will learn—that, as he tells us in the prologue: "contradiction . . . is how the world moves: Not like an arrow, but a boomerang. (Beware of those who speak of the *spiral* of history; they are preparing the boomerang. Keep a steel helmet handy.) I know; I have been boomeranged across my head so much that I now can see the darkness of lightness" (5). In his turnabouts, then, we see another way in which Tod anticipates the invisible man's motion out of darkness into light.

If there is something messianic in this movement, however, it is still marked by violence. If Tod is a Christ figure in that he seems to discover and rebuff the temptations of a Satan figure, and in that his sacrificial death points the way to the invisible man's salvation, he seems more an anti-Christ in that his life is circumscribed by violence that he precipitates. To call Tod an anti-

Christ, however, seems just as inappropriate as discounting or rationalizing his violence in order to call him a Christ figure.

The text captures us in an apparent interpretive paradox, resolved, I think, by accepting the contradictions and simply saying: Ellison's Christ is violent, not nonviolent. This approach takes us to a basic understanding of Ellison's use of allusion. His allusions almost always force us to reconsider the referent; although he gives us enough clues to suggest a specific secret (spiritual) reading, in considering the implications of that reading, we constantly find that we cannot take referents for granted; Ellison's text requires reinterpretation of the constants. In this case, Ellison is making us challenge or suspend our idea of Christ by finding a context in which our reading requires a coherent but different view of the figure. In a larger sense this becomes the direction of the whole book. The alluded-to becomes a network of tradition, the standard assumptions about which are both actively and tacitly challenged to make the reader aware of possibilities. For the purposes of forming a coherent spiritual reading of the Tod Clifton episodes, therefore, we have to entertain the possibility that the black Christ may be violent, or at least ask the question: under what circumstances, is Ellison suggesting, may the black Christ be violent?

Thinking about Tod's role also takes us to some important questions about keeping the faith and about betrayal, as these, too, are themes in the Christ myth challenged directly by our reading of Clifton's story. Ras and the Brotherhood both come to regard Tod as a betrayer, but they also come to regard the invisible man as one. At the same time that the Brotherhood believes he's betrayed them for not following orders, the people of Harlem believe that he's betrayed them by letting the Brotherhood order him elsewhere. After Tod's death, moreover, the invisible man feels betrayed by Tod, but he also considers himself Tod's betrayer. Since the Christ-myth allusions seem to highlight a motif of betrayal in the novel, the invisible black thread that Wilner identifies as the thread of tradition can also be seen as a thread of betrayal. The invisible man's grandfather, whom Wilner associates with the string, was after all a betrayer, "a traitor all my born days, a spy in the enemy's country ever since I give up my gun back in the Reconstruction" (13). "Live with your head in the lion's mouth" he advised the invisible man. "I want you to overcome 'em with yeses, undermine 'em with grins, agree 'em to death and destruction . . ." (13). Having heard his grandfather's advice, the invisible man always felt "guilty and uncomfortable" (14) when things went well for him:

> When I was praised for my conduct I felt guilt that in some way I was really doing something that was against the wishes of the white folks, that if they had understood they would have desired me to act just the opposite, that I should have been sulky and mean and that would have been really what they wanted, even though they were fooled and thought they wanted me to act as I did. It

made me afraid that some day they would look upon me as a traitor and I
would be lost. (14)

Those feelings become a self-fulfilling prophecy. At the battle royal, the
black boys in the ring consider him as much a traitor, when he takes the place
of one of their friends, as the white townsfolk do when he accidentally says
"social equality" in his speech instead of "social responsibility." Similarly,
Bledsoe considers him a betrayer for bringing the white trustee, Mr. Norton,
to the Golden Day, as much as the black vet at the Golden Day considers
him one for identifying with Mr. Norton. At the Liberty Paints factory, the
union fears he is a scab and Lucius Brockway fears he is a union man. Yet at
the same time that he is considered a betrayer, he feels betrayed, betrayed by
the secret agreement among the other blacks in the ring at the battle royal as
well as by the white citizens who compensated him with false coins on an
electrified rug; betrayed by Norton and Bledsoe and Brockway and Wrestrum,
before Tod's turnabout, and later by Brother Jack.

In terms of the folk motifs, this accounts for the invisible man's thinking of
himself as both rabbit and bear, trickster and dupe; in Stephen Dedalus'
terms, he is both kinetic and aesthetic; and in Christian mythology he is both
Jesus and Judas. This doubling of possibilities, this mirroring, forces us to
defer our understanding until we can reconcile the differences. The text continues to evoke Christ comparisons which not so much inform as confront us
with the difficulty of affixing meaning because we cannot be sure what informing assumptions to make about the allusion. The concept of betrayal, for
example, ties inextricably to the concept of faith. If one believes in the
Brotherhood or in black separatist nationalism, the assumptions become
clear. These alternative religions, in fact, are in many ways interchangeable.
The sense of prophesy and ordination in Ras' rhetoric differs little from the
Brothers' faith in the doctrines of "history" and "science." Brother Wrestrum,
for example, talks of the Brotherhood in the language of a born-again Christian, stressing the good fortune of salvation and the need for unremitting
vigilance:

> "I'm fair. I ask myself every day, 'What are you doing against Brotherhood?'
> and when I find it, I root it out, I burn it out like a man cauterizing a mad-
> dog bite. This business of being a brother is a full-time job. You have to be
> pure in heart and you have to be disciplined in body and mind. Brother, you
> understand what I mean?"
> "Yes, I think I do," I said. "Some folks feel that way about religion."
> "Religion?" He blinked his eyes. "Folks like me and you is full of distrust,"
> he said. "We been corrupted 'til it's hard for some of us to believe in Brother-
> hood. And some even want revenge! That's what I'm talking about. We have
> to root it out! We have to learn to trust our other Brothers. After all, didn't
> *they* start the Brotherhood? Didn't *they* come and stretch out their hand to us

black men and say, 'We wan y'all for our brothers?' Didn't they do it? Didn't they, now? Didn't they set out to organize us, and help fight our battle and all like that? Sho they did, and we have to remember it twenty-four hours a day. *Brotherhood*. That's the word we got to keep right in front of our eyes every second. Now this brings me to why I come to see you, Brother." (297)

Brother Jack, moreover, in his final confrontation with the invisible man, allows his glass eye to pop from his head and roll on the table, a grotesquely literal interpretation of Jesus' command, which he uses to intimidate the invisible man. Even more ironically, Jack's need to "cast out the offending eye" enacts Norton's words to Jim Trueblood. Hearing of Trueblood's act of incest, Norton, horrified and fascinated, asks: "You feel no inner turmoil, no need to cast out the offending eye?" (40). For Norton as for Jack (as well as the blind Reverend Homer A. Barbee), faith comes from blindness. The casting out of the offending eye—the failure to see the realities or possibilities of black American experience—allows their religiouslike dedication to their respective causes. Within the realm of their assumptions, marked by the limitations of their vision, the idea of betrayal has meaning. When the invisible man begins, however, to see around corners, those limitations and the meanings they provided start to dissolve, a point that becomes clear in the language of Tod's death scene.

Tod has disappeared for about one month (forty days?). Recalled to Harlem to reorganize the deteriorated Brotherhood chapter, the invisible man, now considered a betrayer by the people, is also betrayed by the Brotherhood, which intentionally holds a strategy meeting without informing him.

While the meeting from which he is barred goes on, he discovers Clifton selling paper Sambo dolls on 42nd Street:

> For a second our eyes met and he gave me a contemptuous smile, then he spieled again. I felt betrayed. I looked at the doll and felt my throat constrict. The rage welled behind the phlegm as I rocked back on my heels and crouched forward. There was a splash of whiteness and a splatter like heavy rain striking a newspaper and I saw the doll go over backwards, wilting into a dripping rag of frilled tissue, the hateful head upturned on its outstretched neck still grinning toward the sky. The crowd turned on me indignantly. The whistle came again. I saw a short, pot-bellied man look down, then up at me with amazement and explode with laughter, pointing from me to the doll, rocking. People backed away from me. (328–29)

As the invisible man describes it, Tod is the betrayer, but the crowd, applying a different set of assumptions, sees a likeness between the doll and the invisible man, a likeness further borne out by his own earlier descriptions: "It was Clifton, riding easily back and forth on his knees, flexing his legs without shifting his feet, his right shoulder raised at an angle and his arm pointing stiffly at the bouncing doll as he spieled from the corner of his mouth" (327). Being soaked in phlegm, the doll also undergoes an experience analogous to that which the invisible man imagined himself experiencing when he recognized Tod: "It was as though I had waded into a shallow pool only to have the bottom drop out and water close over my head" (327).

As a "frill of paper," the doll also resembles all the other papers in this novel, each one a sign of betrayal. Not until he burns them, of course, does the narrator realize how universally this signification holds true. Again the sign has a different meaning for the reader and narrator than for the invisible man. Yet that meaning confounds rather than clarifies when the doll is put in the same pocket "where I carried Brother Tarp's chain link" (238), a broken link which signifies freedom. Our inability to separate the betrayer from the betrayed is further exacerbated by the invisible man's reluctance to face Tod, as though the invisible man were the betrayer, not Tod.

Following this comes language which treats Tod as a fallen angel:

> How on earth could he drop from Brotherhood to this in so short a time? And why if he had to fall back did he try to carry the whole structure with him? What would non-members who knew him say? It was as though he had chosen—how had he put it the night he fought with Ras?—to fall outside of *history*. I stopped in the middle of the walk with the thought. "To Plunge," he had said. But he knew that only in the Brotherhood could we make ourselves known, could we avoid being empty Sambo dolls. Such an obscene flouncing of everything human! My God! And I had been worrying about being left out of a meeting. (328)

This passage starts out treating, with a sense of Christian pity, the fallen ideal who had dropped to earth, fallen back, and was therefore in danger of subverting the system. The "God" in the passage is history, with the Brotherhood its practicing religion. In his praise of the Brotherhood, the invisible man echoes Brother Wrestrum's blind dicta; yet at this point in the text we can also identify Wrestrum with the Sambo dolls, for, as the invisible man noted about him earlier, "Clifton would know how to handle this clown" (304). Wrestrum had betrayed the invisible man by encouraging him to accept a magazine interview and, subsequently, accusing him of disloyalty to the Brotherhood by doing so. So the invisible man was not only adopting Wrestrum's rhetoric but emulating Wrestrum's acts, the acts of someone he knew to be a betrayer. If we identify Wrestrum with the Sambo dolls that Clifton handles, then the invisible man has accurately identified betrayal and done the right thing in spitting on the doll. But since the invisible man can be identified with Wrestrum, his accusations can also be seen as masking his own acts of betrayal.

To complicate matters further, the invisible man, as we have seen, also resembles the doll itself, the doll he renounces as the "obscene flouncing of everything human." Yet "humanity" has been one of his highest values, the trait he associated with his grandfather and his college instructor, Woodridge. It was even the term he first used as a Brotherhood spokesman to describe the effect of the Brotherhood on him. The inhuman, the electrified, and the mechanical, on the other hand—from the electric carpet in the first chapter to the nightmare of the mechanical man in the last—permeate the novel with menace. When the invisible man thus sees the dolls as an "obscene flouncing of everything human," he seems to be renouncing his own values.

This ironic self-incrimination lends even more irony to the term "My God!" Although it seems an appeal to heaven in a kind of shock or horror, we should remember that the invisible man's "God" in this passage is the Brotherhood, which, just before this scene, had again betrayed him. The invisible man, then, is calling to his betrayers (in the language of Wrestrum) about the outrage of flouncing everything human. Grammatically, "My God!" is in apposition to the noun phrase "everything human," and we could say that, at some level, "everything human" is the invisible man's God. "Everything human," however, is part of a larger gerund phrase, itself in apposition to "empty Sambo dolls," and the exclamation at another level can make us see "My God" as a synonym for the dolls, or at least make us ask in what way the two can be equated. The Sambo dolls thus suggest Tod and Wrestrum and the invisible man; they represent betrayer and betrayed, resiliency and emptiness, deity and fallen angel, humanity and mechanization. In other words, the Sambo dolls suggest infinite possibilities and show that the meaning of a black image depends upon its interpreters, just as the meaning of betrayal depends on one's loyalties.

Tod's spiel says so much:

Shake it up! Shake it up!
He's Sambo, the dancing doll, ladies and gentlemen.
Shake him, stretch him by the neck and set him down,
—He'll do the rest. Yes!
He'll make you laugh, he'll make you sigh, si-igh.
He'll make you want to dance, and dance—
Here you are, ladies and gentlemen, Sambo,
The dancing doll.
Buy one for your baby. Take him to your girl friend and she'll love you,
　　loove you!
He'll keep you entertained. He'll make you weep sweet—
Tears from laughing.
Shake him, shake him, you cannot break him
For he's Sambo, the dancing, Sambo, the prancing,
Sambo, the entrancing, Sambo Boogie Woogie paper doll.
And all for twenty-five cents, the quarter part of a dollar . . .

Ladies and gentlemen, he'll bring you joy, step up and meet him,
    Sambo the—. . . .
What makes him happy, what makes him dance,
This Sambo, this jambo, this high-stepping joy boy?
He's more than a toy, ladies and gentlemen, he's Sambo, the dancing doll,
    the twentieth-century miracle.
Look at that rumba, that suzy-q, he's Sambo-Boogie,
Sambo-Woogie, you don't have to feed him, he sleeps collapsed, he'll kill
    your depression
And your dispossession, he lives upon the sunshine of your lordly smile
And only twenty-five cents, the brotherly two bits of a dollar because
    he wants me to eat.
It gives him pleasure to see me eat.
You simply take him and shake him . . . and he does the rest.
Thank you, lady . . . (326–27)

The invisible man, blinded by Tod's act of selling the dolls, apparently doesn't
listen to the spiel, for there is nothing in it with which he would disagree.
Tod accurately describes the images of the black for sale in America. When
Tod suggests, furthermore, that the Sambo doll will "take it on the lambo"
(327), a phrase the invisible man will reiterate, he emphasizes the sacrificial
quality of the manipulated black image, a sacrifice Tod will manifest in human form a few moments later when he confronts the policeman and invites
his own death.

As we noted when we first saw Tod coming out of the shadow into the
light, in many ways he points the direction for the invisible man and thus
anticipates the journey of the novel. In much the same way, Tod's spiel says
what the invisible man will learn—about his image, his tradition, his loyalties
and betrayals—that necessitates his hibernation, his retreat to the underground. His adamant aversion to Tod's spiel also anticipates what he will learn
about the reaction to his own spiels and acts: that "[he] was never more hated
than when [he] tried to be honest" (432).

Just as spiritually and psychologically Tod leads the invisible man to enlightenment, his death physically directs the invisible man underground: "I
wandered down the subway stairs," he says after leaving the scene of Tod's
shooting, "seeing nothing, my mind plunging" (331). This plunge into the
subway also takes the invisible man outside "history," for while he is contem-
plating the meaning of history he sees some young men on the platform:

What about those three boys . . . tall and slender, walking stiffly with swinging shoulders in their well-pressed, too-hot-for-summer suits, their collars
high and tight about their necks, their identical hats of black cheap felt set
upon the crowns of their heads with a severe formality above their hard

conked hair? It was as though I'd never seen their like before: Walking slowly, their shoulders swaying, their legs swinging from their hips in trousers that ballooned upward from cuffs fitting snug about their ankles; their coats long and hip-tight with shoulders far too broad to be those of natural western men. These fellows whose bodies seemed—what had one of my teachers said of me?—"You're like one of these African sculptures, distorted in the interest of design?" Well, what design and whose? (332–33)

This trinity, silent and ritualistic, suggests to the invisible man a new way of reading history. In asking "what design and whose?" the invisible man is starting to confront the basic issue—which I have called hermeneutics—that frames this novel. His question indicates that the terms "accuracy" and "distortion" become bogus once we realize that they presume norms. With different presumption, we find the same object or narrative reveals different distortions which in turn suggest different secrets, different spiritual readings.

The invisible man describes these young men, who for the first time have become significant to him, in language that associates them with some mystery play or pageant about the sacrificial death of Tod Clifton:

> I stared as they seemed to move like dancers in some kind of funeral ceremony, swaying, going forward, their black faces secret, moving slowly down the subway platform, the heavy heel-plated shoes making a rhythmical tapping as they moved. Everyone must have seen them, or heard their muted laughter, or smelled the heavy pomade on their hair—or perhaps failed to see them at all. For they were men outside of historical time, they were untouched, they didn't believe in Brotherhood, no doubt had never heard of it; or perhaps like Clifton would mysteriously have rejected its mysteries; men of transition whose faces were immobile. (333)

The consequences of his new spiritual reading overwhelm the invisible man but also enable him to connect disparate and seemingly irreconcilable details.

> But who knew (and now I began to tremble so violently I had to lean against a refuse can)—who knew but that they were the saviors, the true leaders, the bearers of something precious? The stewards of something uncomfortable, burdensome, which they hated because, living outside the realm of history, there was no one to applaud their value and they themselves failed to understand it. What if Brother Jack were wrong? What if history was a gambler, instead of a force in a laboratory experiment, and the boys his ace in the hole? What if history was not a reasonable citizen, but a madman full of paranoid guile and these boys his agents, his big surprise! His own revenge? For they were outside, in the dark with Sambo, the dancing paper doll; taking it on the lambo with my fallen brother, Tod Clifton (Tod, Tod) running and dodging the forces of history instead of making a dominating stand. (333)

The Sambo dolls, the running man, the underground man, the brothers (Brer) bear and rabbit all come together, in the last sentence, with the three dancerlike boys with taps on their shoes, the sacrificial lamb, and Tod Clifton. With this, the invisible man's language takes on ceremonial formality ("There were many seats and the three sat together" [334]), and the details he notices evoke, in both their symmetry and content, religious connotations:

> I stood, holding onto the center pole, looking down the length of the car. On one side I saw a white nun in black telling her beads, and standing before the door across the aisle there was another dressed completely in white, the exact duplicate of the other except that she was black and her black feet bare. Neither of the nuns was looking at the other but at their crucifixes. . . . (334)

This scene causes the invisible man to paraphrase a verse he had heard "long ago at the Golden Day" which strongly suggests the eucharist:

> *Bread and Wine,*
> *Bread and Wine,*
>   *Your cross ain't nearly so*
>   *Heavy as mine* . . . (334)

He continues to notice the formal aspects of the young men's behavior, which recall again the scene of Tod's death, and we see that Tod, in one more way, anticipated the invisible man's behavior: ". . . Clifton would have known them better than I. He knew them all the time" (334). As they leave, the invisible man again acknowledges their spiritual significance: "I studied them closely until they left the train, their shoulders rocking, their heavy heel plates clicking remote, cryptic messages in the brief silence of the train's stop" (335).

Studying these young men, the invisible man again assumes the role of student, this time not at anyone's direct command, but as the self-willed revolt against the imposed and institutionalized studies which have enslaved and betrayed him. Emerging from the subway, outside the dictates of others' presumptions—because of Clifton's death, outside of their versions of history—he views the people of Harlem differently:

> Now, moving through the crowds along 125th Street, I was painfully aware of other men dressed like the boys, and of girls in dark exotic-colored stockings, their costumes surreal variations of downtown styles. They'd been there all along, but somehow I'd missed them. I'd missed them even when my work had been most successful. They were outside the groove of history, and it was my job to get them in, all of them. I looked into the design of their faces, hardly a one that was unlike someone I'd known down South. Forgotten names sang through my head like forgotten scenes in dreams. I moved with the crowd, the sweat pouring off me, listening to the grinding roar of traffic, the growing sound of a record shop loudspeaker blaring a languid blues. I

stopped. Was this all that would be recorded? Was this the only true history of the times, a mood blared by trumpets, trombones, saxophones and drums, a song with turgid, inadequate words? (335)

The word "design" takes us back to the question about the invisible man's past (what design and whose?), just as the faces themselves return him to it. This forgotten heritage takes the invisible man to the blues which, for Ellison, represent infinite possibilities, the possibilities seen by stepping outside history to repossess the forgotten folk culture, the signs of which can be discovered everywhere, once one understands that the secret is there. So Wilner is correct in seeing the thread as a sign of black cultural ties, but it is a sign intelligible only to those who know to look for the secret.

To reveal that secret, Tod died, and the doll thus becomes the key to interpreting his death. In that regard, one of its significant details is that it had "grinned back at Clifton as it grinned forward at the crowd, and their entertainment had been his death" (337), which is an emblematic restatement of the basic lesson in hermeneutics that I have been claiming is central to this novel.

Another important detail is that Tod had been controlling the doll all along with an invisible black thread. This is the black thread that has perplexed critics. It has raised questions about the informing context, the context which would tell us what the string represents, tell us, in other words, who is manipulating whom. That, however, may be the wrong question, the appropriate one focusing not on the manipulators but on the manipulation itself. Being both black *and* invisible the string becomes an emblematic lesson about the possibilities of black power. Clifton could make the image do anything he wanted it to, but, having gotten control of the invisible black string, he could not discover what to do with it because every choice was subject to interpretation by a world with different assumptions. So long as he lived in the realm of others' assumptions, his life could not have its own meaning, and the only alternative to selling his image was violently to assault the buyers. The only hope for freedom from that double bind—the double bind first acknowledged by the invisible man's grandfather—is to make others aware of that bind in which their sense of meaning is centered. To the cause of that decentering, Tod sacrifices himself and thus begins the invisible man on his road to salvation. "I could think of no justification for Clifton's having sold the dolls," he states, "but there was justification enough for giving him a public funeral, and I seized upon the idea, now, as though it would save my life" (338).

The invisible man's action precedes his understanding, because once he understands Tod's actions, he will already have found his salvation. For the time being, he understands that the dolls signify power: "[The other side] had the power to use a paper doll, first to destroy [Tod's] integrity and then as an excuse for killing him. All right, so we'll use his funeral to put his integrity back together again. . . . For that's all he had had or wanted. And now I could see the doll only vaguely and drops of moisture were thudding down upon its absorbent paper" (338). The doll's transformation, in the invisible man's eyes, from a sign of betrayal to a reminder of Tod's quest for integrity prefigures the invisible man's own transformation, as does the substitution of rainlike tears for the earlier shower of phlegm.

The funeral service itself is also rich with allusions to Christian mythology. Tod's coffin rests "upon the backs of its wobbly carpenter's horses" (343), and the word "mass" is used repeatedly in such a way as to suggest a Catholic service: "The sun shone down upon a mass of unbeared heads" (340); "I could see them winding up in a mass to the muffled sound of the drums" (341); "And now some of the older ones in the mass were joining in" (341); "I felt a wonder at the singing mass" (342). Although the word could also suggest the Brotherhood's call to the masses, it is never used in that way, almost calling our attention to the omission of the plural usage, especially when we remember not only Ellison's Joycean relish for puns but also that, in his own prenovelist days, Ellison published frequently for *New Masses*. Rather the invisible man fixes on individual faces—"a slender black man with his face turned toward the sun, singing through the upturned bells of the horn" (341), "a peanut vendor standing beneath a street lamp upon which pigeons were gathered, and now I saw him stretch out his arms with his palms turned upward, and suddenly he was covered, head, shoulders and outflung arms, with fluttering, feasting birds" (342).

The ritualistic quality, especially of this last crucifix image, would tend to suggest a spiritual reading of the text which reveals the ascension of Clifton's soul. In this context, the invisible man's references to the mountain from which he is speaking evoke associations with the sermon on the mount. The funeral is held in Mount Morris Park, where many of those reaching "the top of the mountain were spreading massed together" (342), and as the mass gathers, "the top of the little mountain bristled with banners, horns and uplifted faces" (342). The invisible man further calls attention to the fact that his nonsermon is given from a mount by saying, "Listen to me standing upon this so-called mountain!" (345).

These mount references, however, suggest that the invisible man, not Tod, is the Christ figure, or they suggest that Christ and/or Tod are somehow like Caesar, or they suggest that Jesus' sermon on the mount should be read as a subtle funeral oration. The content of the speech, moreover, is very different from that of the sermon on the mount. For although the speech suggests the danger in failing to turn the other cheek, it emphasizes more the degradation involved in doing so. Exercising Christian tolerance, the speech implies repeatedly, yields neither earthly nor heavenly reward, and after the funeral we are not allowed to see Tod as risen. Succinctly, the invisible man tells us: "They filled the grave quickly and we left. Tod Clifton was underground" (347). Tod (whose name, critics are quick to point out, means death) is, as the invisible man repeatedly reminded his audience, completely mortal: "do you expect to see some magic and the dead rise up and walk again? Go home, he's as dead as he'll ever die. That's the end in the beginning and there's no encore" (343).

If the end of Tod's funeral oration is in the beginning, then that is one more way in which Tod is like the narrator, who tells us in the prologue about his own narration that "the end is in the beginning and lies far ahead" (5). Thus Tod Clifton, buried in a density of allusion, from which he might or might not rise, as Christ or anti-Christ, to save or reveal his friend or betrayer, the invisible man, speaking a funeral sermon on the so-called mountain after the death of his Tod. I asked early in this chapter: "Who is Tod Clifton?" The answer I now want to suggest is: the enemy of dogma. For dogma is the real devil of *Invisible Man*, no matter whose. When the invisible man subverts his individuality to the cause of dogma, he indeed becomes the devil's hench-man, but when he sees himself or others as individuals he moves toward salvation. Because dogma makes people blind, it causes the narrator's invisi-bility; it blocks the light and limits possibilities. Dogma is the dog that has undone so many in this novel. When Peter Wheatstraw says "oh goddog daddy-o . . . who got the damn dog?" (132) that dog-daddy is a dog-ma, too. Wheatstraw's shift from "oh" to "o" echoes the implied shift in chapter 2, where Ellison transfers his debt from Whitman to what the invisible man o, o, owes those multimillionaires. As the goddog palindrome reminds us, fur-thermore, "god" spelled backwards is "dog"; what we learn later is change the "g" to "t," and God is dead.

Through Tod's death, the invisible man comes to see the victims of dogma everywhere, and Tod's plunge outside that dogma—his route underground—means both violence and finality. For if Tod were guaranteed escape or resur-rection, he would simply be trading the body of one dogma for the spirit of another. At the other extreme in this novel is Rinehart, who instead of re-nouncing all dogma endorses it all. That is his "spiritual technology," his mastery of religion and science, his dominion over every audience. For the invisible man, this yea-saying means chaos, just as Tod's nay-saying means death. The invisible man learns to substitute invisibility for death; that is, he learns to follow his Tod symbolically and to oppose Rinehartism through an awareness of the hidden assumptions that make Rinehartism possible in any of its forms.

Invisibility thus casts a cold eye on the Brotherhood's dogma of the left as it does on the fascist dogma of the right.[4] Invisibility rejects equally the dogma of Bledsoe and that of Brockway, of Norton and of Ras, of Hambro, Kimbro, and Rambo. It also, as I hope to demonstrate in detail, rejects the dogma of historians and literary critics, and, as Joyce did, it challenges dogma about literary conventions themselves. Whereas, in 1952 (and very often today), allusions by convention refer to an accepted understanding, we have seen that potentially they can make us question that understanding and the reasons we might have accepted it.

4. Invisible Man in the Golden Day

The next allusion in *Invisible Man* that I am going to discuss at length is the term "Golden Day." Putting aside, momentarily, the allusory significance of the term, we can safely say that within the structure of the novel, the name, the image, the place haunts the narrator. One of his obsessions is to discover what went wrong in the Golden Day.

Ostensibly the name of a bar/bordello which is the setting for chapter 3, it is mentioned thirty-four times in the novel. Until the day the narrator brought Mr. Norton, the northern trustee, into the Golden Day, his life seemed a model of success, as defined by the world around him. Because he had been the model black in his southern town, the white community leaders had awarded him a scholarship to the "state college for Negroes." There, too, he showed that he could become a model black, that is, one who would not challenge the white power structure. In short, he was conforming to the model he had adopted, Booker T. Washington. But the nameless narrator, the invisible man, was largely unaware that this intricate system of role-playing depended upon lies, depended upon the black's knowing the difference between what the white man *said* he wanted to see and what he *actually* wanted to see. When the invisible man showed Mr. Norton Jim Trueblood and the black life in the Golden Day, he unwittingly precipitated his expulsion from the college, his emigration north, and his involvement with urban life and political organizing. For the first half of his narration, so long as he has hopes of returning to his old way of life, he is obsessed with the incidents in the Golden Day, with the hysteria and turmoil that seemed unfairly to have propelled him out of his way of life. In chapter 10, for example, the invisible man, expelled from college, his hopes of finding a lucrative job destroyed, begins work in the Liberty Paints factory, and thinks, "Damn that Golden Day! But it was strange how life connected up. Because I had carried Mr. Norton to the old run-down building with rotting paint, I was here" (153).

This is virtually the last reference to the Golden Day in the novel, for thirty-two of the thirty-four references occur in chapters 2 through 10. In chapter 11, the invisible man has an electric lobotomy in the factory hospital, after which he abandons all hope of returning to the South, and the Golden Day is only mentioned again once before the epilogue.

In order to examine the allusory significance of the term "Golden Day," we first must consider Lewis Mumford's book by the same name: oversimplification is at its core. It seeks to reduce the course of American literature to one dramatic action. The book is, in fact, organized like a classic tragedy, in which we see enacted a drama whose hero is the individual and antagonist the machine. The "Golden Day," the period from 1830 to 1860 that historians often call the Era of Reform, was, according to Mumford, the period when the individual had the greatest hopes of triumphing. Alas (a stage word Mumford uses more than once), he did not. Industrialism, the machine, the Gilded Age triumphed; materialism, cynicism, shallowness replaced idealism, optimism, depth. Revealing this tragedy is the purpose of Mumford's book.

The opening chapter serves as a prologue and prepares us for the underlying dramatic conceit. In the eighteenth century, we are told, "Distinguished American figures step onto the stage, in turn as if the Muse of History had prepared their entrances and exits. Their arrangement is almost diagrammatic: they form a resume of the European mind. In fact these Edwardses and Franklins seem scarcely living characters: they were Protestantism, Science, Finance, Politics" (12–13).

The masque's processional thus begins. Not only is this a play, but a play with allegorical significance, characters standing for abstract concepts, national, political, moral types: "First on stage was Jonathan Edwards . . . the last great expositor of Calvinism. . . . After Edwards, Protestantism lost its intellectual backbone. It developed into the bloodless Unitarianism of the early Nineteenth century, which is a sort of humanism without courage, or got caught in the orgies of revivalism, and, under the name of evangelical Christianity, threw itself under the hoofs of more than one muddy satyr" (13).

Note in this passage, too, the element of personification, the tendency to treat a whole philosophical/theological movement as though it were of one mind, as though it could be measured, like a tragic hero, against one of Aristotle's heroic ideals. We watch the "life" of American Protestantism as a morality drama: the sad demise of a religion gone astray because of its tragic flaw, lack of courage, lack of "intellectual backbone." In this encapsulation, American Protestantism seems to have found a fate similar to that of many of the characters in the popular fiction and melodrama of the period, rampant with tales of those gone astray for lack of backbone.[1]

The Mumford passage cited above, however, relies also on another device popular on the stage, the use of reductive definitions. "Humanism without courage" is a workable stage definition for Unitarianism. Although, as the Chorus points out at the beginning of *Henry V*, bold reductions are necessary to render the complicated flow of history within the time/space limitations of a stage, the Chorus makes this explanation as a concession, an apology to the audience for the limited credibility of what we are to see. But Mumford seems to believe in the verisimilitude of his conceits, and he invites us to join as credulous spectators in the pageant of American history.

The processional of representative men continues through to the nineteenth century. Even Rousseau—for Mumford the philosophic patriarch of romanticism and, therefore, of the American pioneer—makes an appearance, along with Paul Bunyan, Thomas Jefferson, Rip Van Winkle, Ben Franklin, and Edgar Allan Poe and Leatherstocking. Most strikingly here, Mumford willingly blends fictional characters with real, finding Leatherstocking as representative of the pioneer as he finds Ben Franklin representative of the inventor. When the curtain drops, we see that the pioneer movement has become a war against nature, and in the end find it "as far from Rousseau and Wordsworth as the inventor of poison gas was from the troubadour who sang the song of Roland" (34). "The dream [of Leatherstocking] had become the nightmare of Poe" (38). "The gun and the ax and the pick, alas!, had taught their lessons too well" (38). "The return to nature led, ironically, to the denatured environment" (39).

Thus the scene is set for the next act, the chapter entitled "The Golden Day," which covers the period from 1830 to 1860. This is how Mumford describes it:

An imaginative New World came to birth during this period, a new hemisphere in the geography of the mind. That world was the climax of American experience. What preceded led up to it: what followed, dwindled away from it; and we who think and write today are either continuing the first exploration, or we are disheartened, and relapse into some stale formula, or console ourselves with empty gestures of frivolity. (43)

The structural relationship of the Golden Day to the rest of history has classical tragedy as its paradigm. We have the rising action in which Mumford identifies the confluence of incidents which make the tragedy inevitable; we have unity of place and, by reducing thirty years to one (golden) day, unity of time. Finally, we have recognition of the less than heroic audience—we who think and write today—incapable of the heroic heights or tragic falls, who must live in lesser times, like those which led up to that heroic period or followed from it.

The "Day," too, has its tragic substructure, with literary figures personifying times of day which, in turn, personify the rising action, the climax and the fall. Thus, in the tragic masque, Emerson is "The Morning Star"; Thoreau, "Dawn"; Whitman, "High Noon"; Hawthorne, "Twilight"; and Melville, "Night."

Mumford's insistence on his tragic progression can be seen clearly at the conclusion of his brief "Twilight" section. Preparing a transition from Hawthorne to Melville, he concludes:

There is no surer test of the quality of life in what I have called the Golden
Day, than the two tragedies, *The Scarlet Letter* and *Moby Dick*, which issued
out of it. The sunlight had in Emerson and Whitman penetrated to every
spot, and in its presence, the dark corners became more intense. If one explored the white summits of the glacier with Emerson, one might also fall
into the abyss with Melville. One climbed high; and when one fell, the fall
was deep. (70–71)

To accept this dramatic structure, one must forget that the deep abyss of
Melville and Night, *Moby-Dick*, was published four years before Whitman
first began to show the glimmers of Noon light with the first slim 1855 edition
of *Leaves of Grass*. Ignoring the difficulty of falling from summits not yet
scaled and the oddity of midnight noon, Mumford subjugates all to his dramatic conceit. At the end of the next section, in summing up Melville and
Night and, therefore, the Golden Day, he says: "The American had faced the
tragedy of the White Whale. He was now to retire to nearer and shallower
waters. Emerson, Thoreau, Whitman, Melville, yes, and Hawthorne had
answered the challenge of American experience. Presently, their heroic words
will be forgotten, and their successors, living corpses, too, will look back to
the days of their youth, as to a dream, real only while it lasted" (76–77).
Melville in his tragic state has become the tragic American, destined to live
on, in the Gilded Age, a dormant shell, a blind Oedipus, in the face of crass
materialism, of the machine age.

Here we touch on a particularly problematic aspect of Mumford's book.
The underlying implications of its dramatic structure require that we regard
the Civil War as the crux of the tragedy, the crucial turning point for the
worse. Materialistic and mechanistic, America after the Civil War then stands
triumphant over the fallen American, Melville. We see this negative view of
the outcome of the Civil War as early as "Noon," when Mumford says that
Whitman

> did not see that the great conflict might have a punic ending. As it turned
> out, the war was a struggle between two forms of servitude, the slave and the
> machine. . . . The Machines won; and the war kept on. Its casualties were
> not always buried at Antietam or Gettysburg; they moldered too in libraries,
> studies, offices. The justifiable antebellum optimism of Emerson turned into
> a waxen smile. . . . Among the young men many a corpse was left to go
> through the routine of living. (67–68)

These, in the aftermath of the Civil War, are clearly Waste Land figures.
It is very possible that Mumford's distaste for the Civil War may be displaced
antipathy to World War I, and he may be projecting his own experience of
living in the wake of a devastating war onto life half a century earlier.[2] It is
not unreasonable, furthermore, to assume that Mumford's distaste for war in

general colors his beliefs about the possible good any war can achieve. He may have felt, therefore, that he was serving a useful purpose in questioning the value of a war generally conceded to be justified. (As recent studies have shown, the self-justifying myths about war have far-reaching, often tragic consequences.)[3] But whatever the likelihood of these factors affecting Mumford's approach to the Civil War, to whatever extent he was projecting the Lost Generation cynicism about war, Mumford's chief enemy seems to be the mechanized age, and mechanized war, as one manifestation of it. Mumford intends *The Golden Day* to show that American industrialism, impersonality, and greed ruined American literature. Providing unseen justification for the turn in the dramatic action, the Civil War occupies a role similar to a battle fought offstage, between the acts of a Wagnerian opera. And the sweeping drama here is the fall of American individualism, which was idealistic and optimistic—"justifiably optimistic"—and of which Emerson was the heroic essence. When the curtain rises after the war, therefore, for Mumford the dramatic contrast is complete, the tragedy full:

> The Civil War . . . dramatized in a stroke the changes that had begun to take place during the preceding twenty or thirty years. On one side lay the Golden Day, the period of an Elizabethan daring on the sea, of a well-balanced adjustment of farm and factory in the East, of a thriving regional culture . . . the American mind had flourished and had begun to find itself. When the curtain rose on the post-bellum scene, this old America was for all practical purposes demolished. Industrialism had entered overnight. (79)

But how justifiable was that Emersonian optimism? Even a brief review of 1830 to 1860 reveals it to be nothing like Mumford's Golden Day.[4] The single most significant characteristic of the Era of Reform is that it effected relatively little reform. To understand why this is so, perhaps we should broaden our understanding of the term "reform." If we strip it of its liberal connotations and think of it as the process of "re-forming," shaping anew, we come close to a word which embraces all the activities that went under that name.

America was still a great experiment in democracy and, as such, seemed to inspire and foster numerous individual experiments in the religious, social, and political arenas. There seemed to be ample space to try anything, and a large enough, mobile enough, uneducated enough population to find supporters for almost anything. It would, however, be an error to infer from this that the Era of Reform was an era of tolerance. Quite the contrary.

By contemporary standards, perhaps the best example of this was the anti-Catholic reform movement. Yet it was also one of the most virulent and successful of the period. The artist and inventor Samuel F. B. Morse, for example, published, in 1835, *The Imminent Dangers to the Free Institutions of the United States through Foreign Immigration*, which claimed that Jesuits were sent by the pope and instructed to undermine American liberties. In the same year, Lyman Beecher, a noted reformer, wrote perhaps the most widely read of the anti-Catholic books, A *Plea for the West*, which sought funds for missionaries to save the West for Protestantism and portrayed the Catholic menace as undemocratic and un-American. In 1836, the Protestant Reformation Society was formed. It sought to disseminate anti-Catholic information and convert "Papists to Christianity." Alice Felt Tyler's description of the events surrounding the destruction of the Ursuline Convent school, in Boston, helps reveal the violent degree of anti-Catholic feeling that grew in the 1830s:

> On the night of Sunday, August 10, 1834, Lyman Beecher delivered three violently anti-Catholic sermons. . . . The mob that formed the next day advanced upon the Ursuline convent, and the police were entirely unable—or unwilling—to control it. The convent was burned and the nuns and their pupils were given barely time enough to escape to nearby refuges.
>
> For a number of days rioting mobs roamed the streets, . . . Catholic churches were protected by troops, and Irish laborers guarded their homes, while Harvard students patroled the Yard to protect the college from violence. It was an ominous evidence of the effectiveness of the anti-Catholic propaganda that the trial of the leaders of the mob was a farce in which the nuns were insulted and the Catholic Church reviled, and that legislators were so intimidated by their constituents that they dared make no reparation. (370–71)

(Mumford might have noted that Harvard needed this protection only three years before Emerson gave his famous Divinity School address there.)

This "negative" reform reveals a more tarnished portion of the Golden Day. There were portions, also ignored by Mumford, that were unjustifiably positive—the fool's gold of the day: utopian schemes, millennial visions, and temperance associations. Utopian societies abounded, as did communes of almost every sort, many of which had their foundations in religious beliefs and many in philosophical. The abundance of these communities attests to the fact that many people harbored the belief that an ideal society was possible. What Mumford ignores, however, is that most of them came to discover that it was not. The communities failed because they were poorly conceived or easily subverted by confidence men. Hopedale, for instance, one of the most successful of communal experiments, failed when the Draper Brothers bought up 75 percent of the stock in the cooperative farm community, then sold the community out for a profit. One of the brothers simply decided, after buying the stock in what the other members believed to be good faith, that the socialistic scheme was impractical. Of the forty or fifty Fourierist phalanxes, only one lasted as long as twelve years, and that brought the overall average up to two years. Although, as Perry Miller points out in *The Life of the American Mind*, revivalism and religious zeal have always oscillated between periods of fervor and declension, the mass appeal distinguishes revivalism as more than simply faddish. It focused the American penchant for activism; making what rhetoricians call the emotional appeal as opposed to the rational, it disdained religious institutions and even more the treatises these institutions produced. In place of long syntactically complex arguments refining obscure theological points, irrelevant and inaccessible to the common person, the revivalist relied on a simple message in simple language, an assertion of free will and a call to action.

Revivalism is inextricably linked to the myriad of reforms which sprang up in the period. Much has been written arguing the exact nature of the relationship,[5] but few doubt that the popularizing of the idea that one could and ought to do God's work had a profound effect on the Era of Reform. The Revivalist movement is particularly important, therefore, not only because it actually motivated many other movements of the period, but also because it pioneered and refined the methods of mass promotion which structured the nature of antebellum, nineteenth-century America.

Coupled with revivalist zeal was a spirit of millennialism, perhaps best typified in its most extreme by the Millerite movement. William Miller, a convert to the Calvinist Baptist Church, amassed calculations based on a literal reading of the scriptures, that proved, he felt, the second advent would come in 1843. As 1843 drew closer, Miller rapidly increased his followers and his zeal. Miller unfortunately was subject to a much more immediate and rigorous test than other revivalists.

> As 1843 drew to its close, the dangers of . . . religious excitement and delusion became apparent. Suicides were attributed to despair over the necessity of facing the day of judgment. The state insane asylums reported the admission of several who had been crazed by fear of the end of the world. In Portsmouth, New Hampshire, a Millerite in voluminous white robes climbed a tree, tried to fly when he thought the fatal hour was near, fell, and broke his neck. A Massachusetts farmer cut his wife's throat because she refused to convert to Millerism, and a despairing mother poisoned herself and all her children. The editor of a New Bedford paper described the somewhat amusing anguish of a mechanic whom he had seen kneeling in the snow with a Millerite pamphlet in each hand, praying and blaspheming in a "most piteous manner." In Wilkes-Barre, Pennsylvania, a storekeeper requested the sheriff to give all his goods to anyone who would take them away, and in New York another merchant offered to give a pair of shoes to anyone who needed them, since "he had no further use for them." (75)

The great impact of the Fox sisters, who invented the seance, also attests to the high level of public credulousness in the period. The sisters' popularity as public, fee-charging mediums spread rapidly, and spiritualist circles formed in every town and nearly every village. When the Fox sisters finally admitted their fraudulence, they were not believed by other spiritualists, who charged that the confession, not the spiritualism, was fraudulent. Certainly, seances are still with us, representing one branch of American optimism that Mumford ignores.

He ignores, as well, the period's inconsistent attempts at social reform. The public did not know, for instance, how to deal with the idea of poverty, considered separate from, albeit related to, the problem of dealing with the poor. The urban, industrial poverty of nineteenth-century America was unprecedented, but at what point was one to be considered "poor"—that is, in need of help from others—as opposed to living humbly? Who, furthermore, was to be held responsible for an individual's poverty? Americans tended ambivalently to hold to the idea that, in a land of abundance, poverty was a moral problem as well as an economic one. The chief form of charity during this period, therefore, was moral instruction. Although some exceptional, systematic social measures were taken that laid the foundation for modern social work, the predominant attitude was that "moral and religious culture," as William Ellery Channing wrote in 1835, "is the greatest blessing to be bestowed upon the poor" (Nye, *Society and Culture in America*, 43).

All this Mumford overlooks, instead presenting his private vision of what America was like. *The Golden Day* is a fictive conception, an ode to a period that never existed. And, as in all poetic conceptions, the genre and the conceit dominate the content. In the exercise of Mumford's poetic license, the question of slavery perhaps suffers the most. Simply, if one addresses the problem of slavery, it is difficult to assert that antebellum America is preferable to postbellum. For the most part, he avoids the issue completely, but he does warn against assuming that too much good came of the Civil War:

> The Civil War arose in a mess of muddy issues. The abolitionists' attack on slavery, full of moral righteousness and oblivious to the new varieties of slavery that were being practiced under industrialism, stiffened the South into a spasm even more self-righteous. . . . Twenty years of fierce debate found the Southerner frequently denying that the Negro was a human being: it also found the abolitionist denying that the slaveholder was a human being. . . . to muddle matters worse, the issue was mixed up with Centralism versus State's rights. . . . After the war the slave question had disappeared but the "Negro" question remained. (78)

Mumford is absolutely right in pointing out that the issues surrounding the Civil War are not clear-cut, nor were the consequences uniformly beneficial. It is remarkable, however, to see the above passage in the middle of a book so structurally dependent on the oversimplification inherent in dramatic hyperbole. Mumford is in a bind: to pursue the issue of slavery any further would be to force the discussion into the book. Were that to happen, he would either have to contradict his thesis or pronounce and support blatant racism. Since the tone and structure of his book permit no other means of discussion, Mumford simply does not discuss. In a book of well over 50,000 words, aimed at comparing the antebellum American mind to the postbellum, there are not 500 words dealing with slavery and/or blacks.

Mumford thus overlooks the obvious polarization of America and sees the basic split to be East/West instead of North/South. This is, for him, a convenient oversight because it allows him to ignore the large bundle of energies which, by the 1850s, the end of the Golden Day, contributed to a massive, brutal war. Revivalists, millennialists, Transcendentalists, nativists, utopians, anti-Catholics, social reformers, temperance reformers, and abolitionists all found their energies diverted or subsumed during the 1850s by a movement toward an unavoidable, bloody conflict over one basic question: did a state or states in the United States of America have the right to permit slavery?

If America was a great experiment, it was an experiment in, above all else, morality. Could people be expected to behave morally without a state-mandated religion? Could people, left to their own devices, choose leaders and create institutions that would protect the rights of all? An experiment of this size and daring was unprecedented in modern history. Yet it was undertaken with perhaps an unwarranted degree of optimism. Mumford stresses this optimistic strain, but ignores the sad, ironic, and often brutal consequences of unchecked optimism and of unjustifiable faith in effecting millennial changes in one or two generations. He ignores the numerous ways civil liberties fall victim to a highly credulous, easily swayed public. He ignores the scapegoating and factionalism that resulted from impatience and too strong an expectation of immediate results. Finally, he ignores the facts that this American experiment was undertaken in the face of an overwhelming problem, which initially almost prevented the forming of the union: the presence of slavery in half the colonies.

I have briefly shown that 1830 to 1860 was not the Golden Day Mumford described. Were it not for the slave question, we could perhaps write it off as a period of naive and fanatical tunnel vision. But slavery was the one question which absorbed all the others, the most obvious proof of which is the Civil War, which compelled most Americans, regardless of their personal beliefs, to align themselves with one of two great causes. By 1860 all the tunnels led to one clearing.

The Era of Reform reflected the climate set by the American religious/ moral experiment. When Lincoln said, at Gettysburg, in perhaps the most famous speech in American history, "Now we are engaged in a great Civil War testing whether that nation or any other nation so conceived and so dedicated can long endure," he was reflecting the American awareness that the Era of Reform had come to an end. The whole American experiment was under test. All reforms had to yield to the question of union, which was inextricably linked to the question of slavery. To miss this fact, as Mumford has done, is to misunderstand a whole era and, consequently, the experience of writers living in that era. And that misunderstanding of history, literary history, and literature, for decades, remained the legacy of Lewis Mumford's *The Golden Day.*

Despite its flaws, or perhaps because of them, *The Golden Day* did significantly help alter our literary consciousness. And one tribute to its success is that we no longer use the book. Melville, Hawthorne, Emerson, Thoreau, and Whitman now seem so inherent a part of the landscape that we no longer know their origin in our history. We now seek ways of looking at and understanding that landscape for which *The Golden Day* gives little help. F. O. Matthiessen's *American Renaissance* (1941) is six or seven times longer than *The Golden Day*; and since it starts by presuming much of what *The Golden Day* was trying to prove, it is fully understandable that *American Renaissance* is of much greater value to current readers. It is further understandable that, because it was one of the first and most comprehensive books of its sort, the name "American Renaissance" has supplanted the name "Golden Day" to describe the same literary period.

But, although Matthiessen takes issue with some of Mumford's work—especially his book *Herman Melville*—quite clearly Matthiessen owes much to Mumford. He limits his study to the same five authors as Mumford did and his title also has the connotation of a golden age. Matthiessen, moreover, openly acknowledges his debt to Mumford in his introduction: "the appearance of Lewis Mumford's *The Golden Day* (1926) was a major event in my experience. Through Mumford I became aware of the body of ideas he was popularizing, with their first expression in Brooks' *America's Coming of Age* (1915)" (xvii). *The Golden Day* is an appropriate target for Ellison, therefore, not because it was the most significant book of its type but because it was one of the earliest and most typical: one that represents a typical whitewashing of American history, one that flows from exactly that social/historical consciousness that forced the black into invisibility.[6]

In this light, we can now examine the term "Golden Day" as Ellison uses it. The invisible man first thinks of the Golden Day when he is looking for a place to revive Mr. Norton. Norton is a trustee of the black college at which the invisible man is in his junior year. The invisible man has been assigned as Norton's chauffeur on the trustee's annual visit to the southern campus. Because the invisible man drives Norton off the main paths, Norton comes in contact with Jim Trueblood, a black farmer who impregnated his own daughter. The detailed account of Trueblood's incest shocks Norton, who has unconsciously harbored incestuous desires for his own daughter. Seeing that the farmer has actually acted out Norton's deepest fantasies, Norton rewards the man with a $100 bill and then lapses into semiconsciousness, his face chalk white. As they drive away from Trueblood's, Norton requests whiskey:

"I must have a stimulant, young man. A little whiskey" (54). The invisible man asks if he is all right, and Norton repeats his request for stimulation; the invisible man concludes: "There was only one place, the Golden Day." If this is meant to suggest Mumford's Golden Day, we can infer a step back in time, an entrance into a historical period and/or a historical text. The use of the term thus becomes an implicit criticism of Mumford; and in the working out of the similarities and differences between the two Golden Days, we are forced constantly to sharpen our understanding of Ellison's criticism, its degree and its intent.

The first suggestion that Ellison is presenting a sharply alternative view comes on the next page, the beginning of chapter 3, when we discover that the road to the Golden Day has been obstructed by a group of black veterans from the local asylum. Because they are "blocking the way from the white line to the frazzled weeds" (55), they force the invisible man to drive over to the other side of the white line. We see that if Mr. Norton is going to see the Golden Day, he is going to approach it from the wrong side of the white line: "I shot the car across the line to avoid the men and stayed there on the wrong side as I headed for the Golden Day" (56). The invisible man, however, still acting as the agent of the school, intends to make sure Mr. Norton will not see the Golden Day: "I would run in, get a pint, and run out again, I thought. Then he wouldn't see the Golden Day" (56–57).

We are thus beginning to see two worlds, one of white trustees and schools, and one of bars, bordellos, and tenant farmers. The invisible man's charge has been to keep the two separate. The school, in other words, wants to present a façade of black life and—if the Golden Day stands for a historical text—of history as well. "The school," we are told, "had tried to make the Golden Day respectable, but the local white folks had a hand in it somehow and they got nowhere. The best the school could do was make it hot for any student caught going there" (57). Ellison's Golden Day, then, must not be Mumford's, in that Mumford's is the version *acceptable* to the school. Any student who goes there for himself, who compares for himself the Golden Day to its "respectable" version, and, especially, anyone who shows a white trustee what the Golden Day is really like is in for trouble. The invisible man thus commits the first transgression by entering the Golden Day himself, but tries to avoid the second, hoping to bring the stimulant out to Norton in the car.

The Golden Day that the invisible man enters has none of the clarity and optimism of the ideal era Mumford described. When entering, the invisible man first meets a millennialist:

> "It will occur at 5:30," he said, looking straight through me.
> "What?"
> "The great all-embracing, absolute Armistice, the end of the world!" (57)

The Golden Day is also filled with black professionals:

> Many of the men had been doctors, lawyers, teachers, Civil Service workers;
> there were several cooks, a preacher, a politician and an artist. One very nutty
> one had been a psychiatrist. Whenever I saw them I felt uncomfortable. They
> were supposed to be members of the professions toward which at various times
> I vaguely aspired myself, and even though they never seemed to see me I
> could never believe that they were really patients. (57)

The relationship between the invisible man and the others in the Golden
Day is not equal. Although he sees them, they seem not to see him but to
look through him. His position is therefore analogous to any historian's, literary historian's, or literary critic's in that he must make order from experi-
ences and people with whom he cannot communicate directly. He must,
moreover, reconcile what he sees both to his preconceptions and to the expectations of his society, that is, the audience which authorizes his position
as historian or critic. His job in this case becomes to see the Golden Day
without letting the school know he has, and to get Mr. Norton the stimulation
he needs without letting him actually know what the Golden Day is like.[7] For
the Golden Day has both the stimulation Norton needs and truths too dangerous—at least in the eyes of the school—for Norton to have. The problem
for the invisible man (or any black who wants to be successful in the eyes of
the school) is to provide the stimulation without revealing the truths which
created it. He realizes this: "Mr. Norton wouldn't want to come in here. He
was too sick. And besides I didn't want him to see the patients and the girls"
(58–59). When he shares his dilemma with the bartender, the bartender reminds him that his role as college student demands he solve that problem
himself: " 'You're going to college, figure it out,' he said" (59).

Remembering again that the Golden Day can refer both to Mumford's
book and to the period that book names, we are forced to suspend our understanding of both. For the Golden Day bordello is a stimulating place as,
according to Mumford, 1830–1860 was a stimulating era. But the bordello
stimulates for very different reasons, reasons that seem connected to those
aspects of the era that Mumford ignored: the fanatic tunnel vision, the "reformers" absorbed with their own causes, the zeal.

Although the invisible man runs back and forth between the bar and the
car, he finally fails to keep the two worlds separate and, with the help of one
of the vets, brings Norton into the Golden Day. As the vets carry him in,
another aspect of the Golden Day's complexity and vitality, ignored by Mumford, emerges—miscegenation:

> As we carried him toward the Golden Day, one of the men stopped suddenly
> and Mr. Norton's head hung down, his white hair dragging in the dust.
>   "Gentlemen, this is my grandfather!"

"But he's *white*, his name's Norton."

"I should know my own grandfather! He's Thomas Jefferson and I'm his grandson—on the 'field-nigger' side," the tall man said.

"Sylvester, I do believe that you're right. I certainly do," he said, staring at Mr. Norton. "Look at those features. Exactly like yours—from the identical mold." (60)

They revive the unconscious Norton with some brandy.

"You were unconscious, sir," I said.

"Where am I, young man?" he asked wearily.

"This is the Golden Day, sir."

"What?"

"The Golden Day. It's a kind of sporting-and-gambling house," I added reluctantly.

"Now give him another drinka brandy," Halley said. I poured a drink and handed it to him. He sniffed it, closed his eyes as in puzzlement, then drank; his cheeks swelled out like small bellows; he was rinsing his mouth.

"Thank you," he said, a little stronger now. "What is this place?"

"The Golden Day," said several patients in unison.

He looked slowly around him, up to the balcony, with its scrolled and carved wood. A large flag hung lank above the floor. He frowned.

"What was this building used for in the past?" he said.

"It was a church, then a bank, then it was a restaurant and a fancy gambling house, and now *we* got it," Halley explained. "I think somebody said it used to be a jailhouse too." (61–62)

This exchange gives meaning to the scene in that it emphasizes the dream/ nightmare journey of Mr. Norton. He has been dislocated, taken to a strange, protean place, thoroughly alien to him, the name of which has special significance. The name has now been repeated thirteen times in eleven pages, building to this string of Golden Day responses, which shouts at the reader as well as at Mr. Norton.

The first leap would seem to be to Mumford. If, in other words, we have so far resisted seeing the name "Golden Day" as an allusion, it seems necessary that we do so now to explain its repetitions. The problem with simply assuming an allusion to Mumford, however, is that it makes us realize Ellison's bordello is much more dissimilar than similar to Mumford's text. This makes necessary our conceiving of a revised or criticized Mumford text, so that the text alluded to becomes not "Mumford's-history," but "Mumford's-distorted-history" and by extension "the-tradition-of-Mumford's-distorted-history," both the tradition from which it came and the tradition which it helped propagate. Yet in our revision of Mumford, in our comparison of his history to others, we find Mumford both right and wrong, for the era may not

have been one exclusively of harmony and optimism, but it was one of great
energy and creativity; it *was* the Golden Day of American letters, so that
Mumford's book becomes one which confers the right name for the wrong
reasons. The right reason, Ellison would assert, is the great moral awareness
of the period, an awareness deeply connected with the issue of slavery.

From 1776 to 1876, Ellison points out, in the *New Republic*:

> there was a conception of democracy current in this country that allowed the
> writer to identify himself with the Negro; and that had such an anthology of
> writings on the Negro situation as seen by both white and Negro authors been
> conceivable during the nineteenth century it would have included such writ-
> ers as Whitman, Emerson, Thoreau, Hawthorne, Melville and Mark Twain.
> For slavery (it was not termed a "Negro problem" then) was a vital issue in the
> American consciousness, symbolic of the condition of Man, and a valid as-
> pect of the writer's reality. Only after the Emancipation and the return of the
> Southern ruling class to power in the counter-revolution of 1876, was the Ne-
> gro issue pushed into the underground of the American conscience and ig-
> nored. (SA, 107–8)

And in his acceptance speech for the National Book Award, he explains
further:

> The writers of [the mid-nineteenth century] took a much greater responsibility
> for the condition of democracy and, indeed, their works were imaginative
> projections of the conflicts within the human heart which arose when the
> sacred principles of the Constitution and the Bill of Rights clashed with the
> practical exigencies of human greed and fear, hate and love. Naturally I was
> attracted to these writers as a Negro. Whatever they thought of my people per
> se, in their imaginary economy the Negro symbolized both the man lowest
> down and the mysterious, underground aspect of human personality. In a
> sense the Negro was the gauge of human condition as it waxed and waned in
> our democracy. These writers were willing to confront the broad complexities
> of American life. . . . (SA, 112–13)

The complexity, too, the protean aspects of the period contribute to both
its pain and energy, energy that teetered on the verge of explosion. Burdened
with the growing problem of an oppressed people, the Golden Day was on
the brink of chaos which the tradition of American criticism erased. The
school—or the academy—made it "respectable" for the eyes of Mr. Norton.
But Mr. Norton's presence creates a rebellion, and the vets riot, overthrowing
their overseer, Supercargo, and beating him. "The Golden Day was in an
uproar" (64), the invisible man tells us, but watching the turmoil, the invisible man forgets Norton. This suggests some relationship between the invisible man's attention to Norton and the nature of the Golden Day. As long as
the invisible man shares with Norton and the school the idea that the past

ought to be made respectable for the Nortons, then the institutions have power over him, command his attention. When he attends to the turmoil, the chaos, the pain and confusion, he is momentarily free of the authority figures whose sense of respectability he tries to share. In this sense, it is appropriate to see "Supercargo," as Ellison has indicated, as a pun on "superego," and the scene takes on aspects of the invisible man's internal struggle with authority figures, the repression and guilt that have become the internal mechanism for his invisibility, his bondage to anonymity.

Remembering Foucault's insights about the mad, furthermore, we can see the appropriateness of the metaphoric comparison between blacks and the mad. For, as Foucault points out, those in the asylum are those who have not succeeded in suppressing their identity adequately enough to return to society as permanent prisoners of their own invisibility. The invisible man, then, differs from the vets in that he has almost completely internalized his otherness, organized his guilt. But the chaos of the Golden Day has shocked the invisible man, has "deorganized" him, so that he not only forgets about Norton but also, seeing the overthrow of Supercargo, hearing Mr. Norton cry out in Supercargo's defense, hearing one of the vets respond " 'He's [Supercargo] the white folk's man!' " (64), and seeing men jumping up and down upon Supercargo with both feet, the invisible man thinks, "I felt such an excitement that I wanted to join them" (64). Although he never actually does join them, he becomes very attentive to the specifics of the beating until Supercargo is laid out unconscious on the bar and "the men whirled about like maniacs" (65).

This identification between the disenfranchised blacks, fighting to maintain their identity, and members of an asylum takes on larger significance when we realize that the invisible man's brief release from authority is made possible only by his entrance into the Golden Day, which represents a privileged piece of the past. Again we get the simultaneous acceptance and denial of the allusion. For it was Mumford's thesis that in the Golden Day the individual had the greatest chance of triumphing, and certainly this is true for the invisible man, in that only while he remains in the Golden Day can he lose sight of Norton and admit his desire to overthrow Supercargo. Leaving the Golden Day for the present day can only be done at the price of his identity. The irony, of course, comes in the simultaneous recognition that the reason the Golden Day occupies such a privileged position is that it was made invisible by the same literary-historical tradition that defined it. Mumford's fictive creation, *The Golden Day*, in other words, created another Golden Day through what that fiction excluded. In the things that Mumford omitted, in the discourse waiting to be retrieved, lay the truth about Norton: "With his eyes closed he seemed more threatening than with them open. He was like a formless white death, suddenly appeared before me, a death which had been there all the time and which had now revealed itself in the madness of the

Golden Day" (66). But in this revelation lay also the truth of the relationship between Norton and the invisible man, a truth which the invisible man is so incapable of facing that he screams without even realizing it:

> "Stop screaming," a voice commanded, and I felt myself pulled away. It was the short fat man. . . .
> "That's better," he shouted into my ear. "He's only a man. Remember that. He's only a man."
> "I wanted to tell him that Mr. Norton was much more than that, that he was a rich white man and in my charge; but the very idea that I was responsible for him was too much for me to put into words." (66)

The fat vet, who had been a surgeon, helps the invisible man to bring Norton upstairs and explains that Norton has had a mild shock. "This here Golden Day is enough to shock anybody," a girl says. The vet helps revive Norton and relates his personal history: the vet had been a surgeon who served in World War I, lived in Paris, performed some brain surgery, and finally returned to the United States where he came to realize what he had forgotten: "I learned . . . that my work could bring me no dignity" (71). The invisible man regards this conversation with great ambivalence:

> "You look better, sir," I said, anxious to get out of the place. I could understand the vet's words but not what they conveyed, and Mr. Norton looked as uncomfortable as I felt. The one thing which I did know was that the vet was acting toward the white man with a freedom which could only bring on trouble. I wanted to tell Mr. Norton that the man was crazy and yet I received a fearful satisfaction from hearing him talk as he had to a white man. (71)

As Norton returns to consciousness, the invisible man returns to his role and remembers he should keep Norton from the Golden Day. Still within its privileged surroundings, he can take a painful pleasure from seeing a black speak to Norton as an equal. The vet, however, is more than an equal; he is almost an oracle, for he knows the significance of the Golden Day and of Norton's relation to it. To some of the vets, he explains to Norton, "you are the great white father, to others the lyncher of souls, but for all you are confusion come even into the Golden Day" (86).

The vet goes on to tell Norton and the invisible man (and the reader) the nature of their roles and hence of the institutions that define them:

> "You will hardly recognize it, but it is very fitting that you came to the Golden Day with the young fellow," he said.
> "I came out of illness—or rather, he brought me," Mr. Norton said.
> "Of course, but you came, and it was fitting."
> "What do you mean?" Mr. Norton said with irritation.
> "A little child shall lead them," the vet said with a smile. "But seriously,

because you both fail to understand what is happening to you. You cannot see or hear or smell the truth of what you see—and you, looking for destiny! It's classic! And the boy, this automaton, he was made of the very mud of the region and he sees far less than you. Poor stumblers, neither of you can see the other. To you he is a mark on the score-card of your achievement, a thing and not a man; a child, or even less—a black amorphous thing. And you, for all your power, are not a man to him, but a God, a force—"

Mr. Norton stood abruptly. "Let us go, young man," he said angrily.

"No, listen. He believes in you as he believes in the beat of his heart. He believes in that great false wisdom taught slaves and pragmatists alike, that white is right. I can tell you *his* destiny. He'll do your bidding and for that his blindness is his chief asset." (73)

In this context, we see that Norton does indeed find stimulation in the Golden Day, but not in the way he or the invisible man had expected. He finds instead not only riot, chaos, and manic energy but also a voice that sees precisely the irony of their relationship, their symbiotic blindness. This is exactly what Ellison says the *literature* of the Golden Day contains, and what has been lost in the twentieth century. Norton's illness and blindness are one and the same, both deriving from the fact that he lives in a world which insulates him from the moral consequences of his actions. Since the invisible man desires to succeed in that world, he must contribute to the insulation of Norton by making himself invisible. This scene then lets us contrast Ellison's idea of the nineteenth-century American black literary figure—represented by the vet—with the twentieth-century black literary figure—represented by the invisible man. Such a comparison, the chapter suggests, is only possible in a return to the Golden Day. Although we cannot return to the past, per se, we can return to the literature of the period and find there the moral issues inherently linked to blacks and slavery.

As a result, when the invisible man leaves the Golden Day, he reverts to his invisible self and has no understanding of the vet's message, or the meaning of the experience. In chapter 4 he thinks:

Was Mr. Norton angry with *me?* In the Golden Day he seemed more curious than anything else—until the vet had started talking wild. Damn Trueblood. It was his fault. If we hadn't sat in the sun so long Mr. Norton would not have needed whiskey and I wouldn't have gone to the Golden Day. And why would the vets act that way with a white man in the house? (76)

A little later in the chapter he indicates that none of his contemporaries can understand the Golden Day: "To whom could I turn for help? I could think of no one. No one to whom I could even explain what had happened at the Golden Day. Everything was upset inside me" (81).

When Dr. Bledsoe, the college's director, expels the invisible man, he makes clear that the proper way for him to have dealt with Trueblood and the Golden Day was to lie to Norton to keep him from seeing them: " '*Please* him? And here you are a junior in college! Why, the dumbest black bastard in the cotton patch knows the only way to please a white man is to tell him a lie! What kind of education you getting around here?' " (107). He thus connects lying about Trueblood and the Golden Day directly to the function of education. A little later, Bledsoe connects that function of education with the preservation of the institution of the South: " 'And I'll tell you something your sociology teachers are afraid to tell you,' he said. 'If there weren't men like me running schools like this, there'd be no South. Nor North, either. No, and there'd be no country—not as it is today. You think about that, son' " (110). But the irony of that statement is lost on the invisible man, for he is still fully committed to the system which has organized his guilt, made him internalize it and, consequently, reject the message of the Golden Day:

> How had I come to this? I had kept unswervingly to the path placed before me, had tried to be exactly what I was expected to be, had done exactly what I was expected to do—yet, instead of winning the expected reward, here I was stumbling along. . . . For, despite my anguish and anger, I knew of no other way of living, nor other forms of success available to such as me. I was so completely part of that existence that in the end I had to make my peace . . . though I still believed myself innocent, I saw that the only alternative to permanently facing the world of Trueblood and the Golden Day was to accept responsibility for what had happened. Somehow, I convinced myself, I had violated the code and thus would have to submit to punishment. Dr. Bledsoe is right, I told myself, he's right; the school and what it stands for have to be protected. (113)

In chapter 7, understandably, the invisible man reiterates that he "wanted to remember nothing connected with Trueblood or the Golden Day" (116), and the name is mentioned only twice more before the epilogue, including the scene in the Liberty Paints factory cited at the beginning of this chapter. If we look at a larger piece of that passage, we can see that we are being prepared to move away from the Golden Day. Struggling to remove the lid of some Liberty paint, he remembers the whiteness of the college buildings, which were painted regularly, unlike the other local buildings, which

> were left untouched to become the dull grained gray of weathered wood. And I remember how the splinters in some of the boards were raised from the grain by the wind, the sun and the rain until the clapboards shone with a satiny, silvery, silver-fish sheen. Like Trueblood's cabin, or the Golden Day. . . . The Golden Day had once been painted white; now its paint was flaking away with the years, the scratch of a finger being enough to send it down. Damn that Golden Day! But it was strange how life connected up.

Because I had carried Mr. Norton to the old run-down building with rotten paint, I was here. If, I thought, one could slow down his heartbeats and memory to the tempo of the black drops falling so slowly into the bucket yet reacting so swiftly, it would seem like a sequence in a feverish dream. (153)

The passage contrasts the Golden Day, which shone from exposure to natural elements, with the school, which was artificially whitened. The contrast reinforces the school's concern with maintaining a respectable appearance; the passage indicates that the same concern had been expressed by the Golden Day—it, too, "had once been painted white." The passage, however, also indicates a change has taken place. Unlike the school, it had lost its all-white façade: "now its paint was flaking away with the years, the scratch of a finger being enough to send it down." Again we can return to Mumford's text, in its literary-historical context: Mumford like many of his contemporaries painted the Golden Day all white, which, as we have seen, has had profound effects *on* American institutions just as, simultaneously, it manifested the effects *of* those institutions. Ellison suggests here, however, a change in consciousness (last to reach the school) which has already begun to expose the real nature of the Golden Day. This works two ways and thereby encapsulates the interrelation between literary and social criticism: any information or perspective that sheds more light on the era of the Golden Day, exposes the flaws in the book *The Golden Day*, and gives us a new reading of that book, changing it and the tradition it helped create, in the same way that the book changed American literature by creating that tradition. Finally, the American literature—the substance of the Golden Day—Ellison suggests—outlasts and outshines the façade of whiteness.

Having made this half-peace with the Golden Day, the invisible man is ready to move on. Shortly after this scene, he will be caught in an explosion, given an electric lobotomy, and released from the factory hospital, bewildered, but with the realization that he will never return to the South again, that he is, for better or worse, a northern, urban black. I believe that this represents, in the structure of the book, not only the motion of American blacks from the South to the North and from the farm to the city, but also from the nineteenth to the twentieth century. The overwhelming preponderance of references to the nineteenth-century American writers occurs before the invisible man is released from the factory hospital. The next chapter looks specifically at Ellison's allusions to Melville and Emerson, concentrating on the way he uses these allusions to amend some of the criticism of those authors fostered by *The Golden Day* tradition.

5. Invisible Criticism: Melville and Emerson Revised

N ow that we have seen how Ellison's allusions to Lewis Mumford force us to reevaluate Mumford's text, we have a context wherein we can examine the effect of his allusions on the two authors who represent, for Mumford, the major figures at the opposite ends of his golden spectrum: Melville and Emerson.

I am going to begin with Melville because Ellison does. An inscription from the last pages of "Benito Cereno," the final interview between Delano and Cereno, prefaces *Invisible Man*. That interview is pivotal in understanding the racial/political implications of Melville's story. Although general critical consensus today holds that Delano does not share or voice Melville's opinions, that he spends his time aboard the slave ship as much a captive of his own stereotyping and prejudice about slavery as Cereno is a captive of the actual slaves,[1] we nevertheless must decide the effect on Delano of seeing his stereotypes shattered, and decide if he remains as much a victim of his prejudice—one critic calls him an American fool[2]—at the conclusion as at the outset. If he stands, furthermore, for optimistic, Yankee America, what does his close bond with the decadent Old World—represented by Cereno[3]—portend for that America; and, more specifically, since "Benito Cereno" was written on the verge of the Civil War, what does it suggest about the attitude of America toward slavery? If Delano understands Cereno's complicity in a corrupt system and therefore its violent ramifications, then why is he so cheerful and why does he consider Cereno saved? If, on the other hand, he does not understand the nature of the system he has helped to preserve, what credibility can be given his belief that he is innocent and/or a savior? These questions and problems take us, I believe, to the heart of "Benito Cereno," to the moral dilemma the black represents for the Democratic Experiment.

Most appropriately, therefore, Ellison begins *Invisible Man* with an inscription quoting Delano's final question to Cereno: " 'You are saved,' cried Captain Delano, more and more astonished and pained; 'you are saved: what has cast such a shadow upon you?' " To make the question even more open, to make its answer, by implication, the text which will follow, Ellison leaves out Cereno's response, "The Negro." If *Invisible Man* then implicitly answers

Delano's question by revealing the ramifications of his dilemma, the book is a critique on American blindness masked as American optimism. This merely puts in a slightly different historical context the generally accepted idea that *Invisible Man* contains strong social commentary that systematically exposes the way American institutions have erased a people. Within this context of social criticism lies a body of literary criticism that both flows out of the social criticism and contributes to it. Despite the fact, therefore, that an issue from "Benito Cereno" frames the novel, the story "Benito Cereno" is reinterpreted in the novel through the use of allusions. I intend, therefore, to examine the allusions to "Benito Cereno" in the same way I did the allusions to *The Golden Day*, to see both how those allusions alter the reader's understanding of Melville and the way the altered Melville reverberates in Ellison's text. This will point us directly at the differences between Melville's vision and Emerson's (originally emphasized in a largely apolitical context by F. O. Matthiessen) and prepare us to examine Ellison's allusions to Emerson.

Chapter 3 of *Invisible Man*—the "Golden Day" chapter—is also an extended allusion to "Benito Cereno." Like "Benito Cereno," the Golden Day chapter contains an uprising of enslaved blacks, in which they overthrow their oppressors and take part in a few moments of ultimately futile chaos. Their overseer, furthermore, bears the name "Supercargo," which is the title for the financial overseer on a ship. Melville, moreover, allows for the comparison between the ship and a strange house.

> Always upon first boarding a large and populous ship at sea, especially a foreign one . . . the impression varies in a peculiar way from that produced by first entering a strange house with strange inmates in a strange land. Both house and ship—the one by its walls and blinds, the other by its high bulwarks like ramparts—hoard from view their interiors till the last moment: but in the case of the ship there is this addition; that the living spectacle it contains, upon its sudden and complete disclosure, has, in contrast with the blank ocean which zones it, something of the effect of enchantment. The ship seems unreal; these strange costumes, gestures, and faces, but a shadowy tableau just emerged from the deep, which directly must receive back what it gave.[4]

Ellison similarly tries for a surreal effect in the Golden Day sequence.

Mr. Norton also bears a resemblance to Cereno. Like Cereno, he represents the old order, the white power structure, and yet, suffering from exhaustion and/or a form of shock, he is at the mercy of the blacks who must carry him around: "The debility, constitutional or induced by hardships, bodily and mental, of the Spanish Captain was too obvious to be overlooked. . . . His mind appeared unstrung, if not still more seriously affected. . . . This distempered body was lodged, as before hinted, in a distempered frame"

(122–23). And a "tendency to some pulmonary complaint appeared to have been lately confirmed. . . . No wonder that, as in this state he tottered about, his private servant apprehensively followed him. Sometimes the Negro gave his master his arm, or took his handkerchief out of his pocket for him" (123). His "pale face" is noted (137), and later we are told "the Spaniard was a pale invalid" (153).

Norton seems to be in a similar condition. "He stood shakily, still staring intently at Trueblood" (53). After leaving Trueblood, the invisible man tells us Norton "stumbled a bit climbing in [the car] and I gave him my arm. His face was still chalk white" (53). A little later he raised himself "weak and white-faced from the car" (56).

Both men have a tendency toward unconsciousness and semiconsciousness. Cereno, who "seemed the involuntary victim of mental disorder" (129), faints a number of times ("Here there was a sudden fainting attack" [131], "he fell heavily against his supporter" [132], "Here again he fell faint back" [134], "once more the faintness returned" [135]). When the invisible man first ran into the Golden Day, Norton "lay like a man asleep" (57), and when he returned to the car, Norton "lay like a figure of chalk" (59). During the riot that overthrows Supercargo, Norton gets pushed under the stairs, and when the invisible man finds him, we are told "he was out again" (66).

Like Cereno he relies on the blacks around him to support and revive him, and in both cases they use alcohol. During one of Cereno's spells, Babo

> sustained him, and drawing a cordial from his pocket placed it to his lips. He a little revived. But unwilling to leave him unsupported while yet imperfectly restored, the black with one arm still encircled his master, at the same time keeping his eye fixed on his face, as if to watch for the first sign of complete restoration, or relapse, as the event might prove. (131)

In a somewhat similar scene, the invisible man tells us,

> tilting Mr. Norton's head back, I put the glass to his lips and poured. A brown stream ran from the corner of his mouth, down his delicate chin. The room was suddenly quiet. I felt a slight movement against my hand, like a child's breast when it whimpers at the end of a spell of crying. The fine-veined eyelids flickered. He coughed. I saw a slow flush creep, then spurt, up his neck, spreading over his face.
> "Hold it under his nose, school-boy. Let 'im smell it."
> I waved the glass beneath Mr. Norton's nose. He opened his pale blue eyes. They seemed watery now in the red flush that bathed his face. He tried to sit up, his right hand fluttering to his chin. His eyes widened, moved quickly from face to face. Then coming to mine the moist eyes focused with recognition.
> "You were unconscious, sir," I said. (61)

We thus have a general set of parallels: a pale, traumatized aristocrat, in the grip of imprisoned blacks who have violently overthrown their overseer, is both sustained and abused by those blacks. He faints a number of times, is forced to confront the nature of his authority, and eventually escapes. When the limp body of Norton is being passed between the vets, furthermore, "a short, pock-marked man appeared and took Mr. Norton's head between his hands, tilting it at arm's length and then, pinching the chin gently like a barber about to apply a razor, gave a sharp, swift movement" (60–61).

This strange event echoes strongly the emblematic shaving scene in "Benito Cereno," when Cereno, draped in the flag of Spain, talks to Delano while his secret captor, Babo, lathers his face, and with a razor draws blood, "spots of which stained the creamy lather under the throat" (205). The scene is one of the story's most memorable because it vividly encapsulates the odd relationship between the three characters: Cereno the trembling victim, wearing the flag of his nation now reduced to a rag which catches his blood; Babo the secret ruler and terrorist, subjugating both Cereno and Cereno's flag; Delano the obtuse American, not understanding this relationship even while he watches Babo slit (albeit not seriously) Cereno's throat. By now Delano has all the evidence before him and in fact understands that Cereno and Babo have been role-playing, but Delano is so bound by his prejudices that he cannot envisage the people before him outside of the roles he believes definitive, and therefore he dismisses his doubts:

> To Captain Delano's imagination, now again not wholly at rest, there was something so hollow in the Spaniard's manner, with apparently some reciprocal hollowness in the servant's dusky comment of silence, that the idea flashed across him, that possibly master and man, for some unknown purpose, were acting out, both in word and deed, nay to the very tremour of Don Benito's limbs, some juggling play before him. Neither did the suspicion of collusion lack apparent support, from the fact of those whispered conferences before mentioned. But then, what could be the object of enacting this play of the barber before him? At last regarding the notion as a whimsy, insensibly suggested, perhaps, by the theatrical aspect of Don Benito in his harlequin ensign, Captain Delano speedily banished it. (207–8)

This paragraph—framed from the first words within Delano's "imagination"— becomes a clear demonstration of the severe limits of that imagination. The inability to imagine evil prevents him from seeing it where he does not expect to.

With the shaving detail, then, Ellison seems to force us to consider the possibility that he is alluding to "Benito Cereno," but in working out the other aspects of that allusion, we must deal with a number of startling departures. First, we must account for the narrator. At times, as Norton's servant and aide, he seems to be analogous to Babo, but as the persona through which the scene is filtered, and finally as the one who rescues Norton, he seems to parallel Delano. If he does parallel Delano, however, the other vets not only parallel Babo but multiply him: Babos are everywhere in the Golden Day. It is hard to consider this possibility without eventually considering the ways in which the vets and the slaves of the San Dominick are similar. The most striking similarity is that both have refused to conform to the roles set for them by white society. Ellison makes clear that this failure forces the vets into the asylum, and, by implication, the parallel lets us see that it is slavery which has forced the San Dominick slaves into rebellion. Ellison has, in other words, answered Matthiessen's charge that Melville failed to reckon with the evil that had originally been done to the slaves. For if we see all of the aberrant acts of the vets as a struggle to maintain the vestiges of their dignity, their personal freedom, then the same holds true of the slaves, no matter how peculiarly they behave.

The Golden Day chapter makes clear that finding behavior aberrant implies a point of view, and understanding the point of view is indeed essential to Ellison's chapter. Blinded by racial role-playing, by the implicit rules which govern interaction between races in a segregated society, the invisible man clearly does not understand what he sees. Numerous times he tells the reader that blacks aren't supposed to treat or look at or talk to a white man the way the vets do to Norton. He understands neither the vets' actions nor Norton's motivations. He believes that Norton is suffering from overlong exposure to the sun and not from having faced the implications of his own incestuous drives while listening to Jim Trueblood's incest story. He doesn't understand why Norton gives Trueblood instead of him the money, or why the vets rebel when Norton enters the Golden Day, any more than he understands the implications of the specific remarks the vets make. Most important, he identifies with Norton in that they both represent the school-approved ideas about the acceptable role for blacks, the preservation of the status quo. Although sometimes tempted or lured by the social freedom the vets express, the invisible man finally cannot free himself enough from social roles to see Norton as *just* a man or see himself as *even* a man.

Reflecting his aversion to "understatement," Ellison makes this explicit by having a vet articulate the relationship after it has been dramatized. I cited the vet's statements in the preceding chapter and refer to them now only to show that Ellison emphasizes both implicitly and explicitly the invisible man's naivete and reliance on defined roles. He is so naive, in other words, that he is unable to recognize his blindness, *even after the vet explains it*.

In the context of the allusions to "Benito Cereno" and the state of Melville criticism when Ellison wrote, this chapter has profound implications. For if this Golden Day retelling casts the invisible man in the role of Delano—a possibility we have to consider since, like Delano, he is the consciousness through which the story is filtered—then we can no longer miss Delano's naivete; we can no longer see him as representing the author's viewpoint, or as representing an American ideal. Yet here the allusion gains in complication because the reason, ironically, that the invisible man doesn't represent an American ideal and/or an ideal American is that he is doing everything he believes he ought to preserve that ideal. In this way he is not different from Delano but exactly like him, *despite the difference in their race.* The invisible man, with a vague belief in the values society espouses—and not the ones it follows—endorses the role-playing out of self-interest: he wants to succeed, and this is what the school—with Bledsoe the prime example—has taught him is necessary. He thus embodies the best and worst of the American character: if he is shallow, the shallowness permits a shallow idealism; if he is unable to recognize contradiction, he is incapable of duplicity. Like Delano, he is an American fool, but because he is black, his complicity in the foolhardiness of his position is harder to miss, in that we see even more clearly how much he actually fails his own interests in the largest sense. The differences between the invisible man and Delano thus come to accentuate their similarities. In this way, Ellison emulates a technique pervasive in Melville. As Carolyn Karcher points out, Melville's mode

> was an indirect one, relying on many ingenious techniques of subverting his readers' racial prejudices and inducing them to identify with victims of oppression, regardless of race. Initially, Melville seems to have believed that if his compatriots could be aroused to a sense of fellowship with the Negro, a solution to the slavery problem would naturally follow. *Moby-Dick,* in which he dramatizes a love marriage between the races as the means of averting apocalyptic doom for the nation, marks the climax of this hope. As the decade inaugurated by the Fugitive Slave Law of 1850 wore on, Melville's vision of America grew increasingly pessimistic. His later novels and tales no longer seek to convert readers to an ideal of human brotherhood. Instead, they exhibit a perverse relish for entrapping readers in the toils of their own racism and for impelling them to experience the consequences of blinding themselves to the humanity of their non-white victims. (*Shadow over the Promised Land,* xi–xii)

When we see a Delano figure adhering to views which discriminate against him, we are forced to see Delano's beliefs in their self-destructive light. Perhaps the most self-destructive aspect of Delano's blindness—his inability to see what he does not expect—is not his resulting failure to understand Babo and the other slaves, but his inability to understand himself. He thus ambles on with a pervasive sense that no harm can come to him because he is innocent:

> "What, I, Amasa Delano—Jack of the Beach, as they called me when a lad—I, Amasa; the same that, duck-satchel in hand, I used to paddle along

the waterside to the school-house made from the old hulk—I little Jack of the Beach, that used to go berrying with cousin Nat and the rest; I had to be murdered here at the ends of the earth, on board a haunted pirate-ship by a horrible Spaniard? Too nonsensical to think of! Who would murder Amasa Delano? His conscience is clean. There is someone above. Fie, fie, Jack of the Beach! You are a child indeed; a child of the second childhood, old boy; you are beginning to dote and drule, I'm afraid." (184–85)

Although the invisible man, similarly, believes in his own innocence, harm does come to him. Ironically, it comes not from his complicity in a corrupt system, but from his *ineffective* complicity in it. In this way he differs from Delano, who ostensibly succeeds, but here again we are forced by the comparison to measure their relative success and failure. Whatever the invisible man learns about the American ideal in theory and in practice, whatever he comes to discover about social and personal responsibility, it is the result of his "failure" at the Golden Day, which causes him to question the presumptions around which he has structured his life. Nothing, on the other hand, forces Delano to such a self-confrontation.

Ellison, in other words, seems to be suggesting a reading of Melville which had eluded previous critics because, as we have seen, criticism had been clouded for many years by the belief that the important writers of the "Golden Day" were not very aware of or concerned about the issue of slavery. Yvor Winters' opinion was typical, when he wrote in *Maule's Curse:* "The morality of slavery is not an issue in the story; the issue is this, that through a series of acts of performance and of negligence, the fundamental evil of a group of men, evil which normally would have been kept in abeyance, was freed to act. The story is a portrait of that evil in action, as shown in the negroes, and the effect of the action, as shown in Cereno" (77). F. O. Matthiessen was the first to realize that the racial implications of the story could not be ignored, and therefore found the story ultimately superficial because it showed the evil of the slave rebellion, and not the evil of the institution against which they rebelled (508). In the 1950s and 1960s, the question of race became more hotly debated, with some critics accusing Melville of racism and others calling "Benito Cereno" an assault on racism.[5] But the most important work to be done on Melville as an antislavery writer is Karcher's. Karcher has returned Melville to the context of his time, that "Era of Reform" so strongly occupied with the idea of America as millennial experiment, the moral complexity of which, for Melville, as for the majority of his contemporaries during the 1850s, united in and embodied the slave question. Karcher thus locates Melville's antipathy to slavery at the center of his work, inextricably linked to the questions of religion and evil, natural and civil law, authority and rebellion long seen as central to his canon.

Ralph Ellison, however, understood this about Melville's work much earlier. In his essay on twentieth-century fiction, written in 1946 (and published in 1953), Ellison contrasts that fiction to nineteenth-century fiction:

> This conception of the Negro as a symbol of Man—the reversal of what he represents in most contemporary thought—was organic to Nineteenth Century literature. It occurs not only in Twain but in Emerson, Thoreau, Whitman and Melville (whose symbol of evil, incidentally was white), all of whom were men publicly involved in various forms of deeply personal rebellion. (SA, 49)

> . . . while it is unlikely that American writing will ever retrace the way to the nineteenth century, it might be worth while to point out that for all its technical experimentation it is nevertheless an ethical instrument, and as such it might well exercise some choice in the kind of ethic it prefers to support. The artist is no freer than the society in which he lives, and in the United States the writers who stereotype or ignore the Negro and other minorities in the final analysis stereotype and distort their own humanity. Mark Twain knew that in *his* America humanity masked its face with blackness. (SA, 60)

Of great significance is Ellison's desire for American writing to retrace its way to the nineteenth century. This is another sense in which *Invisible Man* returns us to the Golden Day: Ellison is reestablishing the link between the "Democratic Experiment" and the "Negro Question" and pointing out that the link had firm roots in the tradition of great American writers. Ellison's allusions to "Benito Cereno" thus suggest about a specific text Ellison's reading of Melville in general—that he understood the moral burden that the problem of slavery placed on the ideals of American democracy.

The question of Melville's understanding of the relationship between slavery and evil, upon which any consideration of "Benito Cereno" touches, also points toward the question, in the nineteenth century, of Emersonianism and its implications for reform. The question of Emersonianism, appropriately, also reverberates through the first half of *Invisible Man*, where the allusions work to express the differences between Melville's and Emerson's approach toward evil and also a great tradition of ambivalence about Emersonian ideas and ideals.

Understanding what *Invisible Man* has to say about Emerson requires first understanding that Emerson is both a literary figure and a historical one, both an important stylistic influence on American letters and a public orator. One line of Emerson criticism, therefore, views him as a sculptor of words, a fabricator of a world elsewhere, a visionary. In the context of his time, however, on the verge of the Civil War, faced with the great question of America as blessed nation or damned nation, Emerson was also champion of a basic strain of American rugged individualism, spokesman for and about the national ethic. That Emerson is the "hero" of Mumford's *The Golden Day*.[6]

Appropriately, therefore, *Invisible Man* contains two Emersons, Ralph Waldo and Mr. Emerson, one of the college's trustees. Although neither of the Emersons actually appears in the novel, Mr. Norton, a trustee like Mr. Emerson, is once removed from both Emersons. As the visible representation, he suggests the pragmatic approach to Emersonianism. Norton has, in other words, as he makes quite clear, tried to model his life around Emersonian principles. Norton begins by explaining, for instance, that having been one of the original founders of the school, "it has been my *pleasant fate* to return each spring and observe the changes that the years have wrought. That has been more pleasant and satisfying to me than my own work. It has been a *pleasant fate* indeed" (31; my emphasis). Shortly he returns to this idea of a "pleasant fate" to the point of confusing the invisible man:

> "A pleasant fate," he repeated, "and I hope yours will be as pleasant."
> "Yes, sir. Thank you, sir," I said, pleased that he wished something pleasant for me.
> But at the same time I was puzzled: How could anyone's fate be pleasant? I had always thought of it as something painful. No one I knew spoke of it as pleasant—not even Woodridge, who made us read Greek plays. (31)

Mr. Norton tells the invisible man that he became interested in the school because he felt "that your people were somehow closely connected with my destiny. Do you understand?" (32). The following exchange takes place:

> "Not so clearly, sir," I said ashamed to admit it.
> "You have studied Emerson, haven't you?"
> "Emerson, sir?"
> "Ralph Waldo Emerson."
> I was embarrassed because I hadn't. "Not yet, sir. We haven't come to him yet."
> "No?" he said with a note of surprise. "Well, never mind. I am a New Englander, like Emerson. You must learn about him, for he was important to your people. He had a hand in your destiny. Yes, perhaps that is what I mean. I had a feeling that your people were somehow connected with my destiny. That what happened to you was connected with what would happen to me." (32–33)

Norton explains to the invisible man that their fates are bound together: "If you become a good farmer, a chef, a preacher, doctor, singer, mechanic—whatever you become, and even if you fail, you are my fate. And you must write me and tell me the outcome." The invisible man responds:

> I was relieved to see him smiling through the mirror. My feelings were mixed. Was he kidding me? Was he talking to me like someone in a book just to see how I would take it? Or could it be, I was almost afraid to think, that this rich

man was just the tiniest bit crazy? How could I tell him *his* fate? He raised his head and our eyes met for an instant in the glass, then I lowered mine to the blazing white line that divided the highway. (34)

The text thus presents, accentuated by the reference to the "blazing white line" which divides their path in life, the disparity between ideal audience and actual audience. When the invisible man applies the Emersonian doctrines of "Fate" and "Compensation" to one in his situation, they seem mad. Norton, of course, is not being fair to Emerson; he is oversimplifying him and taking him too literally. He reduces the concept of compensation to an absurdity when he asks the invisible man actually to write his fate to him. Whether this is fair to Emerson or not, however, it remains clear that Norton believes Emerson to be his philosophical patriarch, for he not only invokes Emerson expressly to explain his interest in the invisible man's fate but he also identifies with Emerson in other ways. One can almost laughingly picture Norton, believing himself to be acting in the Emersonian tradition, going to the mail each day to discover anew his "destiny."

In this scene, Norton is taking the Emersonian position on fate, while the invisible man expresses (to himself and the reader) the fatalistic view against which Emerson argues. Early in his essay "Fate," Emerson summarizes what he perceives as cross-cultural fatalism:

> Great men, great nations, have not been boasters and buffoons, but perceivers of the terror of life, and have manned themselves to face it . . . the Turk, the Arab, the Persian, accepts the foreordained fate. . . . Wise men feel there is something that cannot be talked or voted away. . . . The Greek Tragedy expressed the same sense. "Whatever is fated that will take place. The great immense mind of Jove is not to be transgressed." (*Complete Works*, VI:11)

In response to this position, he asserts that Fate is Nature, which is good, and failure to see that good in any given event is the failure of human understanding to penetrate the underlying natural cause; the conclusion he comes to is that "the indwelling necessity plants the rose of beauty on the brow of chaos, and discloses the central intention of Nature to be harmony and joy" (VI:51). The implication here is that all human remedy and redress is attitudinal. Some may regard this as rationalizing, but that may not be a bad choice for problems which admit no other solution. The problem with this philosophy is that it does not differentiate—in fact encourages not differentiating—between natural evils and correctable human error. Such a lack of distinction enables wealthy Mr. Norton to oversimplify Emerson and see "fate" as pleasant, not realizing how inapplicable such a concept is for one not born with all his comforts and advantages, as the invisible man's comment and subsequent "fate" make clear. The disparity between Norton and the invisible man becomes even more apparent as Norton tries ridiculously to show how

little disparity there is, asserting not only that his "fate" is pleasant but also
that the invisible man *is* his destiny.

After the adventures in the Golden Day and the return to the campus, the
invisible man sees Norton one last time. In his parting words to Norton—
his last attempt to win the trustee's goodwill—he returns to their initial
discussion:

> "And maybe next time you come I'll be able to answer some of the ques-
> tions you asked me this afternoon."
> "Questions?" His eyes narrowed.
> "Yes, sir, about . . . about your fate," I said.
> "Ah, yes, yes," he said.
> "And I intend to read Emerson, too . . ."
> "Very good. Self-reliance is a most worthy virtue. I shall look forward with
> the greatest of interest to learning your contribution to my fate." He motioned
> me toward the door. "And don't forget to see Dr. Bledsoe." (83–84)

Ellison is reinforcing the connection between Norton and Emerson, while
also undercutting Norton's Emersonian beliefs by ending the exchange with
the reminder to see Bledsoe. For that reminder points us toward the invisible
man's actual fate, one that does not fit in with either Norton's general philosophy or his specific belief about what will happen to the invisible man. He
believes that, having "explained" everything to Bledsoe, no harm will come
to the invisible man. Lest we forget that he harbors this illusion, we see that
only after the invisible man threatens to tell Mr. Norton of his fate does
Bledsoe devise the plan with the letters of introduction, one of them to Mr.
Emerson. At all costs, Mr. Norton must go on harboring the idea that his
destiny is one with the invisible man's, while all around him the invisible are
meeting with destinies very different from Mr. Norton's. In this sense, Norton
is morally blind, both unaware of the evil in Bledsoe and unaware of his own
complicity.

Leonard Deutsch feels, however, that Ellison is not criticizing Emerson
because Norton does not actually understand Emerson. Even if we agree with
Deutsch, we are still forced by the allusions to make the comparison between
Norton's alleged Emersonianism and actual Emersonianism. If Norton's
speeches allude to Emerson's essays, the difference we notice is that Norton
is overliteral; but in recognizing that, we are forced to ask the larger question:
just how literally are we to take Emerson? "Trustee," we should also remember, is Emerson's name for God, and on numerous occasions Norton is not
only treated as a God, but referred to as one. When the invisible man states
at the Golden Day that Norton is a trustee, the vet who later explains that
Norton is a God to the invisible man makes the link explicit when he says,
ironically, "trustee of consciousness" (69).

By seeing Norton not just as a failed God but as a failed Emersonian God, we are forced to question the nature of his failure on Emersonian terms. If Emerson, then, cannot be taken literally, if that reduces him to absurdity, an alternative is to see him as representing an ideal. To test that approach to Emerson, we have the unseen trustee, Mr. Emerson. We could say in fact that in devising the letter trick, Bledsoe is taking the invisible man out of the auspices of one ersatz version of Emerson and sending him running after another. Mr. Emerson for a while serves, therefore, as the invisible man's hope for success. The invisible man has gone to New York with a letter of introduction to him (and to six other unnamed trustees), believing that one will give him a job which will enable him to return to the college. When the six other trustees fail to respond to the letters, the invisible man decides to deliver the last one (to Emerson) in person; Emerson comes to represent his last hope. Instead of seeing Emerson, he sees Emerson's son, who reveals to him the contents of Bledsoe's letter:

My dear Mr. Emerson:

The bearer of this letter is a former student of ours (I say *former* because he shall never, under any circumstances, be enrolled as a student here again) who has been expelled for a most serious defection from our strictest rules of deportment.

Due, however, to circumstances the nature of which I shall explain to you in person on the occasion of the next meeting of the board, it is to the best interests of the college that this young man have no knowledge of the finality of his expulsion. For it is indeed his hope to return here to his classes in the fall. However, it is to the best interests of the great work which we are dedicated to perform, that he continue undisturbed in these vain hopes while remaining as far as possible from our midst.

This case represents, my dear Mr. Emerson, one of the rare, delicate instances in which one for whom we held great expectations has gone grievously astray, and who in his fall threatens to upset certain delicate relationships between certain interested individuals and the school. Thus, while the bearer is no longer a member of our scholastic family, it is highly important that his severance with the college be executed as painlessly as possible. I beg of you, sir, to help him continue in the direction of that promise which, like the horizon, recedes ever brightly and distantly beyond the hopeful traveler.

Respectfully, I am your humble servant,

A. Hebert Bledsoe (145)

The most significant thing about this letter is that it is not intended to crush the invisible man's hopes—that happens only by accident—but rather to extend them. Bledsoe's letter presents this systematic offer of false hope, furthermore, not as a sadistic joke, not even as a self-interested conspiracy so much as an idealistic act. The unmistakable irony of the phrase "the best interests of the great work which we are dedicated to perform" forces us to wonder what exactly is the nature of that "great work" that Emerson and Bledsoe *share*. The implication that they share a common understanding, are sympathetic to one another, is further emphasized by the salutation, "My dear Mr. Emerson," appearing twice in the letter.

It is unlikely, of course, that Ralph Waldo Emerson would actually sympathize with so cynical and manipulative a character as Bledsoe, if he were to see Bledsoe for what he was. But the allusion then highlights that incongruity and forces us to see Emerson's inability to recognize evil, his blindness to the complicated form it takes in the actual world. One consequence of that failing in his philosophy is that it is easily adapted by intentionally manipulative people. Mr. Emerson, like Emersonianism itself, we see, is easily used to keep the invisible man "in the direction of that promise which, like the horizon, recedes ever brightly and distantly beyond the hopeful traveler."

The relationship between Mr. Emerson and his son further indicates the failure of Emersonianism to communicate to an audience, for Emerson's son is clearly alienated from his father. His first personal reference to his father elliptically suggests this:

> "Ambition is a wonderful force," he said, "but sometimes it can be blinding . . . On the other hand, it can make you successful—like my father . . ." A new edge came into his voice and he frowned and looked down at his hands, which were trembling. "The only trouble with ambition is that it sometimes blinds one to realities . . ." (140)

The reference to his father, accompanied by the trembling and sandwiched between two charges of blindness, achieves three ends. In addition to hinting at the son's alienation, it suggests that his father is blind to realities and, finally, it reflects on the blinding effect of the invisible man's ambition. The son's comment allows us to realize that it is exactly because, in a literal and figurative way, the invisible man is following Emerson that he is blind to realities. His faith in what Emerson would do for him gave him a feeling of confidence, and despite the son's odd behavior, his intimations that all might not be well, the invisible man still believes that all he has to do, to solve his problems, is to see Emerson:

> "We're both frustrated, understand? Both of us, and I want to help you . . ."
> "You mean you'll let me see Mr. Emerson?"
> He frowned. "Please don't seem so happy about it, and don't leap to conclusions. I want to help, but there is a tyranny involved . . ."
> "A *tyranny?*" My lungs tightened.
> "Yes. That's a way of putting it. Because to help you I must disillusion you . . ."

"Oh, I don't think I mind, sir. Once I see Mr. Emerson, it'll be up to me. All I want to do is speak to him."

"*Speak* to him," he said, getting quickly to his feet and mashing his cigarette into the tray with shaking fingers. "No one speaks *to* him. *He* does all the speaking—" Suddenly he broke off. "On second thought, perhaps you'd better leave me your address and I'll mail you Mr. Emerson's reply in the morning. He's really a very busy man."

His whole manner had changed.

"But you said . . ." I stood up completely confused. Was he having fun with me? "Couldn't you let me talk to him for just five minutes?" I pleaded. "I'm sure I can convince him that I'm worthy of a job. And if there's someone who has tampered with my letter, I'll prove my identity . . . Dr. Bledsoe would—" (142)

With the outburst "No one speaks *to* him. *He* does all the speaking," we see the assertiveness of Emerson, his domination, and his failure to communicate with others. This may be read as biographical criticism, but I think that it is more interesting to see it as stylistic commentary, for certainly the unit of organization in Emerson's essays is the assertion. On almost every page sweeping generalizations abound, often paraphrasing one another in intense juxtaposition, as if reiteration were synonymous with proof. Excessive use of the verb "to be" creates an "a priori" tone to which the frequent future tense adds echoes of propheticism. The "organic" organization, furthermore, tends to prevent logical pauses at which one might initiate, even as reader, objections or counter arguments. Emerson's rhetoric, in other words, is very hard to penetrate; so are his arguments themselves, in that they are so all-embracing.

More important, however, than the appropriateness of the implied criticism is the fact that the son, who seems to understand this, is not impressed by Emerson, while the invisible man, who misses all this subtlety, is. This suggests that something in popularized Emersonian abstractions makes him more attractive to those who do not fully understand them.

Despite the son's broad hints and self-indulgent digressions, the invisible man adheres single-mindedly to his faith in Emerson. When the son finally suggests the invisible man forget about college, he demands once more to see Mr. Emerson, and the son tells him it is best not to see him. A number of shocked exchanges take place, in each the invisible man asking for Mr. Emerson by name and using Dr. Bledsoe's name to legitimize the request:

"But I'd like to take my chances, Mr. Emerson, sir. . . . This is very important to me. My whole career depends on it."

"But you *have* no chance," he said.

"But Dr. Bledsoe sent me here," I said, growing more excited. "I *must* have a chance . . ."

"Dr. Bledsoe," he said with distaste. "He's like my . . . he ought to be horsewhipped!" (144)

That faith, of course, is about to be destroyed with the revelation of the Bledsoe-Emerson letter. The letter throws the invisible man into shock; after he leaves the office, he tells us: "My mind flew in circles, to Bledsoe, Emerson and back again" (170). Normally the word "circles" would not attract much attention, but since it appears not only in a sentence mentioning Emerson but also in a chapter which mentions the name *sixteen* times, it is hard to overlook the fact that "Circles" is the title of another Emerson essay, the first sentence of which mentions a major image of *Invisible Man*: "The eye is the first circle; the horizon which it forms is the second; and throughout nature this primary figure is repeated without end" (*Complete Works*, II:281). The eye, then, for Emerson *forms* the horizon, creates, in other words, the limits of what it sees. And that horizon is the circle that Bledsoe, with Emerson's help, wants the invisible man to follow. For Emerson it is the manifestation of universal truth: "Our life is an apprenticeship to the truth that around every circle another can be drawn; that there is no end in nature, but every end is a beginning. . . ." (II:281).

Ellison paraphrases the last phrase here at the end of the last chapter before the epilogue. Having finally stopped running, the invisible man tells us: "I would take up residence underground. The end was in the beginning" (431). At some points, then, Ellison seems to be agreeing with Emerson, and the circular patterns in human events, as Emerson describes them, do reflect the nightmare way in which the invisible man moves toward the light and truth. Only after he finds out the truth about Emerson and Bledsoe, for example, can he say his mind moves in circles so that, ironically, he learns this Emersonian principle through a rejection of Emerson. (Nor can we have any doubt that Emerson is rejected, for throughout the rest of the novel, he is mentioned in association with the other characters who have betrayed the invisible man—Norton, Bledsoe, and, later, Brother Jack.) The invisible man then constructs imaginary Bledsoe-Emerson correspondence:

"My dear Mr. Emerson," I said aloud. "The Robin bearing this letter is a former student. Please hope him to death, and keep him running. Your most humble and obedient servant, A. H. Bledsoe . . ." . . . And Emerson would write in reply? Sure: "Dear Bled, have met Robin and shaved tail. Signed, Emerson." (147–48)

Clearly, then, the invisible man represents Emerson as the author of false hopes.

After the explosion in the paint factory, the electric lobotomy in the factory hospital, and the subsequent identity therapy, the invisible man is severed from his past, to the extent that he realizes he cannot go south again, for either success or revenge. When released from the factory hospital, he is told not to work for a while, that he will be "compensated." The issue of "compensation" confuses him, even more so when he discovers that in order to receive his compensation, he has to sign papers releasing the company from responsibility. Finally, in his perplexity, "It came out of itself: 'Do you know Mr. Norton, sir?' I said" (188). The linking of the "compensation" papers to Mr. Norton takes us full circle back to the pragmatic applications of Emersonianism, and Norton's overliteral interpretation of "Fate" and "Self-Reliance" connects here with the overliteral approach to "Compensation."

Emerson writes in that essay:

> The true life and satisfactions of man seem to elude the utmost rigors or felicities of condition and to establish themselves with great indifference under all varieties of circumstances. Under all governments the influence of character remains the same—in Turkey and in New England about alike. Under the primeval despots of Egypt, history honestly confesses that man must have been as free as culture could make him. (*Complete Works*, II:98)

But for the invisible man, money has been substituted for "true life" satisfactions, for money is the medium of compensation that the Mr. Nortons and the Dr. Bledsoes and the Mr. Emersons understand. This inadequate compensation indicates both the blindness of the characters and also the fallibility of the philosophy they have adopted and adapted. This couldn't be more clear when we see that the explosion of the invisible man's life, the rupturing of his hopes, the shattering of his identity, finds compensation in money. Ironically, he now has the money he had come to New York to earn, but he has been deprived of any goal toward which to apply it. As long as the institutions can be absolved of their responsibility, their/his money is worthless. He realizes, subconsciously, that he is once more being appeased with a worthless promise, and he cannot shake the image of Norton:

> Then I heard myself say, "Do you know him?" my voice rising.
> "Who?"
> "Mr. Norton," I said. "Mr. Norton!"
> "Oh, why, no."
> "No," I said, "no one knows anybody and it was too long a time ago."
> He frowned and I laughed. "They picked poor Robin clean," I said. "Do you happen to know Bled?"
> He looked at me, his head to one side. "Are these people friends of yours?"
> "Friends? Oh, yes," I said, "we're all good friends. Buddies from way back. But I don't suppose we get around in the same circles." (188)

The persistent association here with Norton and circles and, finally, with Emerson himself—"I thought of asking him about Emerson" (189)—links the two by means of the Emersonian principle through which he would escape them: "I *was* no longer afraid. Not of important men, not of trustees and such; for knowing now that there was nothing which I could expect from them, there was no reason to be afraid" (189).

At the same time, in other words, that the invisible man indicates the impracticality of Emerson's idea of compensation, he is also learning one of Emerson's principles. For in "Compensation," Emerson also explains:

> All infractions of love and equity in our social relations are speedily punished. They are punished by fear. . . . All the old abuses in society, social and particular, all unjust accumulations of property and power, are avenged in the same manner. Fear is an instructor of great sagacity and the herald of all revolutions. (II:107–8)

At this point, his liberation becomes transcendent: "My mind went alternately bright and blank in slow rolling waves. We, he, him—my mind and I—were no longer getting around in the same circles. Nor my body either" (190).

Emerson is not mentioned again until the end of chapter 23, when the invisible man, betrayed by the Brotherhood and pursued through Harlem by Ras' gang, has just left Hambro's apartment. Hambro has urged him to accept the Brotherhood's decisions: " 'You must, therefore, have confidence in those who lead you—in the collective wisdom of the Brotherhood' " (382).

> Sacrifice and leadership, I thought. For him it was simple. For *them* it was simple. But hell, I was both. Both sacrificer and victim. I couldn't get away from that and Hambro didn't have to deal with it. That was reality, too, my reality. He didn't have to put the knife blade to his own throat. What would he say if *he* were the victim? (382)

This situation recalls again Emerson, who is associated with his infamous correspondent, Bledsoe: "Otherwise there was nothing but betrayal, and that meant going back to serve Bledsoe, and Emerson, jumping from the pot of absurdity into the fire of the ridiculous. And either was a self-betrayal" (382). His thoughts then turn to the Brotherhood, which he realizes didn't see him at all, and

> now I lashed around a corner of my mind and saw Jack and Norton and Emerson merge into one single white figure. They were very much the same, each attempting to force his picture of reality upon me, and neither giving a hoot in hell for how things looked to me. I was simply a material, a natural resource to be used. I had switched from the arrogant absurdity of Norton and Emerson to that of Jack and the Brotherhood, and it all came out the same—except I now realized my invisibility. (384)

This disavowal of Emerson is modified slightly in chapter 25, the last before the epilogue: ". . . I had no longer to run for or from the Jacks and the Emersons and the Bledsoes and Nortons, but only from their confusion, impatience, and refusal to recognize the beautiful absurdity of their American identity and mine" (422). Ellison is thus acknowledging their shared identity, an identity they are too blind to see.

The chapter ends with a dream in which Jack, Emerson, Bledsoe, and Norton are joined by "Ras, the school superintendent and a number of others whom I failed to recognize, but all of whom had run me" (429). They surround the invisible man and, led by Jack, castrate him, throwing his testicles over the bridge, where they "curve up and catch beneath the apex of the curving arch of the bridge, to hang there dripping down through the sunlight into the dark red water" (430).

" 'Now you're free of illusions,' Jack said, pointing to my seed wasting on the air. 'How does it feel to be free of one's illusions?' " (430). In his pain and emptiness, however, he gets an insight:

> "Why do you *laugh?*" he said.
> "Because at a price I now see that which I couldn't see," I said.
> "What does he think he sees?" they said.
> And Jack came closer, threatening, and I laughed. "I'm not afraid now," I said. "But if you'll look, you'll see . . . I'm not invisible . . ."
> "See what?" they said.
> "That there hang not only my generations wasting upon the water—" And now the pain welled up and I could no longer see them.
> "But what? Go on," they said.
> "But your sun . . ."
> "Yes?"
> "And your moon . . ."
> "He's crazy."
> "Your world . . ."
> "I knew he was a mystic idealist!" Tobitt said.
> "Still," I said, "there's your universe, and that drip-drop upon the water you hear is all the history you've made, all you're going to make. Now laugh, you scientists. Let's hear you laugh!"
> And high above me now the bridge seemed to move off to where I could not see, striding like a robot, an iron man, whose iron legs clanged doomfully as it moved. And then I struggled up, full of sorrow and pain, shouting, "No, no, we must stop him!" (430–31)

The mechanical man thus becomes for the invisible man both his revenge and his nightmare, but this nightmare has an oddly Emersonian character: first, the generation of the mechanical man in a grotesque way parallels the process described in the poem at the beginning of "Circles":

> Nature centers into balls,
> And her proud ephemerals,

> Fast to surface and outside,
> Scan the profile of the sphere;
> Knew they what that signified,
> A new genesis were here.

In a more full way, too, the invisible man's position embraces—or perhaps it is better to say fails to escape—the principles of "Self-Reliance" and the world view of "Circles." If this is so, it seems the criticism of these aspects of Emersonianism is lodged in the fact that those aspects of optimism and individuality, so much a part of the American character to which Emerson gave form, are shared even by those he implicitly or ignorantly excluded. As we have seen, much of Emerson is absurd, even cruel, when we change the audience. Despite this, however, he partakes of a tradition which includes—whether he acknowledges it or not—a vast invisible subculture. Whether or not he sees the invisible American population, he is one with it; whether or not his words are used to keep that population invisible, his words also betray their shared American heritage.

Ellison's final position on Emerson is thus filled with ambivalence.[7] Without fully rejecting him, Ellison suggests, through his allusions, great problems with either the pragmatic approach to Emerson or the idealistic. Certainly the invisible man finally realizes his ideal of "self-reliance," but he does so at the price of complete removal from the social world, an option that an invisible man has in the way, for instance, that an enslaved one does not. Ellison's allusions, therefore, make us conscious of the audience, and that consciousness changes our understanding of Emerson's text.

In "Self-Reliance" Emerson states:

> Whoso would be a man must be a non-conformist. He who would gather immortal palms must not be hindered by the name of goodness, but must explore if it be goodness. Nothing is at last sacred but the integrity of your own mind. Absolve you to yourself and you shall have the suffrage of the world. (*Complete Works*, II:51–52)

If we imagined this delivered to an audience of slaves, we have a text not about democracy but about blindness.

In a way, then, Ellison is reiterating Melville's objections to Emerson— that he failed to confront evil. Mumford failed to see this difference between Emerson and Melville, and Matthiessen failed to see it in its political/historical context, which wedded the question of slavery to the question of evil. When Ellison has the Emersonian, Mr. Norton, enter the Golden Day to play the role of Don Benito Cereno, he has in one densely allusive dream scene rewritten a literary tradition. Ellison has created a world in which the allusions comment not only on tradition, but constantly on one another.

Out of that commentary comes a strain of Emersonianism honed on the distortions propagated by the ersatz followers of Emerson, those whom Whitman might call "the linguists and contenders." Or what Twain might call the propagators of "the Gilded Age," the postbellum period which, as we have seen, distorted that Emersonian Americanism as it forced the black into segregation and invisibility. The next chapter discusses the way Ellison's allusions to Twain examine Twain's view of the postbellum treatment of the black.

6. Invisible Man, Huck, and Jim

lbert Bigelow Paine, in his 1912 three-volume biography of Mark Twain, said of *Huckleberry Finn*, "it is built of indestructible blocks of human nature; and if the blocks do not always fit, and the ornaments do not always agree, we need not fear. Time will blur the incongruities and moss over the mistakes" (798). Despite Paine's prediction, time, like the novel's Mississippi, has flowed unavoidably toward conflict, not resolution. In 1945, therefore, when Ellison wrote about *Huckleberry Finn*, in his essay "Twentieth-Century Fiction and the Black Mask of Humanity," he was responding to what was already significant controversy about the book. The controversy related most directly to the interpretations of the last third of the novel. In that section Huck has abandoned the river to live in disguise on the Phelps farm so that he may set free the recaptured Jim. Huck is able (perhaps fortuitously, perhaps not so fortuitously) to assume as his disguise the identity of Tom Sawyer. Tom very shortly arrives, takes the identity of his own brother, Sid, and joins in Huck's escape plot, almost immediately taking charge and directing Huck's and Jim's activities so that they become a child's distorted replication of historical romances in the style of Scott and Dumas.

Van Wyck Brooks and Lewis Mumford, in keeping with their thesis that the Gilded Age after the Civil War created an environment in which artists could not function, find Twain's work deficient.[1] In *The Ordeal of Mark Twain*, Brooks sees Twain's work as a case of arrested development and considers *Huckleberry Finn* a book lacking adult emotions, a book for boys out of the mind of a boy. Bernard DeVoto rests his extensive rebuttal of Brooks largely on the first two-thirds of *Huckleberry Finn*, which DeVoto considers a panorama of uniquely American life, an exploration of society

> from the Grangerfords at the top, through the many-personed middle class, down to the squatters and the river-drifters, and below them to the raw stuff of mobs and such creatures of darkness and dream as the two rogues. An exploration made dangerous by the unseen powers which the ghosts cry about out of the midnight woods and which are forever hinting their menace in signs

and portents—but made much more dangerous by the human violence that is always threatening to break through. (*Mark Twain's America*, 100)

The last third of the novel DeVoto considers a sharp falling off into burlesque. "In the whole reach of the English novel," he states, "there is no more abrupt or more chilling descent" (92). DeVoto argues, nevertheless, that the last third of the novel is excellent in its kind and attributes its misplacement in *Huckleberry Finn* to Twain's lack of self-discipline, his incapacity for self-criticism: "Precisely there is the central limitation of Mark Twain's genius. He felt no difference in value between the highest truths of fiction and merely literary burlesque—if in fact he could at all discriminate between them. . . . He was in the antique sense a genius: he wrote in obedience to an inner drive, he exercised little voluntary control over it, and he was unable to criticize what he had written" (91).

Ernest Hemingway, along the same line, in *The Green Hills of Africa*, renounced the last third of the novel with his famous statement that all modern American literature comes from *Huckleberry Finn*. "If you read it you must stop where the Nigger Jim is stolen from the boys. That is the real end. The rest is just cheating" (22).

In an essay, Ellison responds directly to Hemingway as he does indirectly to DeVoto (as well as Van Wyck Brooks and Lewis Mumford), by defending the complete text of *Huckleberry Finn* and asserting a level of self-awareness in Twain that the others denied:

After Twain's compelling image of black and white fraternity the Negro generally disappears from fiction as a rounded human being. And if already in Twain's time a novel which was optimistic concerning a democracy which would include all men could not escape being banned from public libraries, by our day his great drama of interracial fraternity had become, for most Americans at least, an amusing boy's story and nothing more. But, while a boy, Huck Finn has become the somersault motion of what William Empson terms "pastoral," an embodiment of the heroic, and an exponent of humanism. Indeed, the historical and artistic justification for his adolescence lies in the fact that Twain was depicting a transitional period of American life; its artistic justification is that adolescence is the time of the "great confusion" during which both individuals and nations flounder between accepting and rejecting the responsibilities of adulthood. Accordingly, Huck's relationship to Jim, the river, and all they symbolize, is that of a humanist; in his relation to the community he is an individualist. He embodies the two major conflicting drives operating in nineteenth-century America. And if humanism is man's basic attitude toward a social order which he accepts, and individualism his basic attitude toward one he rejects, one might say that Twain, by allowing these two attitudes to argue dialectically in his work of art, was as highly moral an artist as he was a believer in democracy, and vice versa. (SA, 50–51)

It was Hemingway who pointed out that all modern American writing springs from *Huckleberry Finn*. . . . But by the twenties the element of rejection implicit in Twain had become so dominant an attitude of the American writer that Hemingway goes on to warn us to "stop where the Nigger Jim is stolen from the boys. That is the real end. The rest is just cheating."
So thoroughly had the Negro, both as man and as a symbol of man, been pushed into the underground of the American conscience that Hemingway missed completely the structural, symbolic and moral necessity for that part of the plot in which the boys rescue Jim. Yet it is precisely this part which gives the novel its significance. Without it, except as a boy's tale, the novel is meaningless. Yet Hemingway, a great artist in his own right, speaks as a victim of that culture of which he is himself so critical, for by his time that growing rift in the ethical fabric pointed out by Twain had become completely sundered—snagged upon the irrepressible moral reality of the Negro. Instead of the single democratic ethic for every man, there now existed two: one, the idealized ethic of the Constitution and the Declaration of Independence, reserved for white men; and the other, the pragmatic ethic designed for Negroes and other minorities, which took the form of discrimination. Twain had dramatized the conflict leading to this division in its earlier historical form. (SA, 51)

Hemingway's blindness to the moral values of *Huckleberry Finn* despite his sensitivity to its technical aspects duplicated the one-sided vision of the twenties. Where Twain, seeking for what Melville called "the common continent of man," drew upon the rich folklore of the frontier (not omitting the Negro's) in order to "Americanize" his idiom, thus broadening his stylistic appeal, Hemingway was alert only to Twain's technical discoveries—the flexible colloquial language, the sharp naturalism, the thematic potentialities of adolescence. Thus what for Twain was a means to a moral end became for Hemingway an end in itself. (SA, 52)

These excerpts give us a clear sense of Ellison's attitude toward *Huckleberry Finn* at exactly the time he was starting to write *Invisible Man*.[2] They indicate, not surprisingly, that Ellison once more opposed the general critical consensus of his day, that same consciousness which, we have seen, erased the significance of the black in nineteenth-century literature. Despite Ellison's admiration for Hemingway, expressed in many interviews and essays, he still sees in Hemingway's work, as in his criticism of *Huckleberry Finn*, the manifestation of those twentieth-century attitudes we have examined at great length.

For Ellison, Twain was the last great American author to see the full implications of the connection between the black and the fundamentals of democracy. He was the last writer in the spirit of the Golden Day as Ellison, not Mumford, interpreted the era. The invisible man's plight—to discover what went wrong in the Golden Day—therefore mirrors Ellison's own desire to return American fiction to the sense of moral responsibility manifested by the great writers of that era and culminating in Huck's accepting the tragedy of his journey as well as the necessity of masking it in comic irony. "Huck Finn's acceptance," he tells us, "of the evil implicit in his 'emancipation' of Jim represents Twain's acceptance of his personal responsibility in the condition of society. This was the tragic face behind his comic mask" (*SA*, 50).

While Ellison was in the middle of writing *Invisible Man*, yet another perspective would be added to the body of criticism surrounding *Huckleberry Finn*. In 1948, Leslie Fiedler published in *Partisan Review* his famous essay "Come Back to the Raft Ag'in, Huck Honey!" In that essay he argues that *Huckleberry Finn* is a quintessential American novel because it is a "boy's book," by which Fiedler means one that idealizes homosexual love. This idealized homosexual love, which he also finds in *Moby-Dick* and the Leatherstocking Tales, reflects a preference of the American young man for bonding with the exotic (black) outcast. Fiedler sees this relationship as "the regressiveness, in a technical sense, of American life, its implacable nostalgia for the infantile, at once wrong-headed and somehow admirable" (414–15). Fiedler makes his argument as a call for tolerance, a call for Americans to realize what their great literature has told them about themselves:

> Of the infantile, the homoerotic aspects of these stories we are, though vaguely, aware; but it is only with an effort that we can wake to a consciousness of how, among us who at the level of adulthood find a difference in color sufficient provocation for distrust and hatred, they celebrate, all of them, the mutual love of *a white man and a colored*. So buried at a level of acceptance which does not touch reason, so desperately repressed from overt recognition, so contrary to what is usually thought of as our ultimate level of taboo—the sense of that love can survive only in the obliquity of a symbol, persistent, obsessive, in short, an archetype: the boy's homoerotic crush, the love of the black fused at this level into a single thing. (416)

Ten years later, also in *Partisan Review*, Ellison responded directly to Fiedler, but an earlier and in some ways more detailed response can be found in the critical subtext created by the allusions in *Invisible Man*'s chapter 9. In that chapter, the invisible man meets Emerson's son, who, at one point, asks him if he has ever been to the Club Calamus, "a rendezvous for writers, artists and all kinds of celebrities. There's nothing like it in the city, and by some strange twist it has a truly continental flavor" (141). The name "Calamus," as

I noted earlier, suggests young Emerson's homosexuality by alluding to Whitman's homosexual Calamus poems. Ellison's use of the Whitman allusion to name an integrated, gay night club alludes, in turn, to Fiedler's essay, which mentions "the special night club: the 'queer' cafe, the black-and-tan joint, in which fairy or Negro exhibit their fairyness" (414–15), and later Fiedler associates that milieu with Whitman when he says that Lorca "grasped instinctively . . . the kinship of Harlem and Walt Whitman, the fairy bard" (419).

Like Fiedler, young Emerson also associates this milieu with Huck Finn when, later in his talk with the invisible man, he proclaims himself to be Huckleberry:

> "I was trying to tell you that I know many things about you—not you personally, but fellows like you. Not much, either, but still more than the average. With us it's still Jim and Huck Finn. A number of my friends are jazz musicians, and I've been around. I know the conditions under which you live—Why go back, fellow? There is so much you could do here where there is more freedom. You won't find what you're looking for when you return anyway; because so much is involved that you can't possibly know. Please don't misunderstand me; I don't say all this to impress you. Or to give myself some kind of sadistic catharsis. Truly, I don't. But I do know this world you're trying to contact—all its virtues and all its unspeakables—Ha, yes, unspeakables. I'm afraid my father considers *me* one of the unspeakables . . . I'm Huckleberry, you see . . ." (143)

Young Emerson, of course, is not Huck unless we have a very strange view of Huck, one which sees him as a "boy" in Fiedler's sense of the word, that is as a male with an underdeveloped ego, who desires to escape patriarchal tyranny by running away from responsibility and violating social and psychological taboos. This implicitly Freudian interpretation of Huck shared by Fiedler and young Emerson would suggest that both these literary critics had read *Totem and Taboo*. Young Emerson was in fact reading that book when the invisible man entered his life ("He must have been sitting there when I came in, for on a table that held a beautiful dwarf tree I saw smoke rising from a cigarette in a jade ash tray. An open book, something called *Totem and Taboo*, lay beside it" [137]).

Although Ellison's allusions thus accurately suggest the source of Fiedler's interpretation, the critical subtext not only locates Fiedler in terms of intellectual history but also helps highlight some problems with Fiedler's argument. Young Emerson's persistent immaturity, his inability to move beyond the barely cloaked demands of his id, reflects one premise of Fiedler's argument—that *Huckleberry Finn* is not about a boy's growing up but about his willfully arrested development. The book for Fiedler is about a taboo violated as an alternative to living under the patriarchal life on the shore; it is about the escape to a mythic and timeless world where males can manifest their mutual attraction guiltlessly. Since guilt will always intrude, however, the book for Fiedler is not really about escape, but rather the dream of escape; it is the sublimated fantasy of male love.

Young Emerson accurately fits Fiedler's description of Huck. He languishes in a state of arrested development, fantasizing about the freedom provided by the Harlem club where black and white homosexuals commingle. His "real" life is filled with anxiety and guilt because he seems incapable of separating his ego from his father's, a point Ellison emphasizes by withholding young Emerson's name. We know him only as Emerson's son and by the name he gives himself in his fantasy life—"Huckleberry." "Huckleberry" (as opposed to "Huck"), moreover, is the name used by Miss Watson, the self-righteous old woman who wants to "sivilize" Huck and who sells Jim down the river. The artificial formality of "Huckleberry" contrasts, to comic effect, with the informality of the "Huck" it artificially formalizes. We, like Jim, know that Huck is "Huck," and we have to distrust anyone who fails even that simple a test of identity by trying to make "Huckleberry" out of him.

Ellison achieves the same comic effect when he has young Emerson call himself "Huckleberry." A reader of Twain knows that "Huckleberry" doesn't name Huck but Miss Watson's misguided idea of him. In *Invisible Man*, it also names Leslie Fiedler's idea of Huck, at the comic expense, therefore, not only of young Emerson but also of Fiedler. In a perfect ironic reversal, moreover, the invisible man responds to young Emerson's pronouncements exactly as Fiedler would have him: "*Huckleberry?* Why did he keep talking about a kid's story?" (143). Substituting the word "kid" for "boy," the invisible man is, indeed, agreeing with Fiedler, who insists that the genre he is describing be called the "boy's book." As Ellison sets it up, furthermore, one tends to agree with Fiedler's and the invisible man's judgment—the "Huckleberry" whom young Emerson resembles does belong in a childish fantasy.

For Ellison—as for Twain himself—*Adventures of Huckleberry Finn* is not a child's book because it represents a boy's learning to make independent, responsible decisions in the face of a pervasively corrupt society.[3] Ellison has stressed the importance of that decision not as *fantasy* but as *action*. Huck does not feel guilt about Jim's enslavement nearly so much as he does about his desire to end that enslavement, and Huck's act of personal responsibility is defined by what he does in spite of his guilt, not because of it. We know Huck hasn't forgotten about Jim's fate, therefore, not because Huck *feels* guilt but because he *acts* on Jim's behalf. Fiedler, on the other hand, does not see in Huck's story that his action defies his guilt so much as that his guilt substitutes for action.

If Fiedler is right, Ellison suggests through his use of young Emerson, Huck's wish to free the black is meaningless. Young Emerson insists repeatedly that he wants to help the invisible man and, near the end of their talk, pronounces him free:

He stammered guiltily, "Please, I must ask you never to mention this conversation to anyone."

"No," I said.

"I wouldn't mind, but my father would consider my revelation the most extreme treason . . . You're free of him now. I'm still his prisoner. You have been freed, don't you understand? I've still my battle." (146)

The invisible man's freedom is, of course, ironic: he has no money, no job, no hopes of returning to college, and no recourse but to accept Bledsoe's decision about his fate. Still, his freedom is more real than young Emerson's "battle," which is completely fantasized. Incapable of acting against his father, Emerson battles only in his mind, and his need for secrecy underscores his incapacity to fight his battle. Like his identity and his relationship with the invisible man, his battle remains secret, a fantasy that cannot take the form of action, clear and overt, with social ramifications. Incapable of acting in the social world on the invisible man's (or even on his own) behalf, young Emerson can only "help" the invisible man by bringing him into his (and Fiedler's) fantasy. He thus invites the invisible man to a party at Club Calamus and/or offers him a job as personal valet. When the invisible man rejects these offers—refuses to come back to Fiedler's raft—young Emerson is helpless. He mentions a possible job at Liberty Paints not as part of his own domain but as a place where his father has sent several fellows. Thus, to Emerson's site of liberty, rather than to Fiedler's vision of freedom, Ellison sends the invisible man. If at that site problems arise, they are not, Ellison's allusions suggest, problems as easily rejected as those posed by Fiedler's boy.

This is not to suggest that Ellison wholly endorses Twain's depiction of the relationship between Huck and Jim. He says, in fact, that some of the problems with that depiction create a reader's discomfort with the text which, in turn, caused Fiedler's misreading:

It is not at all odd that this black-faced figure of white fun is for Negroes a symbol of everything they rejected in the white man's thinking about race, in themselves and in their own group. When he appears, for example, in the guise of Nigger Jim, the Negro is made uncomfortable. Writing at a time when the blackfaced minstrel was still popular, and shortly after a war which left even the abolitionists weary of those problems associated with the Negro, Twain fitted Jim into the outlines of the minstrel tradition, and it is from behind this stereotype mask that we see Jim's dignity and human capacity—and Twain's complexity—emerge. Yet it is his source in this same tradition which creates that ambivalence between his identification as an adult and parent and his "boyish" naiveté, and which by contrast makes Huck, with his street-sparrow sophistication, seem more adult. Certainly it upsets a Negro reader, and it offers a less psychoanalytical explanation of the discomfort which lay behind Leslie Fiedler's thesis concerning the relation of Jim and Huck in his essay "Come Back to the Raft Ag'in, Huck Honey!"

. . . Twain, standing closer to the Reconstruction and to the oral tradition, was not so free of the white dictum that Negro males must be treated either as boys or "uncles"—never as men. Jim's friendship for Huck comes across as that of a boy for another boy rather than as the friendship of an adult for a junior; thus there is implicit in it not only a violation of the manners sanctioned by society for relations between Negroes and whites, there is a violation of our conception of adult maleness.

In Jim the extremes of the private and the public come to focus, and before our eyes an "archetypal" figure gives way before the realism implicit in the form of the novel. Here we have, I believe, an explanation in the novel's own terms of that ambiguity which bothered Fiedler. Fiedler was accused of mere sensationalism when he named the friendship homosexual, yet I believe him so profoundly disturbed by the manner in which the deep dichotomies symbolized by blackness and whiteness are resolved that, forgetting to look at the specific form of the novel, he leaped squarely into the middle of that tangle of symbolism which he is dedicated to unsnarling, and yelled out his most terrifying name for chaos. Other things being equal, he might have called it "rape," "incest," "parricide" or—"miscegenation." It is ironic that what to a Negro appears to be a lost fall in Twain's otherwise successful wrestle with the ambiguous figure in black face is viewed by a critic as a symbolic loss of sexual identity. Surely for literature there is some rare richness here. (SA, 65–66)

In this context, we can examine Ellison's most important allusions to *Huckleberry Finn*, which come in chapter 10, the Liberty Paints factory episode. The chapter begins: "The plant was in Long Island, and I crossed a bridge in the fog to get there and came down in a stream of workers. Ahead of me a huge electric sign announced its message through the drifting strands of fog: KEEP AMERICA PURE WITH LIBERTY PAINTS" (149). A few paragraphs later, the invisible man's name is entered on the "shipping department's payroll." The words "island," "bridge," "stream," "drifting," and "shipping," together with the three appearances in the first paragraph of the word "fog"—not a common image in *Invisible Man*—suggest a stream or a river in the fog. Passing through this fog, the invisible man finds himself mixing black dope into the white paint, made white by the unseen presence of that dope. "Slowly," he says, "I measured the glistening black drops, seeing them settle upon the surface and become blacker still, spreading suddenly out to the edges" (152). Though diminished and reversed, this replicates the famous image of the white Ohio River trailing along the edge of the muddy Mississippi before disappearing into it.[4]

In *Huckleberry Finn* that image appears as a sign that Huck and Jim have passed the point of turning back, of going up the Ohio into the free states. It tells them they must have passed Cairo in the fog. The events in the paint factory, similarly, end the invisible man's hopes of reversing the direction of his journey. He had entered the factory as a way of earning money to return to the college to kill Bledsoe. The image of the white paint absorbing the black dope, however, hints that the invisible man, too, will be absorbed in the white world to which he has come rather than return for any reason to the black college. It also foreshadows his story in a more literal way. At the end of the paint factory episode, having fallen for Brockway's trick, he will be absorbed in the exploding white paint. Then he will be given an electric lobotomy and left, with small compensation, to be lost in the dark periphery of New York. As the white Ohio does in *Huckleberry Finn*, the black dope in *Invisible Man* provides a visual image which both tells the reader that a character has passed the point of turning back and signifies his plight.

By reversing the imagery, Ellison shows us once again that an allusion is always both same and different. The differences in this case can remind us that the direction of the journeys are opposite, that in a manner of speaking the invisible man is fulfilling Jim's wish to go north. Considering *Huckleberry Finn* in these terms raises the possibility that the promise of the Ohio was no more likely to meet Jim's expectations than his hopeless drifting to the South. The clear water of the Ohio may have represented the purity of freedom, as the mud of the Mississippi may have the impurity of slavery, but the white in the factory is paint, an impure substance made under the misleading sign of purity, a bogus purity which covers up, whitewashes, makes the black dope invisible.

In many ways, Jim, too, is an invisible man, not the fully realized character that Huck is. As Ellison, among others, has noted, *Huckleberry Finn* is not Jim's story.[5] Huck and Jim have different goals on the raft, and while Huck wants in some ways to remain on the raft forever, Jim wants to get off it and to be free. The moral burden of Jim's quest makes Huck abandon his own, and Jim's primary importance is in what he represents for Huck. Despite his great symbolic importance, however, Ellison, as we have seen, finds Jim as a character in his own right greatly lacking.

By associating Jim with the invisible man, therefore, Ellison points out the ways in which Jim is invisible. At the same time, however, Ellison's imagery highlights the dilemma of which both he and Twain were well aware—that there was no place for Jim to go. In seeing, as the paint-bucket reversal suggests, that the journey north is only another way of going downriver, we see in yet another version the true impossibility of Jim's situation, and we see that the problem of *Huckleberry Finn* is not that Twain is caught in the flow of a river heading only toward enslavement. Rather, especially writing from the perspective of the failure of Reconstruction, Twain understood the problem was not regional but an illness of the shore, of being "sivilized." The Brothers up north, as Ellison will show us, are just latter-day Tom Sawyers. James Cox succinctly explains that in the end of *Huckleberry Finn*, "the narrative movement changes from one of adventure to burlesque—a burlesque which, in place of Huck's sincere but helpless involvement in freeing a real slave, puts Tom's relatively cruel yet successful lark of freeing a slave already free. It is not Mark Twain's failure to distinguish between the two actions which jeopardizes his book; rather, it is his ironic exposure of Tom's action which threatens the humor of the book and produces the inharmonious burlesque DeVoto regrets" (*Mark Twain*, 174).

The diminishing in size from river to bucket also serves to underscore Jim's symbolic status. The invisible man must lose ten drops of black dope in each of many white buckets, all heading for the national monument. The one drop of black dope is one of many, each invisible, all serving myriad goals, in many proper places making the white surface look whiter. In this way, Ellison comments on those who would discount Huck's lesson on the raft. Certainly Huck has not turned into an abolitionist, has not abandoned his ideas about race and slavery. Yet both Twain and Ellison understood the symbolic importance of Huck's commitment to Jim in that both authors knew that any commitment is meaningless in the form of dogma. The power of Huck's commitment comes from its arising out of an understanding between human beings, which contrasts sharply with Tom's inhumane commitments. As Tom is capable only of seeing through books, Huck is incapable of doing so. Thus he cannot learn the lesson of Moses and the Bullrushes from a book, but learns it in practice, being cast out upon the water for salvation, taken for dead, reborn, and eventually taking the slave from Cairo to freedom.[6]

The end of chapter 10 also closely parallels a scene in *Huckleberry Finn*, the sinking of the raft. Very shortly after discovering the traces of the Ohio in the Mississippi, Huck and Jim formulate a new plan—to buy passage up the river—but that, too, is ruined when a riverboat sinks their raft; this first puts them in a state of limbo, then abruptly changes their plans. The explosion in the boiler room has a similar effect on the invisible man at exactly the same point in his story. In many ways, moreover, the details and imagery in the two scenes are very similar. In describing the riverboat Huck concentrates on its furnace:

> We could hear her pounding along, but we didn't see her good till she was close. She aimed right for us. Often they do that and try to see how close they can come without touching; sometimes the wheel bites off a sweep, and then the pilot sticks his head out and laughs, and thinks he's mighty smart. Well, here she comes, and we said she was going to try to shave us; but she didn't seem to be sheering off a bit. She was a big one, and she was coming in a hurry, too, looking like a black cloud with rows of glow-worms around it; but

all of a sudden she bulged out, big and scary, with a long row of wide-open
furnace doors shining like red-hot teeth, and her monstrous bows and guards
hanging right over us. There was a yell at us, and a jingling of bells to stop
the engines, a pow-wow of cussing, and whistling of steam—and as Jim went
overboard on one side and I on the other, she came smashing straight through
the raft.

I dived—and I aimed to find the bottom, too, for a thirty-foot wheel had
got to go over me, and I wanted it to have plenty of room. I could always stay
under water a minute; this time I reckon I staid under water a minute and a
half. Then I bounced for the top in a hurry, for I was nearly busting. I popped
out to my arm-pits and blowed the water out of my nose, and puffed a bit. Of
course there was a booming current; and of course that boat started her engines again ten seconds after she stopped them, for they never cared much for
raftsmen; so now she was churning along up the river, out of sight in the thick
weather, though I could hear her. (78–79)

The exploding furnace is, of course, also the focus in *Invisible Man:*

I heard a shrill hissing from the boilers behind me and turned, hearing Brockway yell, "I tole you to watch them gauges. Git over to the big valves, quick!"

I dashed for where a series of valve wheels projected from the wall near the
crusher, seeing Brockway scrambling away in the other direction, thinking,
Where's he going? as I reached the valves, and hearing him yell, "Turn it!
Turn it!"

"Which?" I yelled, reaching.

"The white one, fool, the white one!"

I jumped, catching it and pulling down with all my weight, feeling it give.
But this only increased the noise and I seemed to hear Brockway laugh as I
looked around to see him scrambling for the stairs, his hands clasping the
back of his head, and his neck pulled in close, like a small boy who has
thrown a brick into the air.

"Hey you! Hey you!" I yelled. "Hey!" But it was too late. All my movements seemed too slow, ran together. I felt the wheel resisting and tried vainly
to reverse it and tried to let go, and it sticking to my palms and my fingers stiff
and sticky, and I turned, running now, seeing the needle on one of the gauges
swinging madly, like a beacon gone out of control, and trying to think clearly,
my eyes darting here and there through the room of tanks and machines
and up the stairs so far away and hearing the clear new note arising while I
seemed to run swiftly up an incline and shot forward with sudden acceleration
into a wet blast of black emptiness that was somehow a bath of whiteness.

It was a fall into space that seemed not a fall but a suspension. Then a
great weight landed upon me and I seemed to sprawl in an interval of clarity
beneath a pile of broken machinery, my head pressed back against a huge
wheel, my body splattered with a stinking goo. Somewhere an engine ground

in furious futility, grating loudly until a pain shot around the curve of my head and bounced me off into blackness for a distance, only to strike another pain that lobbed me back. And in that clear instant of consciousness I opened my eyes to a blinding flash. (174–75)

Clearly, this passage has many of the details and images of Huck's description. In both passages, the narrator is trying to avoid a dangerous and unavoidable accident, sees steam and wheels, hears someone laugh, and hears engine noises which stop and then resume after the accident. Both narrators also have companions with them who escape by going in a different direction and of whose fate the narrators remain unsure; after the explosion or collision, both narrators get submerged in liquid.

If these similarities call our attention to the allusion, they also signal some particularly striking differences. One is that Huck successfully avoids being hit by the wheel, whereas the invisible man does not. In some way, in other words, Huck has succeeded where the invisible man has failed. Perhaps then, in this scene, the invisible man corresponds not to Huck but to Jim, who "got hurt a little" (92). This would be consistent with our earlier reading of the allusions, but it presents an even more disturbing problem, for if the invisible man corresponds to Jim, then Lucius Brockway corresponds to Huck. Since Brockway's deceit caused the explosion and his relationship with the invisible man is one of mutual antipathy and distrust, the possibility that he is a surrogate Huck requires a serious reconsideration of the relationship between the raft partners.

Other details in the text, nevertheless, would suggest this parallel. The invisible man, for example, often associates Brockway with his own grandfather. These associations connect Brockway to all the black trickster surrogates in the novel—Brer Rabbit, Jim Trueblood, the Golden Day vet, and Peter Wheatstraw. Floyd Horowitz has pointed out that Brockway even resembles a rabbit physically, being small and wiry and having cottony white hair.[7] In talking about his own literary education, Ellison has associated these trickster figures directly with Huck:

> I knew the trickster Ulysses just as early as I knew the wily rabbit of Negro American lore, and I could easily imagine myself a pint-sized Ulysses but hardly a rabbit, no matter how human and resourceful or Negro. And a little later I could imagine myself as Huck Finn (I so nicknamed my brother) but not, though I racially identified with him, as Nigger Jim, who struck me as a white man's inadequate portrait of a slave. (SA, 72)

The invisible man's grandfather also resembles Huck in that, like Huck, he does not laugh at circus clowns. After the shooting of the drunken Boggs, Huck goes to the circus, where he sees an apparent drunk insist on riding a horse:

And at last, sure enough, all the circus men could do, the horse broke loose, and away he went like the very nation, round and round the ring, with that sot laying down on him and hanging to his neck, with first one leg hanging most to the ground on one side, and then t'other one on t'other side, and the people just crazy. It warn't funny to me, though; I was all of a tremble to see his danger. (120)

After the battle royal, when the invisible man dreams he is at a circus, his grandfather similarly "refused to laugh at the clowns no matter what they did" (26). In this case, as in Huck's, however, the refusal does not indicate a trickster but a person with compassion, with humanity. Huck, having just seen the drunken Boggs ranting on horseback and then murdered because of his foolhardiness, can no longer laugh at the antics of a drunk. At the battle royal, the invisible man himself had been the clown, tricked by the white citizens into entertaining them at the expense of his own pain and humiliation. As Huck understands the folly of Boggs' drunken bravura, the invisible man's grandfather understands the pain behind the antics in the battle royal and thus cannot laugh.

The invisible man's dream continues:

Then later he told me to open my brief case and read what was inside and I did, finding an official envelope stamped with the state seal; and inside the envelope I found another and another, endlessly, and I thought I would fall of weariness. "Them's years," he said. "Now open that one." And I did and in it I found an engraved document containing a short message in letters of gold. "Read it," my grandfather said. "Out loud!"
"To Whom It May Concern," I intoned. "Keep This Nigger-Boy Running."
I awoke with the old man's laughter ringing in my ears. (26)

At the end of the dream, in other words, the trickster side of the grandfather emerges. Although he refuses to laugh at the clowns in the circus, he will laugh at the invisible man's deluded sense of his own future. Here the invisible man has fallen for the trick in not knowing the difference between the clown and the victim, in not knowing that his grandfather's refusal to laugh was a way of showing him this secret. Unable to recognize the figure of Hermes, he cannot receive the secret message, cannot discover that against his will he had been a clown. But the end, this book always reminds us, is in the beginning, and so the invisible man's inability to see that he had been a clown is also his fate to remain one, without his consent, in spite of his delusions.

In the dream sequence, the grandfather signifies both aspects of the invisible man's heritage—guile and humanity. Huck also embodies both these traits. He starts out with the guile; the humanity he learns from associating with Jim. And only through his knowledge of Jim's humanity does he discover his own. In many ways, then, the grandfather is not only the trickster, Huck, but also the symbol of humanity, Jim. Just before beginning *Invisible Man*, Ellison concluded his essay on twentieth-century fiction with the reminder that, unlike contemporary authors, Twain "knew that in *his* America humanity masked its face with blackness" (SA, 60). At various points in the novel, then, when the invisible man sees a glint of his grandfather's smile and associates that with becoming more human, we could say that Ellison is in some way alluding to Jim.

The nature of those allusions, however, is far from simplistic, often operating in complicated ways to make us distinguish between symbolic humanity and human beings. At his first speech for the Brotherhood, the invisible man finds himself, almost inadvertently, confessing that "suddenly I have become *more human*" (261). Late that night he reviewed the speech in his mind:

> Words, phrases, skipped through my mind; I saw the blue haze again. What had I meant by saying that I had become "more human"? Was it a phrase that I had picked up from some preceding speaker, or a slip of the tongue? For a moment I thought of my grandfather and quickly dismissed him. What had an old slave to do with humanity? (267–68)

That unconscious outburst, drawn from the hidden resources that the grandfather symbolized, was the source both of the speech's success and of its failure. While the audience cheered wildly and Brother Jack congratulated the invisible man enthusiastically, an unnamed Brother who smoked a pipe (with Brother Wrestrum, who looked like Supercargo, agreeing) found the speech *"incorrect"* (" 'In my opinion the speech was wild, hysterical, politically irresponsible and dangerous,' he snapped. 'And worse than that, it was *incorrect!*' He pronounced 'incorrect' as though the term described the most heinous crime imaginable, and I stared at him openmouthed, feeling a vague guilt" [264]). The Brothers decide to send the invisible man to Brother Hambro to learn the proper way to work for the Brotherhood, the "scientific" way. The invisible man's appeal to the heart, the emotions of his audience, the appeal made through his sense of his own humanity, thus has to be modified, the invisible man to be trained. This reversal and the subsequent effects of his training on his humanity create a discomfort similar to the one created when Tom decides to show Huck the "proper" way to free Jim.

Tom's behavior, in fact, in many ways parallels the Brotherhood's treatment of the invisible man. In the name of helping blacks, the Brotherhood thwarts and undermines the progress of their liberation. First it denies human emotions, choosing to see humanity as operating according to the prescriptions of theoretical books. These books, as we have seen, define history and exclude from it those who don't confirm their theories. For the Brotherhood, as for Tom, the proper way of doing things is that which follows the written prescriptions, regardless of empirical evidence. Tom, like the Brotherhood, uses his sense of propriety to suppress another's individuality and divert that person's energies and desires to his own ends.

Many of the specific events in *Invisible Man*, moreover, parallel the trials that Tom puts Jim through in order to prevent Jim from becoming free too easily. Not only does Tom force Jim to conform to the "poetic" dictates of literature by writing nonsensical messages, but he also dresses Jim as a woman, something that both humiliates him and hampers his capacity to flee. In a similar act of humiliation, the Brotherhood transfers the invisible man, when he has mastered their theoretical training, to the "Woman Question," which is a way of diverting his energies and preventing him from achieving the goals that they allegedly share with him. Finally, and most significantly, Tom sends anonymous notes warning Jim's captors of the planned escape. This act of betrayal has a direct parallel in *Invisible Man*, for Brother Jack, ostensibly the invisible man's sponsor and ally, sends him an anonymous note:

> Brother,
> This is advice from a friend who has been watching you closely. *Do not go too fast*. Keep working for the people but remember that you are one of *us* and do not forget if you get too big *they* will cut you down. You are from the South and you know that this is a *white man's world*. So take a friendly advice and go easy so that you can keep on helping the colored people. *They* do not want you to go too fast and will cut you down if you do. Be smart . . . (289)

These parallels make us compare the way that the Brotherhood functions in *Invisible Man* to the way Tom does in *Huckleberry Finn*. It makes us see that the Brotherhood is, like all the people on the shore, more interested in preserving its own "sivilized" values than meeting its commitment to others or even seeing those others as people. At the same time, it asks us to see Tom's actions in *Huckleberry Finn* clearly as acts of betrayal. The parallels call our attention toward rather than away from the last third of *Huckleberry Finn*. It further impels us to see Tom's activities not as a burlesque, not as Twain's attempt to be humorous, but as his way of showing the seriousness of Huck's and Jim's dilemma, the full implications of recognizing Jim's humanity.

Let us again remember that Twain began *Huckleberry Finn* after witnessing the failure of Reconstruction. In many ways, then, Jim's escape preparations parody the *de facto* slavery of the Jim Crow South.[8] Tom knows that Jim is free, but he can't let him act like a free person or, for that matter, realize the extent of his freedom, until Jim can do it the proper way. The literacy laws and the poll taxes, the dependence on the black's physical strength to meet the needs of his ostensive benefactors, all find their parallels in the tests that Tom devises for Jim, as if Jim must prove his worthiness to Tom or Tom will not fulfill his commitment. Tom then is the southern gentleman not of the antebellum but of the post-Reconstruction South. The marked similarity between these two types is one of Twain's points, and given Twain's faith in the importance of upbringing, it should be no surprise that Tom would fulfill as an adult, after Reconstruction, the role he was trained for as a child. In the child Tom, then, we see the adult he will become, for like true nobility, southern ersatz nobility cannot overcome their upbringing, if they have been brought up properly enough. As Huck explains to Jim, "All I say is, kings is kings, and you got to make allowances. Take them all round, they're a mighty ornery lot. It's the way they're raised" (124). In their love of hierarchy, propriety, paternalism, these latter-day Tom Sawyers, Ellison's allusions suggest, are not a lot different from Brother Jack, or all the other authority figures with which he is aligned in the novel. As Neil Schmitz points out, Tom's whitewashing of the fence—the prank that resolves to nothing—becomes the ultimate whitewashing of Jim at the end of *Huckleberry Finn.*[9]

One crucial difference between the anonymous notes in the respective texts, however, is that Tom's are directed at the captors while Brother Jack's is directed at the captive. Jack assumes the persona of a black writing to another black to warn him about whites, while Tom assumes the persona of a reformed cutthroat warning upstanding slaveholders. Juxtaposing these two, we can see that Ellison's allusion asks us to see Jim as the real audience for Tom's antics. All of Tom's betrayals are ways of reminding Jim that he's not on the raft any more but on the shore, that his identity, his humanity, is of no value there. Rather, his freedom depends on his conforming to the roles—no matter how ludicrous or humiliating—defined for him by others. *Huckleberry Finn* is structured so that we see Jim at the outset as the comic butt of practical jokes, but as the book develops Jim's role changes so that he becomes Huck's equal in their minstrel show–like dialogues. The practical jokes purely at his expense cease to be funny; therefore, when Tom wants him to return to the "Sambo" role, we no longer laugh. Chadwick Hansen, in "The Character of Jim and the Ending of *Huckleberry Finn*," sees this lesson about Jim's humanity as a strategy of the novel.

Again, Ellison's allusions suggest something similar by letting us see that what Tom disguises as a joke is nothing but a betrayal, a clear renunciation of the black man's humanity. Ellison underscores this by having the invisible man turn directly to Brother Tarp after reading the anonymous note. Tarp is an old black who escaped a chain gang in the South and still bears a limp from the leg chain he once wore, a limp that suggests he's never achieved complete freedom. He reminds the invisible man of that old ex-slave his grandfather, who, like Jim, connotes humanity. Tarp tells the invisible man the story of his escape and concludes:

> "I've been looking for freedom ever since, son. And sometimes I've done all right. Up to these here hard times I did very well, considering that I'm a

man whose health is not too good. But even when times were best for me I
remembered. Because I didn't want to forget those nineteen years I just kind
of held on to this as a keepsake and a reminder." (293)

He then gives the invisible man the filed chain link which signified his
escape.

> "I'd like to pass it on to you, son. There," he said, handing it to me.
> "Funny thing to give somebody, but I think it's got a heap of signifying
> wrapped up in it and it might help you remember what we're really fighting
> against. I don't think of it in terms of but two words, *yes* and *no*; but it signi-
> fies a heap more . . ."
>   I saw him place his hand on the desk. "Brother," he said, calling me
> "Brother" for the first time, "I want you to take it. I guess it's a kind of luck
> piece. Anyway, it's the one I filed to get away."
>   I took it in my hand, a thick dark, oily piece of filed steel that had been
> twisted open and forced partly back into place, on which I saw marks that
> might have been made by the blade of a hatchet. It was such a link as I had
> seen on Bledsoe's desk, only while that one had been smooth, Tarp's bore the
> marks of haste and violence, looking as though it had been attacked and con-
> quered before it stubbornly yielded. (293)

The link's significance calls us to the larger question of signifying itself.
The polar opposites *yes* and *no*, in conjunction with the contrast between
Bledsoe's unbroken link and Tarp's which was filed, twisted open and forced
partly back into place, highlight the dichotomy of affirmation and negation
which permeates the novel. Both links represent approaches to the same problem, reminders of the same dilemma, Jim's dilemma, that of wanting both to
be free and to live on the "sivilized" shore, a place where not even Huck will
find freedom. The paradox of Jim's flight, then, is not that he must go up-
river, but that he must go ashore, a paradox only emphasized by the fact that
the shore on which he ultimately alights is further physically, if equally dis-
tant socially and psychologically, from his desired goal. The problem of Jim's
flight is that he is moving, although he will never be closer to freedom than
if he can manage to stay still, not leave the raft. Yet that means settling for a
very unsatisfactory version of freedom. This, too, is the invisible man's dilemma, in that the closest he can come to freedom is standing still. Each
time he runs toward a goal, he finds himself helping to fulfill Bledsoe's desire for his fate, that he "continue in the direction of that promise which,
like the horizon, recedes ever brightly and distantly beyond the hopeful
traveler" (145).

At the first Brotherhood party that he attends, for example, a drunken
white man asks him to sing, and is abruptly informed, "The brother *does not
sing!*" (237). After he receives many apologies, the invisible man wonders:

"Shouldn't there be some way for us to be asked to sing? Shouldn't the short man have the right to make a mistake without his motives being considered consciously or unconsciously malicious? After all, *he* was singing, or trying to. What if I asked *him* to sing?" (239). In playing the role created for him by one "brother" he had to renounce that created by another; in the process, his freedom—to sing or not to sing—was lost. This entrapment is echoed in sexual terms, as well, throughout the novel. At the beginning, some whites threaten the black boys at the battle royal if they look at the naked blonde dancer, while some threaten them if they do not, and near the end of the novel the invisible man's sexual encounter with Sybil is predicated on his denying his own desires in order to act out the role of rapist.

Perhaps the most emblematic representation in sexual terms of the dilemma shared by Jim and the invisible man is the condition in which Jim Trueblood finds himself when he awakes to discover he has penetrated his own daughter. He reasons that so long as he doesn't move, he hasn't committed a sin, and yet he also knows it hopeless to remain where he is:

> "But once a man gits hisself in a tight spot like that there ain't much he can do. It ain't up to him no longer. There I was, tryin' to git away with all my might, yet having to move *without* movin'. I flew in but I had to walk out. I had to move without movin'. I done thought 'bout it since a heap, and when you think right hard you see that that's the way things is always been with me. That's just about been my life. . . . Everything was happenin' inside of me like a fight was goin' on. Then just the very thought of the fix I'm in puts the iron back in me.
>
> "Then if that ain't bad enough, Matty Lou can't hold out no longer and gits to movin' herself. First she was tryin' to push me away and I'm tryin' to hold her down to keep from sinnin'. Then I'm pullin' away and shushin' her to be quiet so's not to wake her Ma, when she grabs hold to me and holds tight. She didn't want me to go then—and to tell the honest-to-God truth I found out that I didn't want to go neither. I guess I felt then, at that time—and although I been sorry since—just 'bout like that fellow did down in Birmingham. That one what locked hisself in his house and shot at them police until they set fire to the house and burned him up. I was lost. The more wringlin' and twistin' we done tryin' to git away, the more we wanted to stay. So like that fellow, I stayed, I had to fight it on out to the end. He mighta died, but I suspects now that he got a heapa satisfaction before he went." (46–47)

Jim Trueblood's plight, like that of Twain's Jim, is that only by remaining in a completely untenable position can he avoid sinning; that any attempt to escape his situation makes that situation worse, both in its physical consequences and in his own degree of culpability. By taking personal responsibility for his actions, Trueblood therefore converts the sin of situation into the sin of volition.

This is also what Huck does when he decides to violate the dictates of his conscience and commit a sin by making his tacit assistance of Jim active. He wrestles with conscience in rhetoric not greatly dissimilar from Trueblood's. Huck in fact calls his predicament "a close place" (169), while Trueblood calls his a tight spot. For both Huck and Trueblood, however, their decision in their moral confinement to take personal responsibility for their actions has political implications. Although Huck ignores these implications, Trueblood acknowledges them by drawing the parallel between his motion and the fellow in Birmingham who attacked the police. When Trueblood then says that the more wriggling he did to escape the more he wanted to stay, staying has been converted from the undesirable predicament it was at the outset of his contemplation to a pleasure worth defying death for. That it has become more attractive by virtue of trying to escape it gives us a gloss equally on Huck's situation, on Jim's, and on the invisible man's. They are all caught in the same problem of running to something that doesn't exist; for all, the journey must culminate in their surrendering their identities so that they can affirm someone else's definition of themselves.

Ellison leaves unclear, therefore, to what Tarp refers, when he says *yes* and *no*. Is Tarp saying *no* to enslavement with his rent chain, while Bledsoe is saying *yes* with his solid link? Or is Tarp affirming his freedom and humanity, while Bledsoe is denying them? Does Tarp's chain link signify yes or no? The answer, of course, depends on who is doing the signifying and the interpreting. Like Tarp, Jim wore a leg chain on the Phelps Farm. Because of it, Tom considered making Jim saw his leg off but concluded that Jim wouldn't see the necessity. The contrast between Bledsoe's chain and Tarp's, between Tarp's way of freeing himself and Tom's way of freeing Jim, highlights again for us the way Jim functions for some as a symbol of humanity and for others as an inhuman fixture.

This returns us again to the confusing parallels between the paint factory explosion and the raft-sinking. The invisible man is Huck and/or Jim, tricked by the hostile Brockway, who in another sense is like the invisible man's grandfather and Huck and/or Jim. We should remember, in addition, that Huck was the person who delivered Tom's anonymous letters, so that he, too, becomes a betrayer, a trickster like Brockway. The invisible man, however, had also tricked Kimbro by sending out slightly greyer paint under the "Optic White" label. Since that paint was heading for the national monument, in a way he had tricked the whole nation. In another way, he had tricked Mr. Norton into meeting Trueblood by playing the role of the naive chauffeur. In that case, of course, we would have to say the trick was subconscious but, then, so was Trueblood's incest. The point is that at various stages throughout the book, the invisible man plays Huck and at others Jim, as often subconsciously as consciously.

The problem for Ellison at the time he was writing *Invisible Man* was that we didn't have a literature which permitted those roles for blacks. This is the problem he found with most American literature after Twain. After the paint factory explosion, the injured invisible man hears "an old man's garrulous voice saying, 'I tole 'em these young Nineteen-Hundred boys ain't no good for the job. They ain't got the nerves. Naw, sir, they just ain't got the nerves.' " Hearing this pronouncement, the invisible man thinks, "I tried to speak, to answer, but something heavy moved again, and I was understanding something fully and trying again to answer but seemed to sink to the center of a lake of heavy water and pause, transfixed and numb with the sense that I had lost irrevocably an important victory" (175). That important victory was the Civil War, lost in what Ellison has termed the counterrevolution of 1876 (i.e., the end of Reconstruction), a defeat marked elegiacally for Ellison by *Huckleberry Finn*, a book structured to find enlightenment through endless cycles of betrayal and resurrection.

Ellison adapted this rigid structure. Both *Invisible Man* and *Huckleberry Finn* divide the flight into three parts. In his *Paris Review* interview, Ellison discussed the tripartite structure of his novel:

> The three parts represent the narrator's movement from, using Kenneth Burke's terms, purpose to passion to perception. These three major sections are built up of smaller units of three which mark the course of the action and which depend for their development upon what I hoped was a consistent and developing motivation. However, you'll note that the maximum insight on the hero's part isn't reached until the final section. After all, it's a novel about innocence and human error, a struggle through illusion to reality. Each section begins with a sheet of paper; each piece of paper is exchanged for another and contains a definition of his identity, or the social role he is to play as defined for him by others. But all say essentially the same thing. "Keep this nigger boy running." Before he could have some voice in his own destiny he had to discard these old identities and illusions; his enlightenment couldn't come until then. Once he recognizes the hole of darkness into which these papers put him, he has to burn them. That's the plan and the intention; whether I achieved this is something else. (SA, 177)

Victor Doyno, in "Over Twain's Shoulder," has accurately noted a similar pattern in *Huckleberry Finn*. Each of the three parts, he points out, begin with Huck's meeting someone who thinks he is dead, first Jim on Jackson's Island, then Jim on the raft after Huck disappeared in the fog, and finally Tom at the Phelps Farm. After Huck resurrects himself in the eyes of this person, he formulates a plan for Jim's escape, a plan which fails and is followed by the exchange of forty dollars. The two men on the skiff each give Huck twenty-dollar gold pieces rather than board Huck's raft, where they believe someone has smallpox. When the Duke and King sell Jim they get forty dollars, and at the end of the novel Tom gives Jim forty dollars for his trouble.

This cycle of resurrection, aspiration, and betrayal, however, bears thematic as well as structural similarity to *Invisible Man*. The invisible man's paper identity becomes his resurrection just as Huck's recognition becomes a form of his. But, like Huck, the invisible man is not seeking his resurrections. They are fortuitous and impressed upon him. Yet also, like Huck, he gladly accepts them because each saves him from a precarious situation and offers the promise of community. As some have noted, Huck craves a kind of primitive community.[10] His hopes, however, like the invisible man's, are impossible, given his predicament which keeps worsening, no matter how much he deludes himself to the contrary. The struggle in *Huckleberry Finn*— one which has been mistakenly seen as Twain's struggle to keep his book comic—is Huck's struggle to delude himself, in the face of overwhelming evidence to the contrary, that his journey can be successful, that is, that he can escape to a world both safe and honest (to Huck mutually exclusive qualities in the "sivilized" society from which he has fled). All Huck wants is an identity of which he does not have to be ashamed, and yet anywhere he turns he finds something which shames him. When Jim tells him, therefore, that a raft is not a place where people make one another ashamed, it becomes Huck's haven. When Mary Jane Wilkes chastises her sister for making their guest, Huck, ashamed, he pledges his loyalty to Mary Jane and risks telling her the truth, and when Tom tells him that he doesn't have to be ashamed of wanting to steal Jim, Huck pledges his loyalty to Tom.

Despite Tom's reassurances, however, the price of Huck's not being ashamed before Jim is to be forever ashamed before "sivilization." At the end, therefore, Huck has to light out for the territories, another place where he wouldn't have to be ashamed. Ellison understood this when he noted "writers have made much of the north star, but they forget that a hell of a lot of slaves were running to the West, 'going to the nation, going to the territory,' because as Mark Twain knew that was an area of Negro freedom."[11] Like the pastoral sections of the book, Huck's language in general is an escape from the realities of the "sivilized" shore. Schmitz, in his brilliant discussion of humorous writing in America, *Of Huck and Alice*, analyzes the nature of "huck-speech" to show how its spelling and diction are an act of conversion which changes painful realities into their nonreal ideals.[12]

Ellison, whose language is also stylized, converts the invisible man's catastrophes not into humor so much as into black humor, that is, humor which reveals the grim sensibility behind at the same time as the comic mask in front, humor which shows the double edge to every joke, the setting in which burlesque is indistinguishable from nightmare. In the world of the invisible man's language, the impending catastrophes seem nearer, more ominous. We expect jokes to backfire, illusions to be exploded; and we distrust the invisible man's optimism when he expresses it. When we see, therefore, that the invisible man's new identities—his release from shame only to move through plans for escape which end in betrayal—parallel Huck's releases, plans, and betrayals, Huck's humorousness less successfully hides his self-delusiveness. We are more able to see that the desire to keep the story humorous and its failure is not Twain's but Huck's, for Huck is the victim of a river the direction of which Twain knew very well. More important, Huck was the victim of a shore without which the river could not exist, and of a moral burden created by that shore which he could not escape. Just as the shore ultimately created and defined the river, so the racism and enslavement on that shore made the raft a place where Huck and Jim, escaping for different reasons, could not make one another ashamed. If there had been no slavery on the shore, then the raft would not have, could not have, the special significance which Jim gives it as a haven from shame. Slavery thus creates Huck's shame as a precondition to creating a place free from being shamed. Twain must have known that—that the river flows south, that boys grow up, and that even the best-intentioned (i.e., the most "unsivilized") people will allow a lot to avoid being shamed. They will swindle, lie, tar-and-feather, kill cold-bloodedly, or even hand over forty dollars. The structure of *Huckleberry Finn* emphasizes this time and again.

William Schafer, in "Irony from Underground," points out that *Invisible Man* has, to use M. C. Bradbrook's phrase, a cumulative plot. By this Schafer means that it presents a series of scenes which illustrate the same theme. In *Invisible Man* that theme in its broadest sense is that the narrator is invisible, that neither he nor others see his humanity. The allusions and parallels to *Huckleberry Finn* thus call our attention to Twain's use of a similar structure, one which illustrates again and again Huck's shame. Just as the invisible man cannot find a world in which he will be visible, Huck cannot find one in which he will be shameless. They both end, therefore, with the promise to continue looking for that world, one outside the boundaries of their imagination.

If Ellison, then, wanted to enter and revive a tradition he saw ending with Twain, he also wanted to broaden that tradition by converting the black from symbol to character. He did not want, in other words, merely to bring a "Jim," a symbolic black, into his work. Rather he wanted to create a character with which he could identify as strongly as he once did with Huck. A black Huck, as we have seen, however, cannot be a Huck; and if Ellison's allusions to *Huckleberry Finn* do nothing else, they explain why a black Huck is as equally impossible an alternative as a "Jim," given twentieth-century literary conventions and the hermeneutics of his audience.

In the realm of these impossibilities and invisibilities, Ellison's allusions have functioned, bearing secrets not only about invisibility and signification, hermeneutics and decentering, tradition and the individual, but also about the nature of allusion itself. What we have found true of the allusions in *Invisible Man* may thus point out some of the properties and potentials of allusion in general. Who knows but that on lower frequencies it speaks the sense of tradition for us all.

Conclusion

Although *Invisible Man*, as we have seen, presents a perfect example of a novel which, through the use of allusions, can contain a literary-critical subtext—and although our understanding of both Ellison's ideas and the literary climate in which he came of age leads us to see such a subtext as intentional—the implications of this study go beyond Ellison or *Invisible Man*. That subtext always already critiques and alters the tradition in which it functions; and this study deals, finally, with the way we think about literature. *Invisible Man* because it is an extreme example accentuates the way new works and old stimulate one another in a constant process of critique and refinement. This stimulation, furthermore, is not a rebellion against tradition but the process of embracing it, and hence not an attempt to undermine meaning but rather an attempt to stabilize it. If allusions, therefore, make us slightly more aware of the instability that thought and language require, they also make us slightly more aware of the ways we cope with these instabilities. Recognizing this may be, furthermore, a means not of inviting chaos but of opening literature to the vitality of other voices, a means that may permit us to hear the voices of otherness.

One last consideration of *Invisible Man* may make this clearer. First we must take a brief look at Melville's *The Confidence Man*, in which the unidentified title character assumes a number of disguises which enable him to act as foil for the passengers on the riverboat *Fidèle* as it moves deeper and deeper into slave territory. One of the first roles the Confidence Man assumes is that of Black Guinea, the crippled black beggar who catches coins in his mouth. He is accused of being an impostor and a debate ensues, during which three passengers come to his defense. But "all three of Black Guinea's benefactors give him some reason to suspect his charity," Karcher points out, "and to test their motives in befriending him. All three, as we shall see, will ultimately negate their seeming benevolence toward the Negro by betraying a racism as thoroughgoing as that of the passengers who have spurned Guinea" (*Shadow over the Promised Land*, 205).

Karcher goes on to examine the significance of Black Guinea and "what his 'game of charity' as a crippled black beggar tells us about the part Melville perceived the Negro to be playing on America's historical stage":

> First of all, on the level of individual behavior, Black Guinea acts out the dual role assumed by every slave, as a victim of oppression who in turn victimizes his white oppressors by dissimulating his vengefulness under the grinning mask they want him to wear. . . . Second, on the collective level, Black Guinea represents the apocalyptic retribution that Melville expected America's four million slave victims to wreak upon her. . . . Third, on the level of Melville's racial discourse, Black Guinea, who may after all be only a white masquerading as a black, incarnates the Confidence Man's joke on America: that the phantasm of race, in whose name Americans had refused to extricate themselves from the slave system that was destroying them, may not exist except in the white mind. Even more subversively, Guinea's masquerade indicates that there is no way of ascertaining whether he is black or white—hence no way of being sure that the treatment American society has reserved for him as a black may not have been "mistakenly" inflicted on a white. (206)

In her analysis of *The Confidence Man*, Karcher convincingly argues slavery is central to the book's meaning:

> Reappearing as "a man in mourning" with "a long weed on his hat," "Guinea" accosts the merchant "with the familiarity of an old acquaintance" (CM, 27). Having appropriated the merchant's business card, he knows the merchant by name. He also recognizes the merchant's face, of course, and seeks to ascertain whether the merchant will recognize his underneath the superficial difference in skin color. . . . Three times he appeals to the merchant to acknowledge his identity with his black predecessor, and by extension their common humanity. Three times the merchant demurs, despite having heard Guinea accused of being a white man masquerading as a black:
> "Don't you know me?"
> "No, certainly." . . .
> "Don't you recall me, now? Look harder."
> "In my conscience—truly—I protest . . . bless my soul, sir, I don't know you—really, really." . . .
> "Still you don't recall my countenance?"
> "Still does truth compel me to say that I cannot, despite my best efforts."
> (209)

This scene between the merchant and the man with the weed is strongly echoed at the end of *Invisible Man*, when the invisible man meets *his* false benefactor, Mr. Norton, on the train station:

> "Don't you know me?" I said.
> "Should I?" he said.

"You see me?" I said, watching him tensely.

"Why, of course—Sir, do you know the way to Centre Street?"

"So. Last time it was the Golden Day, now it's Centre Street. You've re-trenched, sir. But don't you know who I am?"

"Young man, I'm in a hurry," he said, cupping a hand to his ear. "Why should I know you?"

"Because I'm your destiny."

"My destiny, did you say?" He gave me a puzzled stare, backing away. "Young man, are you well? Which train did you say I should take?"

"I didn't say," I said, shaking my head. "Now aren't you ashamed?"

"Ashamed? ASHAMED!" he said indignantly.

I laughed, suddenly taken by the idea. "Because, Mr. Norton, if you don't know *where* you are, you probably don't know *who* you are. So you came to me out of shame. You are ashamed, now aren't you?"

"Young man, I've lived too long in this world to be ashamed of anything. Are you light-headed from hunger? How do you know my name?"

"But I'm your destiny, I made you. Why shouldn't I know you?" I said, walking closer and seeing him back against a pillar. He looked around like a cornered animal. He thought I was mad.

"Don't be afraid, Mr. Norton," I said. "There's a guard down the platform there. You're safe. Take any train; they all go to the Golden D—" (500)

This similarity might not seem worth noting were there not a number of other suggestions of *The Confidence Man*. Frequently, throughout the book, for example, the invisible man is asked for his "confidence," the word being used with the same conspicuousness that abounds in Melville's book. Even more striking is the savings bank that the invisible man finds just before leaving Mary Rambo's. It is a minstrel head: like Black Guinea, it appears to be a black man but is not necessarily one, and like Black Guinea it catches coins in its mouth. This strange image certainly suggests *The Confidence Man*, and it may well be that Ellison has anticipated Karcher by nearly thirty years.

This possibility points us toward a larger point about allusive literature and the modernist tradition. Modernism, as a movement, has come under many attacks of late from all flanks. The structuralists and poststructuralists have attacked its narrowness and cultural bias, while "conservatives" accuse mod-ernism of having led to structuralism and attack the amorality they find im-plicit in its break with what they call "reality." All of this is to be understood, for it is inherent to the nature of thought, in general, that it lives on the ashes of specific beliefs, whether we call this process "faddism" or "dialectics," "prog-ress" or "revisionism," "renaissance" or "superannuation." Bertrand Russell understood this when, in *A History of Western Philosophy*, he wrote:

When an intelligent man expresses a view which seems to us obviously ab-surd, we should not attempt to prove that it is somehow true, but we should try to understand how it even came to *seem* true. This exercise of historical and psychological imagination at once enlarges the scope of our thinking, and helps us to realize how foolish many of our own cherished prejudices will seem to an age which has a different temper of mind. (39)

My intention here, however, is not to launch an argument against Graff et al. or in favor of Derrida et al. Rather, I wish to make one small point, which my study has suggested, about the richness of the allusive literature so closely associated with modernism. As the juxtaposition of Karcher and Ellison again makes clear, allusive literature seems to have an infinite capacity for entering us into a dialogue with tradition, for revivifying the past by changing it. And only in the very narrowest sense is this an escape from or denunciation of reality: our thoughts are real, as is our sense of ourselves, of our individual past and our common tradition; these all bear on our actions and judgments. The fact that *none* of these is permanent does not make *any* of it less real. We have seen how, continually, the way we perceive the past affects the way we receive the present, and the way we perceive the present affects what we retrieve from the past. All our experience tells us, nevertheless, that although this process forms a self-embracing circle, it does not form a closed one. There is enough aberration—or genius—to make each circling unique, and yet there is enough continuity for us to explain the aberration we never would have been able to predict.

As Dr. Johnson noted, *Tristram Shandy* did not last, and yet it is more current today than many of the definitions he believed he had fixed permanently with his dictionary. That outdated dictionary, nevertheless, has been reissued, which is convenient for contemporary readers of *Tristram Shandy*. For without Dr. Johnson's definitions, many of Sterne's subtleties would be lost.

Similarly, as we have seen, Melville, for example, has changed many times because beliefs that had nothing to do with him had everything to do with him. Now there is a Melville tradition, of which *Invisible Man* is a part. *Invisible Man*, too, has undergone many changes, has developed a history and tradition of its own. Like all traditions, it is really a conglomerate of change, an amassing of alterations, a few of which this book has attempted to articulate, thereby making explicit that process of rearrangement which our body of unavoidably self-referential literature always already urges upon us covertly.

Notes

1. The Origins of Invisibility

1. Webster attempts to write a history of twentieth-century American literary criticism by employing a methodology based on Thomas Kuhn's *The Structure of Scientific Revolutions*. Part 1 of Webster's *The Republic of Letters* (3–59) discusses the nature and formation of "charters."

2. Charles A. Beard authored, co-authored, or edited over seventy-five books, pamphlets, and texts. Those germane to this study are *History of the United States* and *The Rise of American Civilization* (with Mary R. Beard), *The History of the American People* (with William C. Bogley), and *American Leviathan: The Republic in the Machine Age* (with William Beard).

3. Webster (*Republic*, 63–206) uses the term "tory formalist" to identify specifically the ideas of, initially, Eliot, Tate, Ransom, Brooks, Blackmur, Winters, and Warren, but I think the term can be used fairly to include many others of the Pound era.

4. According to the statement of principles, agreed to by all twelve authors, one of the purposes of the book was to ask "how far shall the South surrender its moral, social and economic autonomy to the victorious principle of union?" (*I'll Take My Stand*, xxxviii).

5. See *Main Currents*, vol. 2, book 1, part 2, chapter 3, 99–108.

6. Since this topic has been the concern of countless books, my handling it here as part of one chapter no doubt invites overgeneralization. It is important, therefore, to remember that there was a great deal of regionalism within the South, as were there many vying forces, local interests, and political enigmas. To some extent, nevertheless, a body of beliefs united, however loosely, these regions, forces, and interests—beliefs which often correlated less with their sundry lives than with their shared vision of themselves. Since this study does not have space for a segmented history of the South, I don't want to treat the South as a monolith so much as discuss a few specific circumstances which enabled it to ascribe—in the eyes of many of its citizens, adversaries, and historians—to some codes and myths which had specific consequences for blacks and, subsequently, for twentieth-century literary criticism.

7. Although many historians have noted this phenomenon, perhaps nothing reveals the degree of southern uniqueness in this area more clearly than comparing southern criminal statistics with northern. Violent crime was responsible for 61.5 percent of all indictments in the Carolinas, from 1800 to 1860. Ohio County, Virginia, from 1800 to 1810, recorded ninety-one assault indictments, three murders, one robbery, and two breaking-and-enterings. In Massachusetts, however, between 1833 and 1838, burglary charges made up 30.4 percent of all indictments, while crimes of personal violence represented 17.4 percent (Wyatt-Brown, *Southern Honor*, 367).

8. As I stated earlier, any discussion of the South as a whole is prone to overgeneralization. Certainly this does not hold for *all* southern whites. The mountaineer from East Tennessee or the Ozarks, for example, who had little money or desire to buy slaves, probably found his caste "status" as a free white much less important than did the nonslaveholder in Tidewater or the Mississippi delta.

9. Degler: "In a society that puts a premium on mobility and individual achievement it was not an insignificant gain for a white person to know that blacks, as slaves and free people, were kept in an inferior social position. Such a hierarchical arrangement brought not only economic advantages, but social and psychological status as well" (*Place over Time*, 82).

10. Wyatt-Brown: "Ownership of slaves and land [in the nineteenth-century South] continued to offer distinction and moral imprimatur beyond their monetary value" (*Southern Honor*, 73).

11. See *The Archeology of Knowledge and the Discourse on Language, Discipline and Punish: The Birth of the Prison, Madness and Civilization: A History of Insanity in the Age of Reason*, and *The Order of Things: An Archeology of the Human Sciences*. I am also indebted to Edward Said's comments in *Beginnings: Intention and Method*, chapter 5, 279–343.

12. See Lovejoy, *The Great Chain of Being*.

13. See Genovese, *The Political Economy of Slavery: Studies in the Economy and Society of the Slave South* and *The World the Slaveholders Made*; Fogel and Engerman, *Time on the Cross: The Economics of American Negro Slavery*; and *Time on the Cross: Evidence and Methods—A Supplement*, and extensive list of further references, 247–67. For responses to *Time on the Cross*, see Gutman, *Slavery and the Numbers Game: A Critique of Time on the Cross*; and David et al., *Reckoning with Slavery: A Critical Study in the Quantitative History of American Negro Slavery*.

14. This presumes a somewhat controversial idea of continuity in southern society. Both Genovese (*The World the Slaveholders Made*) and Woodward (*Origins of the New South*) see the Civil War as marking a major break in continuity. For Genovese the movement was from precapitalist society to capitalist; for Woodward the rise to power of the lower-class white. In opposition to this view is Cash (*The Mind of the South*), who asserts strong philosophical connections between antebellum and postbellum Southern society. Cash's view, ostensibly re-

futed by Woodward, has come more into favor with recent studies like Degler's *Place over Time*. See also Woodman ("Sequel to Slavery"), Billings (*Planters and the Making of the "New South"*), and Mandle (*The Roots of Black Poverty*). Space and the focus of my study are not amenable to my reconciling or disputing the tenets or nuances of each viewpoint. Suffice it to say that I align with those who see a continuity, for the reasons I am here developing, and that I am not so much concerned with whether the same people or people formerly from the same class continued to hold power as I am that they used that power in a way which conformed to the same beliefs about its organization and distribution, especially as regards race. I find in part circular the reasoning which suggests no "aristocrat" would engage in "redneck" activities, when the distinction between "aristocratic" slaveholding and slave trading and "redneck" lynching, Jim Crow law, and tenant-farmer exploitation rests not in the behavior of the two groups but in the presence or absence of specific legal sanctions.

15. Just as many poor whites suffered near the bottom of the plantation-oriented caste system, poor whites also, of course, became sharecroppers. This is just one more way in which the South replicated the complicated caste hierarchies of antebellum life.

16. See Wade (*Slavery in the Cities*) and Berlin (*Slaves without Masters*).

17. I am not suggesting that the Freedman's Bureau was so sinister as intentionally to desire the reinstitution of slavery, nor that it provided no benefits for the black. Rather, I am merely agreeing with Ransom and Sutch (*One Kind of Freedom*) that it unwittingly participated in creating a system that solidified racial caste, even though the ex-Confederate did not necessarily perceive it as doing so.

18. This is not to suggest that black Americans did not develop their own culture or family structure. See Gutman, *The Black Family in Slavery and Freedom, 1750–1925*. Ellison notes: "Since the beginning of the nation, white Americans have suffered from a deep inner uncertainty as to who they really are. One of the ways that has been used to simplify the answer has been to seize upon the presence of black Americans and use them as a marker, a symbol of limits, a metaphor for the 'outsider.' Many whites could look at the social position of blacks and feel that color formed an easy and reliable gauge for determining to what extent one was or was not American" (*G to the T*, 110–11; see also 174).

19. See Taylor (*Cavalier and Yankee*). In addition to the myth of the "Yankee," or perhaps complementary to it, nonsoutherners mythologized themselves with concepts such as "American Adam," or viewed themselves as fighting the national "sin" of slavery.

20. Ellison notes: "We know now, however, that the freedmen (during the Reconstruction) were actors within a play-within-a-play, and that theirs was a tragic action within a larger drama in which events would convert tragedy into a farce. . . . after the Hayes-Tilden Compromise they were forced to live under a system which was close to, and in some ways worse than, slavery. . . . Within thirteen years Afro-Americans were swept from slavery to a brief period of freedom, to a condition of second-class citizenship. And from a condition of faint

hope, through a period of euphoric optimism, to a condition of despair. The familiar world of slavery was gone, but now they faced a world of ambiguity in which their access to even the most fundamental of life's necessities was regulated strictly on the basis of race and color" (*G to the T*, 130).

21. About Hemingway, for example, Ellison notes that "the personal despair which gave [his] technique its resonance became a means of helping other Americans to avoid those aspects of reality which they no longer had the will to face. This is the tragedy implicit in Hemingway's morality of craftsmanship, the attempt to make a highly personal morality the informing motive of an art form which by its very nature is extremely social and, despite its pose, deeply rooted in the assumption it denied. . . . For although it is seldom mentioned, Hemingway is as obsessed with the Civil War and its aftermath as any Southern writer, and the fact turns up constantly in his work. The children of the good Americans of the 1880s had forgotten the historical problems which made Hemingway's understatement fully meaningful, even it was here exactly that the ideas which were said to be absent were most present and powerful. But many readers, unhappy with the compact we'd made with history, took the novelist's point of view as authority to go on a binge of hooky-playing, as an assurance that there were no new lessons to learn and the old ones were invalid anyway. And this with the Depression only a few years away" (*G to the T*, 256).

22. See *Literature against Itself: Literary Ideas in Modern Society* for a more complete explanation and analysis of the argument which my statements in the text necessarily simplify. Graff's views, moreover, have changed somewhat since 1979, but his book does identify coherently some of the problematic points of continuity between "modernism" and "postmodernism" germane to this discussion. See also Huyssen (*After the Great Divide*).

23. See Klein, "Ralph Ellison," 82–146; Tony Tanner, "The Music of Invisibility," in *Ralph Ellison: A Collection of Critical Essays*, 80–94; and Thomas A. Volger, "*Invisible Man:* Somebody's Protest Novel," 127–50.

24. In many essays and interviews, Ellison notes the influence of Joyce. In an interview with Richard Stern, originally published in *December*, he says that Richard Wright told him "you must learn how Conrad, Joyce, Dostoievsky get their effects" (*SA*, 34). Elsewhere in *Shadow and Act* he explains: "I use folklore in my work not because I am Negro but because writers like Eliot and Joyce made me conscious of the literary value of my folk inheritance" (72). In an interview from *Paris Review* (also reprinted in *Shadow and Act*), Ellison says that while living in Dayton, Ohio, in 1937, with his brother, "at night I practiced writing and studied Joyce, Dostoievsky, Stein and Hemingway" (169). Later he tells those interviewers, "When I started writing I knew that in both *The Waste Land* and *Ulysses* ancient myth and ritual were used to give form and significance to the material; but it took me a few years to realize that the myths and rites which we found functioning in our everyday lives could be used in the same way" (174). And in an interview with John Hersey (*Ralph Ellison: A Collection of Critical Essays*) he explains that Joyce and Eliot "made me aware of the playful possibili-

ties of language. You look at a page of *Finnegans Wake* and see references to all
sorts of American popular music, yet the context gives it an extension from the
popular back to the classical and beyond. This is something that Joyce teaches
you that you can do, and you can abstract the process and apply it to a frame of
reference which is American and historical, and it can refer to class, it can refer
to the fractions and frictions of color, to popular and folk culture—it can do many
things" (14). For more discussion of the relationship between Ellison and Joyce,
see Craig Hansen Werner, *Paradoxical Resolutions: American Fiction since James
Joyce*, 133–43.

2. Translating Tradition

1. See the international annotated bibliography of allusion studies compiled
by Carmela Perri, and Perri's article "On Alluding."

2. Even a partial list of these works would, of course, take several pages.
Readers interested in this subject are advised to begin with Jonathan Culler's discussion, "Structuralism and Linguistic Models," which comprises the first part of
Structuralist Poetics: Structuralism, Linguistics and the Study of Literature,
3–109.

3. Earl Miner, in *Princeton Encyclopedia of Poetry and Poetics*, defines an
allusion as a "tacit reference to another literary work, to another art, to history, to
contemporary figures or the like" (18). Although I am limiting any discussion to
his first category, when I specify literary allusions as those which refer to another
text, I am, however, including implicit texts, such as folktales, myths, and
legends.

4. Brower, of course, has not written a book on "theory" of allusion but rather
one showing how it worked among English Augustans. The theory underlying
that practice, however, typifies more than Augustan use of allusion and provides,
therefore, an excellent reading of not only Augustan but also much prior and
subsequent literary allusion. Without being explicitly "theoretical," Brower thus
provides an exemplary demonstration of a valuable traditional approach to
allusion.

5. This comparison relies on a somewhat radical reading of Eliot's essay.
Brower in fact agreed with Eliot's essay (as does E. D. Hirsch, as *he* interprets it).
Much of Eliot's allusion in his own poetry, furthermore, can be well discussed
with the same approach Brower takes toward the Augustans.

6. In Eliot's essay, therefore, what I have called the artistic sense of tradition
emerged out of a discussion of criticism and returns immediately to it: "No poet,
no artist of any art, has complete meaning alone. His significance, his appreciation is the appreciation of his relation to the dead poets and artists. You cannot
value him alone; you must set him, for contrast and comparison, among the dead.
I mean this as a principle of aesthetic, not merely historical criticism" (*The Sacred
Wood*, 49).

7. Frank Lentricchia does an excellent job of relating this aspect of Frye's book

to the antihumanist romantic tradition of Shelley, as opposed to the humanist
romantic tradition of Coleridge and Wordsworth: "Shelley, we recall, took literally
Milton's deference . . . to the Muse. . . . Again we must not too quickly lord our
sophistication over Shelley: Frye and the structuralists also portray the process of
writing as a passive activity—mere clay in the hands of Frye's archetypal mythoi
or Structuralism's 'languages of man' " ("The Historicity of Frye's *Anatomy*,"
106).

   8. It is interesting to note here that Frye, a Spenser scholar, has adapted the
argument presented in Spenser's "Mutabilitie Cantos." Mutabilitie claims domination over nature, saying all is subject to change, but she loses her claim when
it is pointed out that change, too, is predictable and, therefore, contributes to
maintaining the constancy of nature.

   9. Hartman (*Beyond Formalism*) suggests this, and some of my other remarks.
He concentrates, however, on the various ways Frye's theories fail to relate satis-
factorily the part to the whole.

   10. Fletcher (*Allegory*) is, in a footnote, describing Dr. Johnson's understanding of Milton: "Johnson stresses allusion in Milton: 'the spectacles of books' are a
means of sublimity, since at every point the reader is led from one scene to an
allusive second scene, to a third, and so on. Johnson's Milton has, we might say,
a 'transumptive' style." Bloom sees the allusions, however, as commenting on,
and thereby undermining, one another. From this shift we might infer that Bloom
equates "sublimity" with "triumph."

   11. This analysis of Freudian intervention is developed by Deleuze and Guit-
tari in *Anti-Oedipus* and by Cixous and Clément in *The Newly Born Woman*.

   12. He deals with this most explicitly in his essay "Difference," included in
Speech and Phenomena, 129–60.

   13. This suggests an elegiac quality to allusions. The function of elegy is rec-
onciliatory: the speaker begins by acknowledging the difference between his living
state and the dead state of someone (or something) dear to him; his goal is to
eliminate or diminish the difference by readjusting his sense of what has been
lost. In that they offer not only criticism of the alluded-to but also contexts for
readjustment, therefore, allusions have an elegiac component as well as a critical.
Although I am limiting myself, in this study, to the literary-critical component
(and do not want to go so far as to say all criticism is elegy), I see great potential
for further study of the relationship between allusion and elegy.

   14. Thornton Weldon suggests this approach ("An Allusion List for James
Joyce's Ulysses, Part I, Telemachus").

   15. Pope's *Iliad* provides extensive evidence of the conscious application of
Pope's critical-interpretive faculties. A ten-thousand-word preface explaining the
task of the translation and a twenty-thousand-word essay on the life, writings, and
learnings of Homer are followed not only by the translation but also by a subtext
of footnotes longer than the text itself. The design of the notes, Pope explained,
was "to comment upon *Homer* as a Poet; whatever in them is extracted from
others is constantly own'd; the Remarks of the Ancients are generally set at length,

and the places cited. . . ." (*Poems*, 83). Pope's notes thus provide an extended close reading of Homer which includes justification on interpretive grounds of specific translating choices.

16. "Date Line," in *Literary Essays*, 74, explains in detail how Pound's Provençal poems function as a form of criticism, and Pound himself alludes to this interpretive aspect of translation in a letter to W. H. D. Rouse when he says "Tain't what a man sez, but wot he *means* that the traducer has got to bring over. The *implication* of the word" (*Selected Letters*, 271).

17. See *Validity in Interpretation*, chapter 5, in which Hirsch tries to develop the principle of probability as a validator of interpretation.

18. For discussions of the similarity between the Founder and Booker T. Washington, see Fischer ("*Invisible Man* as History"), Kostelanetz, ("The Politics of Ellison's Booker"), and Gibson (*The Politics of Literary Expression*). Others have noted the similarity in passing.

3. Tod Clifton: Spiritual and Carnal

1. Although I have not done a statistical analysis of name frequency in *Invisible Man*, suffice it to say that simple empirical observation reveals this to be inordinately frequent in the text, much more frequent than any other name, especially given that Clifton does not appear until more than halfway through the novel.

2. See Bone ("Ralph Ellison and the Uses of the Imagination"); also Tischler ("Negro Literature and Classic Form," 352–65) and Cheshire ("*Invisible Man* and the Life of Dialogue," 19–34).

3. See Bennett and Nichols ("Violence in Afro-American Fiction," 173); Rupp (*Celebration in Post-War American Fiction*, 159).

4. Although New York City policemen dress in blue, Ellison makes Clifton's slayer a stiff-armed, black-shirted, solidly (goose?-) stepping man to evoke connotations of fascism: "I could see the cop push Clifton again, stepping solidly forward in his black shirt, his arm shooting out stiffly, sending him in a head-snapping forward stumble . . ." (329).

4. Invisible Man in the Golden Day

1. See Bode (*Anatomy of American Popular Culture*).

2. Weiners notes this ("Anxiety in the Golden Day of Lewis Mumford").

3. See Fussell (*The Great War and Modern Memory*) and Knightley (*The First Casualty*).

4. A great many books have been written on this period. The seminal work is Alice Felt Tyler's *Freedom's Ferment: Phases of American Social History to 1860*. Of the more recent works, Russell Blaine Nye's *Society and Culture in America, 1830–1860* is a good comprehensive study. *The Era of Reform* (ed. Henry Steele Commager) compiles selections from fifty-five primary sources, and *Ante-Bellum*

Reform (ed. David Brion Davis) presents primarily modern essays. Both Davis and Nye have very good bibliographies. See also C. S. Griffin's pamphlet, *The Ferment of Reform*.

5. In addition to Miller, see C. S. Griffin (*Their Brother's Keepers: Moral Stewardship in the United States, 1800–1865*); Foster (*An Errand of Mercy*); Kraditor (*Means and Ends in American Abolitionism*); Bercovitch (*The Puritan Origins of the American Self*); and Karcher (*Shadow over the Promised Land*).

6. "And yet it wasn't that I didn't admire Mumford. I have owned a copy of the sixth Liveright printing of THE GOLDEN DAY since 1937 and own, and have learned from, most of his books. I was simply upset by his implying that the war which freed my grandparents from slavery was of no real consequence to the broader issues of American society and its culture. What else, other than sheer demonic, masochistic hell-raising, was that bloody war all about if not slavery and the contentions which flowed there-from?

"As a self-instructed student I was quite willing for Mumford to play Aeschylus, Jeremiah, or even God, but not at the price of his converting the most tragic incident in American history into bombastic farce. For in doing so he denied my people the sacrificial role which they had played in the drama" (Ralph Ellison, unpublished letter to the author).

7. This is another version of the same dilemma we see throughout the book, wherein the invisible man is constantly required to satisfy a white audience by performing mutually exclusive tasks. The "Battle Royal" chapter is replete with such instances: he is to appear in a boxing match *and* as a clean-cut respectable speaker; he is commanded to look at a naked white woman and threatened for doing so; he is commanded to grab coins off a carpet but given an electric shock when he does.

5. Invisible Criticism: Melville and Emerson Revised

1. Vanderhaar ("A Re-Examination of 'Benito Cereno' ") gives an excellent review of the critical perspectives on the issue of slavery in "Benito Cereno," through 1968. See also Karcher (*Shadow over the Promised Land*, chapter 5). A good selection of articles on the issue can be found in John P. Runden, ed., *Melville's "Benito Cereno": A Text for Guided Research*.

2. See Carlisle ("Captain Amasa Delano").

3. Franklin makes a very strong case for Cereno as symbolic descendant of the dethroned Spanish monarch, Charles V, based on historical and religious allusions in the story. He shows that Melville changed the date from the source material so that the slave rebellion on the ship that Melville renamed the *San Dominick* was contemporaneous with the slave rebellion on Santo Domingo, a territory discovered by Columbus and made, by Charles V, the first large-scale importation site of black slaves in the New World. Don Benito consequently represents the deposed monarch who brought slavery to the New World. Yet Franklin still fails to see the story as a critique of slavery; he states that "the Negroes of the San

Dominick represent not only evil and the destructive force; they represent the church" (" 'Apparent Symbol of Despotic Command,' " 472). Rather than have the slaves represent what they are, Franklin makes them conform to the details of the allusion which they actually critique.

4. "Benito Cereno," in *Piazza Tales*, 117–18 (all page references in the text are to this edition).

5. The major accusation of racism comes from Sidney Kaplan ("Herman Melville and the American National Sin"). See also Runden text (*Melville's "Benito Cereno"*). For arguments against the charge of racism, see the articles by Schiffman, Simpson, Vanderhaar, and Allen Guttmann reprinted in the Runden text.

6. Waggoner, in *Emerson as Poet*, provides in his introductory chapter an excellent summary of the reception of Emerson's poetry, which naturally reflects the general division between aesthetic and historical approaches. More recent books have tried to reconcile the two, but the antecedent strains remain strong. Bercovitch explains the importance of Emerson as a crucial link between the Puritan "Nehemiah" and the American romantic (*The Puritan Origins of the American Self*). Buell looks at the stylistic implications of Emerson's work (*Literary Transcendentalism*). Two more recent books again reflect the division in emphasis: Joel Porte's *Representative Man: Ralph Waldo Emerson in His Time*, and David Porter's *Emerson and Literary Change*. Porte attends to style but is interested in Emerson as historical representative. His conclusion—that Emerson's circle was ultimately comprised of just himself—reflects the influence of the other approach, stressed in Porter's book, dealing with Emerson's writing as a manifestation of his poetics.

7. "Rather than go after Emerson's oracular stance, I went after some of the bombast that has been made of his pronouncements. . . . it might help if you pointed up the distinction you make between my trustee 'Emerson' and ole Waldo; who strikes me, incidentally, as being as difficult to pin down as the narrator's grandfather" (Ralph Ellison, unpublished letter to the author).

6. Invisible Man, Huck, and Jim

1. Brooks, *The Ordeal of Mark Twain*; Mumford, *The Golden Day*, chapter 4.

2. For another discussion of this, see Ellison, *G to the T*, 267–68.

3. Justin Kaplan discusses Twain's oft cited retrospective statement about his book: "Nearly twenty years after he began *Huckleberry Finn* Clemens described it in his notebook as 'a book of mine where a sound heart and a deformed conscience come into collision and the conscience suffers defeat.' Ignoring for the moment the fact that he himself, despite his Hannibal background, had grown up to become the most desouthernized of Southerners, he went on to describe how unquestioned the institution of slavery had been in his boyhood: 'The conscience—that unerring monitor—can be trained to approve any wild thing you

want it to approve if you begin its education early and stick to it' " (*Mr. Clemens and Mark Twain*, 198).

4. In chapter 16, Huck and Jim realize that they passed Cairo in the fog when they see the trace of clear Ohio River water along a bank of the muddy Mississippi: "When it was daylight, here was the clear Ohio water in shore, sure enough, and outside was the old regular Muddy! So it was all up with Cairo" (77). The image is set up and more fully developed in "The Raftsman's Passage" which originally appeared in the 1876 draft of the text but was omitted from the 1884 edition, and printed instead in *Life on the Mississippi* (1883). Beidler argues convincingly for its place in *Adventures of Huckleberry Finn*: "And they talked about how Ohio water didn't like to mix with Mississippi water. Ed said if you take the Mississippi on the rise when the Ohio is low, you'll find a wide band of clear water all the way down the east side of the Mississippi for a hundred mile or more, and the minute you get out a quarter of a mile from shore and pass the line, it is all thick and yaller the rest of the way across" ("The Raft Episode in *Huckleberry Finn*," 236). My reading of this section is somewhat speculative and tests some of the limits of the comparisons. Although all the connections may not have been intentional, *Adventures of Huckleberry Finn* was a text deeply ingrained in Ellison's conscious and subconscious: "I read it so early and at so many points in my life that there's no way in the world for me to know when it is or isn't making itself felt in my work. Thus I wish that I could say that my allusions to fog, bridge, and river in the paint factory section were as intentionally as extensive as you find them to be. I only know for certain that as a novelist I work not only from literary texts but from the sights and scenes around me. Of course these filter-and-feed back to books that have made a strong impression on my imagination. And it is to these that I find myself turning, whether consciously or unconsciously, for clues as to how to give form to my observations. Fortunately, one can draw upon both sources at one and the same time" (Ralph Ellison, unpublished letter to the author).

5. See Cox (*Mark Twain: The Fate of Humor*, 172–84); Egan (*Mark Twain's Huckleberry Finn*); Hansen ("The Character of Jim and the Ending of *Huckleberry Finn*); Johnson (*Mark Twain and the Limits of Power*, 70–119); Poirier (*A World Elsewhere*, 144–207); Rogers (*Mark Twain's Burlesque Patterns*, 150); Schmitz ("The Paradox of Liberation," 125–36); and Tatham (" 'Dismal and Lonesome' ").

6. See Barnes ("Twain's *Adventures of Huckleberry Finn, Chapter I*").

7. See Horowitz ("Ralph Ellison's Modern Version of Brer Bear and Brer Rabbit in *Invisible Man*").

8. See Brown ("*Huckleberry Finn* for Our Time") and Schmitz ("Twain, *Huckleberry Finn*, and the Reconstruction").

9. Schmitz, *Of Huck and Alice*, 68. In the next chapter (122–23), Schmitz connects this whitewashing with the Liberty Paints factory episode of *Invisible Man*; unfortunately he so misrepresents the text of *Invisible Man* by confusing characters and attributing actions and dialogue to the wrong characters in the wrong contexts that his potentially interesting point is very unclear.

10. See Cox (*Mark Twain*); Tatham (" 'Dismal and Lonesome' "); Johnson (*Mark Twain and the Limits of Power*); Schmitz ("The Paradox of Liberation"); and Hoffman ("Huck's Ironic Circle").

11. "Study and Experience: An Interview with Ralph Ellison," Robert B. Septo and Michael S. Harper, interviewers, 422.

12. Schmitz, *Of Huck and Alice*, chapter 4, 96–122.

Works Cited

Baker, Houston A., Jr. "To Move without Moving: An Analysis of Creativity and Commerce in Ralph Ellison's Trueblood Episode." *PMLA*, 98 (1983), 5, 828–45.

Barnes, Daniel. "Twain's *Adventures of Huckleberry Finn, Chapter I*." *Explicator* (1965), Item 62.

Barthes, Roland. *Mythologies*. Trans. Annette Lavers. New York: Hill and Wang, 1978.

Baumbach, Jonathan. *The Landscape of Nightmare: Studies in the Contemporary American Novel*. New York: New York University Press, 1965.

Beard, Charles A., and Mary R. Beard. *A History of the United States*. New York: Macmillan, 1921.

———. *The Rise of American Civilization*. Vol. 2. New York: Macmillan, 1929.

Beard, Charles A., and William Beard. *American Leviathan: The Republic in the Machine Age*. New York: Macmillan, 1930.

Beard, Charles A., and William C. Bogley. *The History of the American People*. New York: Macmillan, 1922.

Beecher, Lyman. *A Plea for the West*. 1835; rpt. New York: Arno, 1977.

Beidler, Peter G. "The Raft Episode in *Huckleberry Finn*." In *Adventures of Huckleberry Finn*, Norton Critical Edition, 2nd ed., ed. Bradley, et al. New York: Norton, 1977.

Bennett, Stephen B., and William W. Nichols. "Violence in Afro-American Fiction: An Hypothesis." In *Ralph Ellison: A Collection of Critical Essays*, ed. John Hersey. Englewood Cliffs, N.J.: Prentice Hall, 1974.

Ben-Porat, Ziva. "The Poetics of Literary Allusion." *PTL: A Journal for Descriptive Poetics and Theory of Literature*, 1 (1976), 106–28.

Bercovitch, Sacvan. *The Puritan Origins of the American Self*. New Haven: Yale University Press, 1975.

Berlin, Ira. *Slaves without Masters*. New York: Pantheon, 1974.

Bernstein, John. " 'Benito Cereno' and the Spanish Inquisition." *Nineteenth-Century Fiction*, 16 (1961), 345–50.

Bigsby, C. W. "The Flight of Words: The Paradox of Ralph Ellison." In *The

Second Black Renaissance: Essays in Black Literature, ed. C. W. Bigsby. Westport, Conn.: Greenwood, 1980.

Billings, Dwight B. *Planters and the Making of the "New South"*. Chapel Hill: University of North Carolina Press, 1979.

Blake, Susan L. "Black Folklore in the Works of Ralph Ellison." *PMLA*, 94:1 (January 1979), 121–35.

Bloom, Harold. *The Anxiety of Influence, A Theory of Poetry*. New York: Oxford University Press, 1973.

————. *A Map of Misreading*. New York: Oxford University Press, 1977.

Bode, Carl. *Anatomy of American Popular Culture 1840–1861*. Berkeley, Cal.: University of California Press, 1959.

Bone, Robert. "Ralph Ellison and the Uses of the Imagination." In *Anger and Beyond*, ed. Herbert Hill. New York: Harper and Row, 1966.

Brooks, Van Wyck. *America's Coming of Age*. 1915; rpt. New York: Farrar, Strauss and Giroux, 1975.

————. *The Flowering of New England, 1815–1865*. New York: Dutton, 1936.

————. *The Ordeal of Mark Twain*. New York: E. P. Dutton, 1920.

Brower, Reuben A. *Alexander Pope—The Poetry of Allusion*. London: Oxford University Press, 1959.

————. "Seven Agamemnons." In *On Translation*, ed. Reuben Brower. Cambridge: Harvard University Press, 1959.

Brown, Spencer. "*Huckleberry Finn* for Our Time: A Rereading of the Concluding Chapters." *Michigan Quarterly Review*, 6 (1967), 41–46.

Bruce, Dickson D. *Violence and Culture in the Antebellum South*. Austin: University of Texas Press, 1974.

Buell, Lawrence. *Literary Transcendentalism: Style and Vision in the American Renaissance*. Ithaca, N.Y.: Cornell University Press, 1973.

Cameron, Kenneth Walter. *Emerson the Essayist*. Raleigh, N.C.: Thistle Press, 1945.

Carlisle, E. F. "Captain Amasa Delano: An American Fool." *Criticism*, 7, 349–62.

Cash, William J. *The Mind of the South*. New York: Knopf, 1941.

Cheshire, Ardner R., Jr. "*Invisible Man* and the Life of Dialogue." *CLA Journal*, 20:1 (1976), 19–34.

Christian, Barbara. "Ralph Ellison: A Critical Study." In *Black Expressions: Essays by and about Black Americans in the Creative Arts*, ed. Addison Gayle. New York: Weybright and Talley, 1969.

Cixous, Hélène, and Catherine Clément. *The Newly Born Woman*. Trans. Betsy Wing. Minneapolis: University of Minnesota Press, 1986.

Clemens, Samuel Langhorne. *Adventures of Huckleberry Finn*. Norton Critical Edition, 2nd ed., ed. Sculley Bradley, et al. New York: Norton, 1977.

Clipper, Lawrence J. "Folkloric and Mythic Elements in *Invisible Man*." *CLA Journal*, 13 (1970), 229–41.

Commager, Henry Steele, ed. *The Era of Reform*. Princeton: D. Van Nostrand Press, 1960.

Cox, James M. *Mark Twain: The Fate of Humor.* Princeton: Princeton University Press, 1966.

Culler, Jonathan. *Structuralist Poetics: Structuralism, Linguistics and the Study of Literature.* Ithaca, N.Y.: Cornell University Press, 1975.

David, Paul, et al. *Reckoning with Slavery: A Critical Study in the Quantitative History of American Negro Slavery.* New York: Oxford University Press, 1976.

Davis, David Brion, ed. *Ante-Bellum Reform.* New York: Harper and Row, 1967.

Degler, Carl N. *Place over Time: The Continuity of Southern Distinctiveness.* Baton Rouge: Louisiana State University Press, 1977.

Deleuze, Gilles, and Felix Guattari. *Anti-Oedipus: Capitalism and Schizophrenia.* Minneapolis: University of Minnesota Press, 1983.

Derrida, Jacques. *Of Grammatology.* Trans. Gayatri Chakrovorty Spivak. Baltimore: Johns Hopkins University Press, 1976.

———. *Speech and Phenomena.* Trans. David B. Allison. Evanston, Ill.: Northwestern University Press, 1976.

Deutsch, Leonard J. "Ralph Waldo Ellison and Ralph Waldo Emerson: A Shared Moral Vision." *CLA Journal,* 16 (1972), 159–78.

DeVoto, Bernard. *Mark Twain's America and Mark Twain at Work.* Cambridge, Mass.: Houghton Mifflin, 1967.

Doyno, Victor. "Over Twain's Shoulder: The Composition and Structure of *Huckleberry Finn.*" *Modern Fiction Studies,* 14:1 (1968), 3–10.

Egan, Michael. *Mark Twain's Huckleberry Finn—Race Class and Society.* London: Sussex University Press, 1977.

Eliot, T. S. *The Sacred Wood.* London: Methuen, 1920.

Ellison, Ralph. *Going to the Territory.* New York: Random House, 1986.

———. Interview. In *Ralph Ellison: A Collection of Critical Essays,* ed. John Hersey. Englewood Cliffs, N.J.: Prentice Hall, 1974.

———. *Invisible Man.* New York: Random House, 1982.

———. *Shadow and Act.* New York: New American Library, 1966.

Emerson, Ralph Waldo. *Complete Works, with General Index and a Memoir by James Elliot Cabot.* 14 vols. Cambridge, Mass.: Riverside, [1883].

Empson, William. *Some Versions of Pastoral.* London: Chatto and Windus, 1950.

Farnsworth, Robert M. "Slavery and Innocence in 'Benito Cereno.'" *Emerson Society Quarterly,* 44 (1967), 94–96.

Fass, Barbara. "Rejection of Paternalism: Hawthorne's 'My Kinsman Major Molineux' and Ellison's *Invisible Man.*" *CLA Journal,* 14 (1971), 313–23.

Feltenstein, Rosalie. "Melville's 'Benito Cereno.'" *American Literature,* 19(1947), 245–55.

Fiedler, Leslie A. "Come Back to the Raft Ag'in, Huck Honey." In *Adventures of Huckleberry Finn,* Norton Critical Edition, second edition, ed. Scully Bradley, et al. New York: Norton, 1977.

Fischer, Russell G. "*Invisible Man* as History." *CLA Journal,* 17 (1974), 338–67.

Fletcher, Angus. *Allegory: The Theory of a Symbolic Mode.* Ithaca, N.Y.: Cornell University Press, 1964.

Fogel, Robert Williams, and Stanley Engerman. *Time on the Cross: The Economics of American Negro Slavery*. Boston: Little, Brown, 1974.

———. *Time on the Cross: Evidence and Methods—A Supplement*. Boston: Little, Brown, 1974.

Fogle, Richard H. "Melville and the Civil War." *Tulane Studies in English*, 9 (1959), 61–89.

———. *Melville's Shorter Fiction*. Norman: University of Oklahoma Press, 1960.

Forrey, Robert. "Herman Melville and the Negro Question." *Mainstream*, 15:2 (1962), 23–32.

Foster, Charles I. *An Errand of Mercy: The Evangelical United Front, 1790–1837*. Chapel Hill: University of North Carolina University Press, 1960.

Foucault, Michel. *The Archeology of Knowledge and the Discourse on Language*. Trans. A. M. Sheridan Smith. New York: Harper and Row, 1976.

———. *Discipline and Punish: The Birth of the Prison*. Trans. Alan Sheridan. New York: Vintage, 1979.

———. *Madness and Civilization: A History of Insanity in the Age of Reason*. Trans. Richard Howard. New York: Vintage, 1973.

———. *The Order of Things: An Archeology of the Human Sciences*. New York: Vintage, 1973.

Franklin, Bruce H. " 'Apparent Symbol of Despotic Command': Melville's 'Benito Cereno.' " *New England Quarterly*, 34 (1961), 462–77.

Frye, Northrop. *Anatomy of Criticism: Four Essays*. Princeton: Princeton University Press, 1957.

———. *Fables of Identity: Fables in Poetic Mythology*. New York: Harcourt, Brace, Jovanovich, 1963.

Fussell, Paul. *The Great War and Modern Memory*. New York: Oxford University Press, 1975.

Gayle, Addison. *The Way of the World: The Black Novel in America*. New York: Doubleday, 1975.

Genovese, Eugene D. *The Political Economy of Slavery: Studies in the Economy and Society of the Slave South*. New York: Pantheon, 1965.

———. *The World the Slaveholders Made*. New York: Pantheon, 1969.

Gibson, Donald. *The Politics of Literary Expression: A Study of Major Black Writers*. Westport, Conn.: Greenwood, 1981.

Goede, William. "On Lower Frequencies: The Buried Men in Wright and Ellison." *Modern Fiction Studies*, 15 (Winter 1969–70), 483–501.

Graff, Gerald. *Literature against Itself: Literary Ideas in Modern Society*. Chicago: University of Chicago Press, 1979.

Griffin, C. S. *The Ferment of Reform*. New York: Crowell, 1967.

———. *Their Brother's Keepers: Moral Stewardship in the United States, 1800–1865*. New Brunswick, N.J.: Rutgers University Press, 1960.

Gutman, Herbert. *The Black Family in Slavery and Freedom, 1750–1925*. New York: Knopf, 1976.

———. *Slavery and the Numbers Game: A Critique of Time on the Cross*. Urbana: University of Illinois Press, 1975.

Guttmann, Allen. "The Enduring Innocence of Captain Amasa Delano." *Boston University Studies in English*, 5 (1961), 35–45.

Hansen, Chadwick. "The Character of Jim and the Ending of *Huckleberry Finn.*" *Massachusetts Review*, 5 (1963), 45–66.

Hartman, Geoffrey. *Beyond Formalism: Literary Essays 1958–1970.* New Haven, Conn.: Yale University Press, 1970.

Hay, Peter L. "The Incest Theme in *Invisible Man.*" *Western Humanities Review*, 23 (1969), 335–39.

Hemingway, Ernest. *The Green Hills of Africa.* New York: Scribner's, 1935.

Hersey, John, ed. *Ralph Ellison: A Collection of Critical Essays.* Englewood Cliffs, N.J.: Prentice-Hall, 1974.

Hicks, Granville. *The Great Tradition.* New York: Macmillan, 1933.

Hirsch, E. D. Rev. of *The Genesis of Secrecy: On the Interpretation of Narrative*, by Frank Kermode. *New York Review of Books*, 14 July 1979, 19.

———. *Validity in Interpretation.* New Haven: Yale University Press, 1967.

Hoffman, Michael J. "Huck's Ironic Circle." *Georgia Review*, 23 (1969), 307–22.

Hollander, John. "Versions, Interpretations, Performances." In *On Translation*, ed. Reuben Brower. Cambridge: Harvard University Press, 1959.

Horowitz, Floyd R. "The Enigma of Ellison's Intellectual Man." *CLA Journal*, 7 (December 1963), 126–31.

———. "Ralph Ellison's Modern Version of Brer Bear and Brer Rabbit in *Invisible Man.*" *Mid-Continent American Studies Journal*, 4:2 (1963), 21–27.

Howe, Irving. "Black Boys and Native Sons." *Dissent*, 10 (Autumn 1963), 353–68.

Huyssen, Andreas. *After the Great Divide: Modernism, Mass Culture, Postmodernism.* Bloomington: Indiana University Press, 1986.

Iser, Wolfgang. *The Implied Reader—Patterns of Communication in Prose Fiction from Bunyan to Beckett.* Baltimore: Johns Hopkins University Press, 1974.

Jackson, Margaret Y. "Melville's Use of a Real Slave Mutiny in 'Benito Cereno.' " *CLA Journal*, 4 (1960), 79–93.

Johnson, James L. *Mark Twain and the Limits of Power: Emerson's God in Ruins.* Knoxville: University of Tennessee Press, 1982.

Kaplan, Justin. *Mr. Clemens and Mark Twain—A Biography.* New York: Simon and Schuster, 1970.

Kaplan, Sidney. "Herman Melville and the American National Sin: The Meaning of *Benito Cereno.*" *Journal of Negro American History*, 41 (1956), 311–38; 42 (1957), 11–37.

Karcher, Carolyn L. *Shadow over the Promised Land: Slavery, Race and Violence in Melville's America.* Baton Rouge: Louisiana State University Press, 1980.

Kent, George E. "Ralph Ellison and Afro American Folk and Cultural Tradition." *CLA Journal*, 13 (1970), 265–76.

Kermode, Frank. *The Genesis of Secrecy: On the Interpretation of Narrative.* Cambridge: Harvard University Press, 1979.

Kirst, E. M. "A Langian Analysis of Blackness in Ralph Ellison's *Invisible Man.*" *Studies in Black American Literature*, 7 (Spring 1976): 21–27.

Klein, Marcus. "Ralph Ellison." In *After Alienation*. New York: World, 1964.

Klotman, Phyllis R. "The Running Man as Metaphor in Ellison's *Invisible Man*." *CLA Journal*, 13 (1970), 277–88.

Knight, Douglas. "Translation: The Augustan Mode." In *On Translation*, ed. Reuben Brower. Cambridge: Harvard University Press, 1959.

Knightley, Philip. *The First Casualty*. New York: Harcourt, Brace, Jovanovich, 1975.

Kostelanetz, Richard. "The Politics of Ellison's Booker: *Invisible Man* as Symbolic History." *Chicago Review*, 19:2 (1967), 5–26.

Kraditor, Aileen S. *Means and Ends in American Abolitionism*. New York: Vintage, 1969.

Kuhn, Thomas A. *The Structure of Scientific Revolutions*. Chicago: University of Chicago Press, 1970.

Lentricchia, Frank. "The Historicity of Frye's *Anatomy*." *Salmagundi*, 40 (1978), 97–121.

Lieber, Todd M. "Ralph Ellison and the Metaphor of Invisibility in Black Literary Tradition." *American Quarterly*, 24 (March 1972), 86–100.

Lillard, Stewart. "Ellison's Ambitious Scope in *Invisible Man*." *English Journal*, 58 (September 1969), 833–39.

List, Robert N. *Dedalus in Harlem: The Joyce-Ellison Connection*. Washington, D.C.: University Press of America, 1982.

Lovejoy, Arthur O. *The Great Chain of Being: A Study of the History of an Idea*. Cambridge: Harvard University Press, 1971.

Magowan, Robin. "Masque and Symbol in Melville's 'Benito Cereno.' " *College English*, 23 (1962), 346–51.

Mandle, Jay R. *The Roots of Black Poverty*. Durham, N.C.: Duke University Press, 1978.

Matthiessen, F. O. *American Renaissance: Art and Expression in the Age of Emerson and Whitman*. 1941; rpt. New York: Oxford University Press, 1974.

McDougal, Stuart Y. *Ezra Pound and the Troubadour Tradition*. Princeton: Princeton University Press, 1972.

Melville, Herman. *Piazza Tales*. New York: Dix and Edwards, 1856.

Mengeling, Marvin E. "Whitman and Ellison: Older Symbols in a Modern Mainstream." *Walt Whitman Review*, 12 (September 1966), 67–70.

Miles, Donald. *The American Novel in the Twentieth Century*. New York: Harper and Row, 1978.

Miller, Perry. *The Life of the American Mind*. New York: Harcourt, Brace, 1965.

———. *The Raven and the Whale: The War of Words and Wits in the Era of Poe and Melville*. New York: Harcourt, Brace, 1956.

Miner, Earl. "Allusion." In *Princeton Encyclopedia of Poetry and Poetics*, ed. Alex Preminger. Princeton: Princeton University Press, 1974.

Mitchell, Louis D., and Henry J. Stauffenberg. "Ellison's B. P. Rinehart: 'Spiritual Technologist.' " *Negro American Literature Forum*, 9:2 (Summer 1975), 51–52.

Morse, Samuel F. B. *The Imminent Dangers to Free Institutions*. 1836; rpt. New York: Arno, 1969.

Mumford, Lewis. *The Golden Day: A Study in American Literature and Culture*. Boston: Beacon, 1957.

——. *Herman Melville*. New York: n.p., 1929.

Murray, Albert. "Something Different, Something More." In *Anger and Beyond*, ed. Herbert Hill. New York: Harper and Row, 1966.

Nye, Russell Blaine. *Society and Culture in America, 1830–1860*. New York: Harper and Row, 1974.

Oakes, James. *The Ruling Class: A History of American Slaveholders*. New York: Knopf, 1982.

O'Meally, Robert G. *The Craft of Ralph Ellison*. Cambridge: Harvard University Press, 1982.

Paine, Albert Bigelow. *Mark Twain—A Biography*. New York: Harper and Bros., 1912.

Parker, Hershel, ed. *The Recognition of Herman Melville: Selected Criticism since 1846*. Ann Arbor: University of Michigan Press, 1967.

Parrington, Vernon L. *Main Currents in American Thought*. Vol. 2. New York: Harcourt, Brace, 1930.

Perri, Carmela. "On Alluding." *Poetics* 7 (1978), 289–307.

Perri, Carmela, et al. "Allusion Studies: An International Annotated Bibliography, 1921–1977." *Style*, 13:2 (1979), 178–227.

Perry, John Oliver. "The Survival of Black Literature and Its Criticism." *Georgia Review*, 35:1 (1981), 169–72.

Pilkington, William T. " 'Benito Cereno' and the American National Character." *Discourse*, 8 (1965), 49–63.

Poirier, Richard. *A World Elsewhere: The Place of Style in American Literature*. New York: Oxford University Press, 1966.

Pope, Alexander. *Poems of Alexander Pope*, ed. Maynard Mack. Vol. 7. New Haven, Conn.: Yale University Press, 1967.

Porte, Joel. *Representative Man: Ralph Waldo Emerson in His Time*. New York: Oxford University Press, 1979.

Porter, David. *Emerson and Literary Change*. Cambridge: Harvard University Press, 1978.

Pound, Ezra. "Date Line." In *Literary Essays of Ezra Pound*, ed. T. S. Eliot. New York: New Directions, 1968.

——. *Selected Letters*, ed. D. D. Paige. New York: New Directions, 1971.

Putzel, Max. "The Source and the Symbols of Melville's 'Benito Cereno.' " *American Literature*, 34 (1964), 191–206.

Ransom, John Crowe, et al. *I'll Take My Stand: The South and the Agrarian Tradition*. 1930; rpt. Baton Rouge: Louisiana State University Press, 1977.

——. *The World's Body*. 1938; rpt. Baton Rouge: Louisiana State University Press, 1968.

Ransom, Roger, and Richard Sutch. *One Kind of Freedom: The Economic Con-

sequences of Emancipation. New York: Cambridge University Press, 1977.

Rice, Duncan. *The Rise and Fall of Black Slavery.* New York: Harper and Row, 1975.

Roark, James L. *Masters without Slaves: Southern Planters in the Civil War and Reconstruction.* New York: Norton, 1977.

Rodnon, Stewart. "*The Adventures of Huckleberry Finn* and *Invisible Man*: Thematic and Structural Comparisons." *Negro American Literature Forum,* 4 (1970), 45–51.

————. "Ralph Ellison's *Invisible Man*: Six Tentative Approaches." *CLA Journal,* 12 (March 1969), 244–56.

Rogers, Franklin R. *Mark Twain's Burlesque Patterns as Seen in the Novels and Narratives.* Dallas: Southern Methodist University Press, 1960.

Rogers, Pat. *The Augustan Vision.* London: Weidenfeld and Nicolson, 1974.

Rovit, Earl. "Ellison and the American Comic Tradition." *Wisconsin Studies in Contemporary Literature,* 1:3 (Fall 1960), 34–42.

Rubin, Louis. Introduction. *I'll Take My Stand: The South and the Agrarian Tradition.* 1930; rpt. Baton Rouge: Louisiana State University Press, 1968.

Runden, John P., ed. *Melville's "Benito Cereno": A Text for Guided Research.* Lexington, Mass.: D. C. Heath, 1965.

Rupp, Richard H. *Celebration in Post-War American Fiction 1945–1967.* Coral Gables, Fla.: University of Miami Press, 1970.

Russell, Bertrand. *A History of Western Philosophy.* New York: Simon and Schuster (Touchstone), 1945.

Said, Edward. *Beginnings: Intention and Method.* New York: Basic Books, 1975.

Sanders, Archie D. "Odysseus in Black." *CLA Journal,* 13 (1970), 217–28.

Schafer, William J. "Irony from Underground—Satiric Elements in *Invisible Man.*" *Satire Newsletter,* 7:1 (Fall 1969), 21–25.

Schiffman, Joseph. "Critical Problems in Melville's 'Benito Cereno.'" *Modern Language Quarterly,* 11 (September 1950), 317–24.

Schlesinger, Arthur M., Sr. *The American as Reformer.* Cambridge: Harvard University Press, 1950.

Schmitz, Neil. *Of Huck and Alice: Humorous Writing in American Literature.* Minneapolis: University of Minnesota Press, 1983.

————. "The Paradox of Liberation in *Huckleberry Finn.*" *Texas Studies in Language and Literature,* 13 (1971), 125–36.

————. "Twain, *Huckleberry Finn,* and the Reconstruction," *American Studies,* 12 (1971), 56–67.

Schudder, Harold. "Melville's *Benito Cereno* and Captain Delano's *Voyages.*" *PMLA,* 43 (June 1928), 502–32.

Scruggs, Charles W. "Ralph Ellison's Use of *The Aeneid* in *Invisible Man.*" *CLA Journal,* 17 (1974), 368–78.

Septo, Robert B., and Michael S. Harper. "Study and Experience: An Interview with Ralph Ellison." *Massachusetts Review,* 18 (1977), 417–35.

Simpson, Eleanor E. "Melville and the Negro: From *Typee* to 'Benito Cereno.'" *American Literature,* 41 (March 1969), 19–38.

Stampp, Kenneth M. *The Peculiar Institution: Slavery in the Ante-Bellum South.* New York: Knopf, 1956.

Stark, John. "*Invisible Man*: Ellison's Black Odyssey." *Negro American Literature Forum*, 7 (1973), 60–63.

Steiner, George. *After Babel: Aspects of Language and Translation.* New York: Oxford University Press, 1975.

Tandy, Jeannette Reid. "Pro-Slavery Propaganda in American Fiction of the Fifties." *South Atlantic Quarterly*, 21 (January/April 1922), 40–50, 170–78.

Tanner, Tony. "The Music of Invisibility." In *Ralph Ellison: A Collection of Critical Essays*, ed. John Hersey. Englewood Cliffs, N.J.: Prentice Hall, 1974.

Tatham, Campbell. " 'Dismal and Lonesome': A New Look at *Huckleberry Finn*." *Modern Fiction Studies*, 14 (1968), 47–55.

Taylor, William R. *Cavalier and Yankee: The Old South and the American National Character.* New York: Harper and Row, 1969.

Tischler, Nancy M. "Negro Literature and Classic Form." *Contemporary Literature*, 10 (Summer 1969), 352–65.

Tyler, Alice Felt. *Freedom's Ferment: Phases of American Social History to 1860.* 1944; rpt. New York: Harper Torchbooks, 1962.

Vanderhaar, Margaret M. "A Re-Examination of 'Benito Cereno.' " *American Literature*, 40 (May 1968), 179–91.

Volger, Thomas A. "*Invisible Man*: Somebody's Protest Novel." *Iowa Review*, 1:2 (Spring 1970), 64–82.

Wade, Richard C. *Slavery in the Cities: The South 1820–1860.* New York: Oxford University Press, 1964.

Waggoner, Hyatt H. *Emerson as Poet.* Princeton: Princeton University Press, 1974.

Wasserman, Jerry. "Embracing the Negative: *Native Son* and *Invisible Man*." *Studies in American Fiction*, 4:1 (Spring 1976), 94–104.

Webster, Grant. *The Republic of Letters: A History of Postwar American Literary Opinion.* Baltimore: Johns Hopkins University Press, 1979.

Weiners, David R. "Anxiety in the Golden Day of Lewis Mumford." *New England Quarterly*, 34 (1963), 179–91.

Weldon, Thornton. "An Allusion List for James Joyce's *Ulysses*, Part I, Telemachus." *James Joyce Quarterly*, 1 (1963), 19–25.

———. *Allusions in Ulysses: An Annotated List.* Chapel Hill: University of North Carolina Press, 1961.

Werner, Craig Hansen. *Paradoxical Resolutions: American Fiction since James Joyce.* Urbana: University of Illinois Press, 1982.

Williams, Stanley T. " 'Follow Your Leader,' Melville's *Benito Cereno*." *Virginia Quarterly Review*, 23 (Winter 1947), 65–76.

Wilner, Eleanor. "The Invisible Black Thread: Identity and Nonentity in *Invisible Man*." *CLA Journal*, 13 (1970), 242–57.

Winters, Yvor. *Maule's Curse.* Norfolk, Conn.: New Directions, 1938.

Woodman, Harold D. "Sequel to Slavery: The New History Views the Postbellum South." *Journal of Southern History*, 43:4 (1977), 523–54.

Woodward, C. Van. *Origins of the New South 1877–1913.* Baton Rouge: Louisiana State University Press, 1951.

Wyatt-Brown, Bertram. *Southern Honor: Ethics and Behavior in the Old South.* New York: Oxford University Press, 1982.

Yip, Wai-Lim. *Ezra Pound's Cathay.* Princeton: Princeton University Press, 1969.

Index

Adolescence, of Huck Finn and United
  States, 125, 126
Adventures of Huckleberry Finn (Twain),
  critical controversy over, 124–128;
  and *Invisible Man*, 138–145; Twain's
  comment on, 159–160n3
Aeneid (Dryden), 41–42
Affirmation/negation dichotomy,
  140–142
Afro-American, Tod Clifton as ideal,
  67–68, 72; values of, and modernism, 24–26. *See also* Blacks
After Babel (Steiner), 49, 50
A la Recherche du Temps Perdu (Proust),
  35
Alexander Pope—The Poetry of Allusion
  (Brower), 27–28, 29, 46
Allusion, acceptance and denial of, 99;
  as act of affirmation, 28; as act of subordination, 28; agitating effect of, 55;
  to Christ and Satan in *Invisible Man*,
  72–83; defined, 155n3; demanding
  conscious attention by, 57–58; and
  elegy, 156n13; Ellison's use of, 73;
  epic, 28; Golden Day in *Invisible
  Man*, 85–86, 94–103; H. Bloom on,
  39–40; as critical subtext of, 127–
  146; limiting reference of, 50–62; as
  literary criticism, 45, 59–62; literary
  versus general, 56; and modernism,
  149–150; overt and covert, 32; to the
  past, 43; promoting stability of text,
  60; referent changed by, 58–62; referent of, 48; R. Brower on, 27–30;
  and simultaneity, 45; as stabilizers of

meaning, 147; studies of, annotated
  bibliography of, 155n1; theory of, 27,
  31, 155n4; and tradition, xii; and
  translation, 45–50; transumptive, 40;
  value of, 53–55
America's Coming of Age (Brooks), 1, 94
American Renaissance (Matthiessen), 94
An American Dilemma (Myrdal), 15
Anatomy of Criticism (Frye), 31, 32, 33,
  34, 36
Animal figures, 32–33
Antebellum America, as ideal world,
  2–4
Antebellum South. *See* Old South
Anxiety of Influence, The (Bloom), 39
Archetypes, 33–34, 37
Aristocracy, and "redneck," 153n14;
  Southern, myth of, 7
Armstrong, Louis, 20
Arnold, Matthew, 30
Ash Wednesday (Eliot), 32
Assumptions, as necessary to meaning,
  19; spheres of, xiii; about tradition,
  33. *See also* Hermeneutics
Augustan poetry, 27–28

Babo, 106, 107
Baker, Houston, 20
Barbee, Homer A., 54–55
Barnes, Daniel, 160n6
Barthes, Roland, 19
Battle Royal, 158n7
Baumbach, Jonathan, 65–66
Beard, Charles A. and Mary R., 1, 2–3,
  151n2